T0360807

statsNotes
Some Statistics for Management Problems

statsNotes

Some Statistics for Management Problems

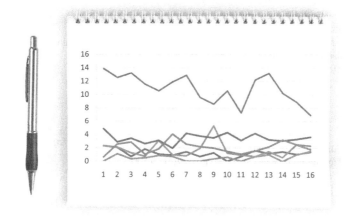

Alan Jessop

Durham University, UK

 **World Scientific**

NEW JERSEY · LONDON · SINGAPORE · BEIJING · SHANGHAI · HONG KONG · TAIPEI · CHENNAI · TOKYO

Published by

World Scientific Publishing Co. Pte. Ltd.

5 Toh Tuck Link, Singapore 596224

USA office: 27 Warren Street, Suite 401-402, Hackensack, NJ 07601

UK office: 57 Shelton Street, Covent Garden, London WC2H 9HE

Library of Congress Cataloging-in-Publication Data

Jessop, Alan.

  StatsNotes : some statistics for management problems / Alan Jessop, Durham University, UK.

    pages cm

  Includes bibliographical references and index.

  ISBN 978-9814696678 (alk. paper)

  1. Mathematical statistics. 2. Measurement uncertainty (Statistics) 3. Instrumental variables (Statistics)

I. Title. II. Title: Stats notes. III. Title: Some statistics for management problems.

  QA279.4.J47 2015

  658.4'033--dc23

                                    20150351512

British Library Cataloguing-in-Publication Data

A catalogue record for this book is available from the British Library.

In-house Editors: Chandrima Maitra/Qi Xiao

Typeset by Stallion Press

Email: enquiries@stallionpress.com

Printed in Singapore

Contents

About the Author

Alan Jessop holds degrees in Civil Engineering from Leeds and Heriot-Watt Universities and in Computer Science from the University of London.

He worked as an urban and transport planner in London, first for a local authority and then for a consultancy where he began an interest in computer modelling and education. After having built forecasting models for cities in the UK and abroad he went to the University of Westminster where he taught transport modelling and statistics as well as undertaking consultancy assignments in planning and highway design.

He then moved to the Business School at Durham University, where he is now, and where he continued to follow his interest in statistics and operational research. He has been Director of the full-time MBA programme on three occasions as well as undertaking other administrative duties.

He has also taught at the European Business School in Germany and at Warwick Business School. His main research interests are in multi-criteria decision making and pattern languages. The twin interests in patterns and teaching modelling to post graduation and experienced managers have resulted in this book.

1

Introduction and guide

The contribution of statistics to business is to be seen everywhere, from risk analysis to big data analytics, from forecasting to process improvement and Six Sigma. Every day managers use reports which include tables, charts, averages and other results of statistical analysis, some simple and some not so simple. Perhaps you just need a useful chart for your PowerPoint presentation.

The main business of statistics is uncertainty and uncertainty is what makes some management decisions difficult. Statistical methods cannot help with all aspects of management uncertainty — will that takeover bid succeed? can we close the deal? — but where uncertainty is due to the variability of output or the availability of only partial information or judgement about some numbers then statistics should be able to help.

Here are two illustrations.

You have to prepare a budget for next year.

The trading company for which you work sells a number of products in different countries.

Some products are in the same sector (tablets, flash drives) but not all (cosmetics, coffee).

The company has not been trading long. It has some data on past sales but it is incomplete.

You rely on the judgement of the product and country managers for sales estimates. They are not always very confident in what they tell you.

Statistical questions: how to describe the judgemental forecasts and make use of them?
what is the effect, if any, of linked sales?
can the data we have help?
how can uncertainties be combined into a forecast for the company?
how should risk be assessed and presented?

Management questions: what should be our pricing policy?
what to negotiate with our suppliers?
should we drop any products and/or introduce new ones?
is the risk too high? how can we manage it?

Are perceptions of our service different in France and in Spain? Informal feedback seems to show they are. If there really is a difference we need to know why. Some market research would be useful but times are tough and we don't want to waste money on unnecessary surveys.

Statistical questions: how should data be collected?
                           how big should the samples be?
                           what is the best way of presenting the results?

Management questions: what do we do if there is a difference?
                           how big a difference would make it worth doing anything?
                           how sure do we need to be?

Statistics can make a contribution by quantifying uncertainty which comes from data and judgement. How useful that contribution is depends on how well the management question has been framed and how well the results are presented.

In this book you will find, among other things,

    how to describe variation
    how to present statistical results in a way useful to managers
    how to describe and use judgement
    how to use evidence to reach a justified conclusion
    how to use models for what-if tests
    how to use data from samples
    how to describe risk and make risky decisions
    how to look for relations and independence
    how to monitor performance with incomplete information

Who should read this book

This book is for managers and management students. Managers are as diverse a group as any other. Some have solid mathematical background and others none. But all manage and so have management problems. Sometimes advice is needed to help decide what to do. Sometimes that advice is statistical.

You have two questions:

    can some statistical method help and, if so, which?
    can I do this?

You aren't a statistician but you can probably do more than you think you can. Having made some statistical analyses you have an awareness of what can be done and the confidence to find out what to do.

Your contribution is that you know the business context and enough of the statistics to make the connection.

So the purpose of this book is twofold, to help you make some statistical analyses and to provide some thoughts on that interface between business problems and statistical problems.

Finding what you need

Management problems are often not straightforward. They don't come pre-labelled.

You will have a good idea of what your management problem is but may be less sure of the sort of statistical advice that best fits, or if there is any such advice. Borrowing from emergency medicine call this task triage, deciding where best to get useful advice.

You need to translate from the language of management to the language of statistics: from uncertainty to probability, from variability to variance.

Then make the statistical calculation.

And then translate the result back to the world of your management problem.

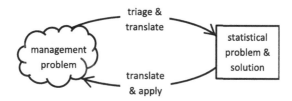

This crossing and re-crossing from the manager's world to the statistical world and back is not trivial and is often the reason why some people find statistics and quantitative methods and the courses that teach them difficult. Once the statistical method is identified it is usually not too hard to make the calculation and provide a statistical answer — the probability is 0.35 — but it may then be hard to decide what this means in practice — the probability is 0.35, so what?

As with any quantitative model a statistical model solves that bit of your problem it *can* solve and leaves *you* with the rest. This means that you have to understand enough about the model to decide whether it will give the help you need, or enough to be useful, and then to communicate the result.

statsNotes are designed to help. Organising the material as a hundred or so discrete modules gives you a hundred or so chances to find a match. Some of the units have names which relate to management problems and some relate to statistical method. Not all contain numerical detail. Some are about why and how your management problem might benefit from a little statistical input.

None of the notes is long. This is to encourage you to use them. Each will tell you of other notes you might find helpful to read and will also give some discussion of underlying ideas from both statistics and management.

The motivation is decision support. The quantitative analyses are there to help you decide, not to take the decision for you. This is always important. It is your decision.

The form of the statsNotes

As you flick through this book you will see that what is written is quite dense. Don't be put off. This is more like a source book. Identify what you need and read around as much as necessary for the job in hand.

Most statsNotes show what to do, then an example of how to do it and then a rationale explaining the context for use and any necessary theoretical points. This is so that you can take what you need quickly. There will also be links to other statsNotes, shown as {B3}, for you to follow as you need or as your curiosity requires.

The design assumption is that you want first to know what to do and then to know the assumptions which justify the recommendation. statsNotes are brief so that you can see at a glance the scope of what is covered and easily pick what *you* want to read. The shape of a statsNote is

---

Title helps you find what you need

Recommendation box shows what to do

Example of application

Rationale

why is this a problem?

what is the question?

Therefore: do this

but these are the assumptions

and these are some related issues

Because the statsNotes are compact it is easy for you quickly to scan the page to pick what you want.

It may be that you are pretty sure what you want to do but cannot recall the method. Look at the Recommendation box first.

Or maybe you are one of those people who prefer to know why before you find out how. Read the Rationale section first.

If you are looking for a good fit to your problem you might find it best to first look at the Example. Does that look like your problem?

Not all statsNotes have the same purpose and so they have different structures. Broadly, there are three types:

Perspectives: an issue with widespread implications
background for recommendations in other notes
Examples {B8, D6}

Business fit: a problem from a business point of view
shows how and why a statistical approach can help
Examples {E1, G1}

Implementation: how to use a particular statistical model or method
Examples {C1, F10}

4

Depending on the purpose of the note some components may not be needed. For example, a *Perspectives* discussion of a background issue will mainly be concerned with Rationale.

You can use these notes to find advice on how to do something and also as an aid for debriefing and learning from your experience.

Find advice

Go to the statsNote or section which you think best matches the problem you have. The names of the statsNotes and of the groups of notes shown in Section 2 should help you find what you need or at least where to start looking. Each section of notes has an overview to give more context.

You have identified a statsNote. For example, you need to analyse some before and after data and so go to {F14} *Testing and reporting differences in means and proportions*.

> Perhaps you have some background in statistics but cannot recall what you did last time. It was a while ago. The first Example looks close enough. You look at the box. Now you remember, always add the variances. The rest makes sense and the Example looks relevant. Read the Rationale. None of the special cases apply to you. You have enough.
>
> Or perhaps you have not so much background in statistics. You recognise the Example as being similar to your problem so want to use the method. You don't know what a standard error is so you follow the link to {F5}. The effect of collecting more data to increase precision makes sense and now you can measure it. But you need to know more about standard deviation so follow the link to {F4}. And so on until you have found enough so that you are confident what to do and why. You have used a subset of notes and may want to keep a record of them.

How much you need other notes will depend on what you already know and what you think relevant for your problem. This will be different for different people.

Debrief and make your own note

You have solved a problem which is particular to you (the you may be a group). Don't lose the experience. Write a statsNote of your own. This has two obvious benefits.

Discussing (even if only with yourself) what worked, why it worked, what didn't work and what to look out for in future is an excellent debrief which will help you and your colleagues internalise what you have learned.

You will also have created a note for future use by yourself or by others.

You may want to include links to sources outside these notes which you found helpful, other books or internal reports or websites. Include them.

Your note may be not so much concerned with the details of the statistical method, which you cover using {} links, but more with the business side of the problem. The experience was *yours* in *your* organisation. It gives a business context relevant for *you*.

When debriefing start wherever seems natural: what was the most useful or the most difficult aspect? Start there. Don't let your notes get too big. Restricting size makes you focus on one topic. If you feel the need to expand to take account of another point just put {} as a reminder that you have to develop another note later.

To illustrate

You have completed your before and after study of process improvement in an engineering company. You started with {F14} and read around other statsNotes as described above. The result was that the reduction of the percentage of rejects was estimated to be between one and six percentage points.

You discuss your findings with a group of colleagues who were involved in the change.

> One of them points out that while the estimated size of the change looks to have been on target the range, from one percentage point to six, looks quite big.
>
> You talk about the effects of larger sample sizes.
>
> There is general agreement that a range of about two percentage points would be better.
>
> After some experimentation on your laptop (only taking a few minutes with everyone joining in) you conclude that two equal samples of about 2,800 would have been needed to get that narrower range.
>
> So, to keep it simple, let us say 3,000. We make these components in volume so that shouldn't be too difficult.
>
> You say that while it isn't necessary that before and after samples are the same size it is easier to give simple advice.
>
> Yes, but suppose the margin of improvement is different? Bigger or smaller samples would be needed to give the same sort of interval.
>
> OK, but for now we'll stick with what we have just decided and keep an eye on what happens.
>
> Well that's alright if you are testing components but I want to bring in some new work practices. I will have to test the performance of my staff and there are nowhere near three thousand of them.
>
> Wait a minute, there is a note about that. If you measure the difference for each worker before and after that should reduce the sampling error.
>
> Yes, let's do that.

And so a note is written. The purpose of the note is to give focussed advice based on your experience.

The language used fits the culture of the business. Rationale was replaced by Notes. This is a common practice for company paperwork.

It was decided to leave in the statsNotes links so that you and anybody else could in future trace the argument behind the recommendation. This is helpful if changes are being considered.

P1. Testing performance improvement using a before and after study

> Decide what to measure and how this can be done.
>
> Collect work samples before a change is made and again afterwards.
>
> Report the change as an interval.

Example

We installed some new cutting machinery (see Production Dept. report PD/207/15) with the aim of increasing accuracy and so reducing the number of rejects.

With the old machinery there were 28 rejects in a batch of 500. With the new machinery there were 10 rejects in a batch of 500.

The reduction achieved is between 1.2 and 6 percentage points against a target of 5.

There was only a 0.3% chance that improvement was due only to differences in samples.

Conclusion: the investment was justified.

Notes

1. Before and after testing monitors improvements after installing new machinery or work practices. {F14}
2. The accuracy of the test gets better if you collect more data. This needs to be considered ahead of the improvement to get a large enough Before sample. {F20}
3. Before and after samples of 3,000 items are recommended.
4. If the change is in work practices use the same operatives in both before and after tests {F17}. There won't be 3,000 operatives so use as big a sample as you can.
5. Report interval: average plus or minus 2 × standard deviation/√sample size. {F19}
6. Queries: contact …

This illustration is written as a workplace application but could just as easily be used to debrief a class exercise or case study analysis.

EXCEL focus

So far as possible algebraic symbols and formulae are not used. EXCEL function names and spreadsheet fragments are used instead.

Function names are shown in small capitals, LIKE THIS.

When used to illustrate their use in computation function names are shown as full capitals like this: MODE (A1:A7)

For some of the statsNotes example spreadsheets are available at my website www.dur.ac.uk/a.t.jessop/statsNotes.

Scope

These notes cover much the same ground as an introductory text on statistics for managers. There are some topics not normally covered and some covered from a different viewpoint to provide a link between the statistics problem and the management problem.

It is assumed that you have a problem: your problem. You are looking for some statistical help but also need to think about the other parts of your problem which are not directly statistical but are important for useful application.

The book is organised like this:

Section 2   gives a listing of the statsNotes with a little commentary to help you see what is there.

Section 3   is the main section and contains the statsNotes in eleven groups.

Section 4   sets out my motivation in designing the book as I did. You may find this of interest (I hope you do) but you do not have to know about this to use the statsNotes.

Section 5   gives a brief listing of variables and functions and where they are defined.

My assumption is that you have a problem. That's what you bring. That and the willingness to invest a little time in finding out if some statistics can help. The modular form of the statsNotes will help you get close to what you need quickly.

The notes have been ordered into groups further to help you find what you want. They are not designed to be read as a continuous piece of prose like book chapters, though you can do that if you want to. The ordering does go from foundational to the more application oriented.

2

Overview of the statsNotes

Most statsNotes have the same simple form:

Name to help you find what you need

Recommend box so that you can see immediately what to do

Example so you can see how to apply the recommendation

Rationale to explain the recommendation and point out limitations and other issues

It will sometimes be useful to emphasise why the recommendation is needed. This is done at the start of the Rationale by describing the context and showing the resolution following a Therefore ... to signal that an argument has been concluded.

Links to other notes are given in braces like this {D4}. A link may point to some knowledge or definition which you might need to make sense of the note. If you already have this knowledge you won't need the link. Other links point to further application of the recommendation which you might find interesting. These forward and backward links emphasise that the notes form a network of advice.

Not all notes are exactly the same. Some provide a background discussion and so may be all Rationale, others are straight calculation and may have no Rationale at all.

Take what you need from each note and read others as necessary. Add links that you find relevant for your problems.

✳✳✳

While the notes are best thought of as a network they have to be printed in some order. They are grouped into sections which resemble the chapters you might find in a popular introductory text on management statistics, starting with some basic ideas and moving towards applications.

Each section starts with a brief overview of the topic.

You do not have to read them in that order (though you may, of course). Go to the note or section that seems most relevant to the task you have.

Here is a listing of the statsNotes with a little guide to why they might be useful.

You need a statistical mindset because you have to deal with quantities which are not constant. They may vary for a number of reasons but they do vary. Having ways to describe these variables is basic for everything statistical.

A. Describing data

A 1. Variables
A 2. How often? The frequency distribution
A 3. Data in groups: the histogram
A 4. Density functions
A 5. No more than that: the cumulative distribution
A 6. Averages
A 7. Spread
A 8. Calculations from tables
A 9. Coefficient of variation
A10. Skew
A11. Picturing more than one distribution with boxplots
A12. Be kind to your audience and keep it simple
A13. Agree/disagree/neither

Variability means uncertainty. How likely or unlikely is any particular outcome? You need a way of talking about this and a way of making calculations so that you can assess these likelihoods. It may be that a fairly simple calculation will do this. For situations which occur frequently a standard model is often useful.

B. Probability: the language of uncertainty

B 1. Probability
B 2. Probability distribution
B 3. Probability of NOT that
B 4. Probability of this OR that
B 5. Independence
B 6. Probability of this AND that
B 7. Expected value
B 8. Words and numbers
B 9. Beware rules of thumb
B10. Not sure? Give a range

C. Probability models: the shapes of uncertainty

C 1. How many in this sample? The Binomial distribution
C 2. How many at this rate? The Poisson distribution
C 3. Normally like this: the Normal distribution
C 4. z values
C 5. Uncertainty about proportions: the Beta distribution
C 6. No negatives: the Gamma distribution
C 7. The negative exponential distribution

C 8. Is the model good enough?
C 9. Degrees of freedom
C10. Modelling your judgement with simple two and three point estimates
C11. Modelling your judgement with MODE
C12. Modelling your judgement with percentiles
C13. Which model for your judgement?

You collect data to find out what is going on. What you see has some diagnostic value. You need a frame-work which ensures that conclusions you draw from data are justified and take account of any well-founded views you have.

D. Evidence and judgement

D 1. Likelihood
D 2. What caused it? Making an inference
D 3. Not all evidence is helpful
D 4. Base rates: what we already know
D 5. More evidence
D 6. Be modest
D 7. maxEnt
D 8. Learning about proportions
D 9. Learning about rates
D10. Learning Normally
D11. Just how important is judgement?

Something bad might happen which affects you or your business. This is a risk. How likely is it? How bad might it get? You need a way of describing the risks you face so that you can decide what, if anything, to do.

E. Risky decisions

E 1. Thinking about risk
E 2. Prioritise risks with a risk matrix
E 3. Screening the alternatives
E 4. Uncertainty and decision
E 5. Risk or uncertainty?
E 6. Risky decision
E 7. Are you risk averse?
E 8. Sensitivity test
E 9. Two summaries: risk and value at risk
E10. Divide and conquer
E11. Correlated risks
E12. Policy constants
E13. Monte Carlo
E14. Find risk through time with a decision tree

A common source of uncertainty is that you only have sample data on which to make a judgement. You have neither the time nor money to inspect everything and so must do what you can with partial information. What are you justified in concluding?

F. Using information from samples

F 1.   Why sample?
F 2.   Inference: test or report?
F 3.   Inference: Normal distribution for test and report
F 4.   Central Limit Theorem
F 5.   Standard error
F 6.   But you don't know the population variance
F 7.   *t* or Normal?
F 8.   Reporting a mean
F 9.   Testing a mean
F10.   Reporting a proportion
F11.   Testing a proportion
F12.   Reporting a variance
F13.   Testing a variance
F14   Testing and reporting differences in means and proportions
F15   Testing and reporting differences with small samples
F16.   Testing and reporting differences in variances
F17.   Before and after in pairs (if you can)
F18.   Sample is large part of population
F19.   Confidence interval
F20.   How big a sample?

You will often want to know whether a system is performing as it should (is a target being met?). Deciding this is not always straightforward. You must distinguish effects (good or bad) which can be attributed to management actions and system variability.

G. Monitoring

G1.   Management by exception
G2.   What to monitor?
G3.   Manager view vs. stats view
G4.   When you win it's skill. When you lose it's bad luck
G5.   League tables
G6.   Comparing intervals is conservative
G7.   Cause for concern? The funnel plot

The same methods used for monitoring are used for testing against an assumption rather than a target.

H. Significance and hypothesis testing

H1.   Hypothesis or target?
H2.   Significance test
H3.   Don't say "statistically significant"
H4. $p=5\%$: sound advice or automation of judgement?
H5.   Hypothesis Testing

Do two variables vary together in a consistent way? Is there a pattern? If they do this may be useful because one can be used to forecast the other. Perhaps this joint variation is not what you want; performance should not vary from one factory to another.

I. Is there a relationship?

I1.   Is there structure in a table?
I2.   Looking for correlation
I3   Inference for the correlation coefficient
I4.   Fitting a straight line
I5.   How useful is the model?
I6.   Regression analysis in EXCEL
I7.   Prediction error with a regression model
I8.   Non-linear models
I9.   Correlation doesn't have to be causal to be useful

Statistical methods help decisions in many management and business problems. Here are some illustrations.

J. Production and operations

J1.   Uncertainty and project duration
J2.   System reliability
J3.   Backups for improved reliability
J4.   Control charts
J5.   Process capability
J6.   Six Sigma

K. Finance

K1.   Risk and reward
K2.   Beta: systematic and unsystematic risks
K3.   Portfolio
K4.   Minimum risk portfolio
K5.   Real options

3

The statsNotes

A. Describing data
B. Probability: the language of uncertainty
C. Probability models: the shapes of uncertainty
D. Evidence and judgement
E. Risky decisions
F. Using information from samples
G. Monitoring
H. Significance and hypothesis testing
I. Is there a relationship?
J. Production and operations
K. Finance

Describing data

---

overview

Faced with unstructured data you need to know what is going on so that you can make a summary as the first stage in some management report.

It is always a good idea to make a picture but you will often need some numeric summary as well: to compare the performance of different organisations or to see if a standard is met.

What pictures and numbers you *can* use will depend on the type of **variable** you are measuring {A1, A13}. How you can describe car sales by model is different to how you can describe the weights of frozen chickens.

The basis for any description is the **distribution** {A2–A5, A11} which shows how frequently each value of your variable occurred.

Once you have the distribution you can decide what else you want to present. This is an editorial decision so you will need to take a view about what is important for your purpose. This is usually pretty clear but just pause and think. Is there a better chart? Is a numeric measure of average {A6} or spread {A7} useful and, if so, which? Would some other summary statistic help in appreciating the possible importance of variation {A9} or the asymmetry of the distribution {A10}.

Summarising is an editing job. The whole point of the summary is that it is easier to understand than the raw data. But this useful simplification is bought at a cost: there may be more than one plausible summary, and different people may make different summaries.

Simplifying necessarily means leaving things out. You might want to try more than one description when making up your mind which account of the data you wish to present.

Use both graphic and numeric summaries carefully, *do not* spew out flashy graphs or lots of numbers just because the software allows you to {A12}. Use the simplest summary that conveys your message. Including the unnecessary will only confuse: think of your audience.

A1. Variables

> The correct methods for summarising, describing and analysing data depend on the type of variable used and how it is measured.

The value of quantities is not fixed; it varies. These quantities are called *variables*. For example:

> The colours of cars sold are not the same.
> The preference for one brand over another is different for different people.
> The time taken to reply to a telephone enquiry is different for each enquiry.

There are four types of measurement scale. The first two scales are not necessarily numerical.

Nominal: We can distinguish one object from another, but that is all. Cars may have different colours and so we may distinguish them but we cannot say that one colour is bigger than another.

Ordinal: Not only can we distinguish objects but we can put them in order. If two clients express satisfaction with a product and one said that she was "satisfied" while the other said that he was "very satisfied" then the second customer is more satisfied that the first, but it makes no sense to say, for instance, that he was twice as satisfied.

Interval: As well as ordering objects we can say something about the size of the differences between them. If the temperatures of three objects are 10°C, 15°C and 20°C we can say that the difference between the first and second, 5°C, is the same as that between the second and third. It makes no sense to say that 20°C is twice as hot as 10°C because the ratio of temperatures would change if a different scale (Fahrenheit, say) was used, although the two differences would still be equal. The two measurement scales have different zero points.

Ratio: As well as being able to say something about the differences between values we can also say something about their relative sizes. If one telephone enquiry is answered in 20 seconds and the other in 30 seconds we can say not only that the second response was 10 seconds longer but also that it was 50% longer (30/20 = 1.5).

As well as differentiating variables by measurement scale we can also distinguish numeric variables according to how many possible values each may take.

Discrete: A variable may take only limited values, commonly whole numbers. The number of people in a car may be 1, 2, 3, 4 and so on. The number of people worldwide drinking a particular soft drink may be very much bigger but is similarly discrete.

Continuous: The variable may take one of an infinity of values. The average number of people per car on a particular highway may be 1 or 1.0000001 or 1.0000002 or 1.0000003 and so on. Even here the number of decimal places given is arbitrarily limited.

It may make sense to treat a discrete variable as continuous when the difference between values, 1, is very small compared to the magnitude (49 million passengers use Madrid Barajas airport annually).

A2. How often? The frequency distribution

> You want a picture of the *shape* of a discrete variable.
>
> List all possible outcomes or values.
>
> Against each value put the *frequency*. The *frequency* is the number of occurrences of each value.
>
> Also give the *relative frequency* as a proportion or a percentage.

Example

You ask 50 people how often they visited the cinema in the last month. Here are the results:

no. of visits	frequency	Relative frequency proportion	Relative frequency %
0	10	0.2	20
1	25	0.5	50
2	12	0.24	24
3 or more	3	0.06	6
	50	1.00	100

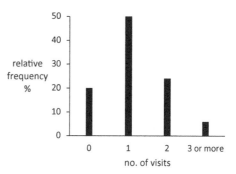

Rationale

You have data about a nominal, ordinal or discrete variable {A1}. The range of values is small (just four in the Example) and you want to describe the *distribution* of data; how often each value occurs.

The number of times each value occurs is called its *frequency*.

If you report that "3 out of 50 people went to the cinema three times last month" the obvious question is "Out of how many?" Reporting that 6% in a sample of 50 went to the cinema three times is much better. You could have reported a proportion of 0.06, but 6% is more easily understood.

You also want to show whether one value occurs more frequently than others and, if so, how much more frequently. Or you may want to show whether the distribution is symmetrical or skewed {A10}.

Therefore:
Count the frequency of each value and calculate the percentage relative frequency. Give the sample size too.
Make a chart of the distribution showing the relative frequencies of each value.

It is important to be consistent in what you report. Percentage and sample size is good. This may seem obvious (it is) but pay attention to radio or television reports which use information from a number of sources. Quite often you will hear inconsistencies, for one source a percentage and for another the frequency. This is confusing. Comparison should be easy, but is not. The reporter has no real idea what (s)he is saying.

Keep the chart simple. You are trying to show how the data are distributed as clearly as you can {A12}.

In EXCEL

1. Highlight the data you want to show.
    Click *Insert/Column* to get a simple chart.
    That is a good start.

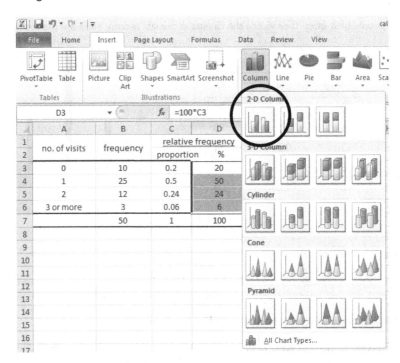

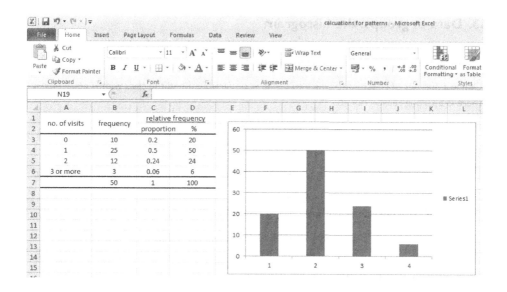

2. Go to *Chart Tools/Layout* to give axis titles and other layout options as you want.
3. Since you have only one series do not forget to delete the key from the right side of the chart.
4. Make the bars thinner.
   Right click on any bar and choose *Format data series* then open the gap.
5. The labels on the horizontal axis are not what you want. You want 0, 1, 2, 3, which are in A3:A6.
   Click on the chart and then
   Chart Tools/Design/Select Data to get the window at right.
   Click *Edit* and then select cells A3:A6.

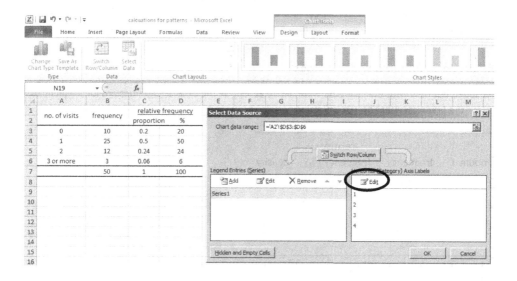

A3. Data in groups: the histogram

You want a picture of the *shape* of a continuous variable.

Define a number of classes into which to divide your variable. Keep the class widths equal unless there is a strong reason not to.

For each class find the *frequency*. The *frequency* is the number of data within that class.

Also give the *relative frequency* as a proportion or a percentage.

If classes are of equal width draw a rectangle for each class, the height being proportional to class frequency.

If the classes have unequal widths make heights proportional to

frequency density = frequency/class width.

Example 1. equal width classes

Five hundred people were interviewed to determine how much they spent when they last visited a garden centre. Nobody spent more than £60. Here are the results:

amount £	frequency	relative frequency (%)
0 to 20	100	20
20 to 40	260	52
40 to 60	140	28
	500	100

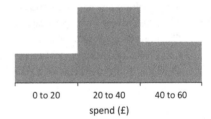

Example 2. unequal width classes

As above, but now with the final class width twice as long as the others. Densities are for frequencies, so for the first class 100/(20 − 0) = 5.

amount £	frequency	relative frequency (%)	density
0 to 20	100	20	5
20 to 40	260	52	13
40 to 80	140	28	3.5
	500	100	

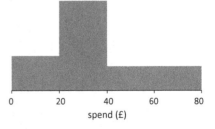

22

Rationale

This is a special case of making a frequency distribution {A2}. The difference is that the variable can take very many values: in Example 1, the expenditure of each customer is one of 6,000 values from £0.00 to £60.00. It is very likely that no value appears more than once — no two customers spent *exactly* the same amounts — so that if you plotted a frequency distribution you would get something like this:

This diagram does not show different frequencies (all frequencies = 1) but you can see that in some regions of the variable data more *dense* than in other regions. This is what you want to show.

Therefore:

Group the data into classes and find the class frequencies.

Make the class widths the same for all classes. For each class draw a rectangle with height proportional to frequency. This is called a *histogram*.

How many classes? There is no correct answer, it is one of those arbitrary but sensible decisions you have to make sometimes. Think of the two extremes. If you have too many classes you will emphasise the variability from class to class and not be much better off than showing the ungrouped data. If you have too few classes you will smooth the picture too much and so not see the shape of the distribution (a histogram of one class would be just a single rectangle). Clearly, the more data you have the more classes you are likely to be able to use while still preserving shape.

Have a look at histograms you see in reports and magazines. Quite often about five or six classes provide a useful picture. This is not a rule, just a thought.

***

Note that in defining class boundaries limiting values appear twice: 0–20, 20–40, so where to put a spend of exactly £20? Choose either class but be consistent.

Using the symbols < for "less than" and ≤ for "less than or equal to" you could define classes unambiguously as, for instance, 0 < spend ≤ 20 and 20 < spend ≤ 40. But for most purposes 0–20, 20–40 communicates more easily. The ambiguity is seldom relevant when presenting a table or chart. So long as *you* know, of course.

***

You will not often want to group data in classes of unequal width (Example 2). You might if you have a highly skewed {A10} distribution or, more likely, you have data already classified by someone else (in a report, say) and you want to make a histogram.

Making the chart as in Example 1, height proportional to frequency, gives the histogram at right.

The story this tells is that there are a lot of data in the last class. But it only looks like this because the class is wider. The eye reads *area*.

This is a false picture.

Plot the histogram with height proportional to density. This is always the right thing to do. Example 1 is a special case of equal width classes so a shortcut is possible. There are two consequences of using density:

First, for the rectangles of a histogram **area is proportional to frequency** — not height but area.

Second, it is simpler and no loss of clarity to omit the vertical axis. If not, what would you call it? Frequency is wrong and density probably confusing. The picture stands without it.

In EXCEL 1. The chart

With equal width classes just repeat the process in {A2} except that at step 4 close the gap between classes.

With unequal width classes you are making EXCEL do something for which it was not built. It only recognises equal width classes so, in Example 2, create 4 classes, the last two each with density 3.5. This gives a four class chart. If you colour all the bars that is fine: it looks like a three class chart as shown.

For the values on the horizontal axis you can just use the same method as in Example 1.

Alternatively, you can cheat again to get the chart in Example 2. Use the *Insert/Shapes* menu again but this time insert a textbox, white background and axis values, and overlay the axis labels EXCEL has given. Again, it is clumsy but it works. Use it or not.

In EXCEL 2. Getting class frequencies from data

You have spend data for 10 customers in A1:A10 and have designed a table with three classes each of width 5.

Select the cells where you want the frequencies to be shown, F3:F5.

Use the f_x button to get the FREQUENCY function from the *Statistics* menu.

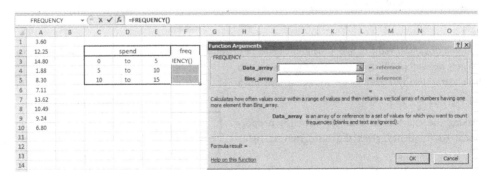

Select the data in Data_array.

EXCEL calls classes bins. In Bins_array select all the upper class bounds except the last. The first and last classes are open-ended; less than or equal to 5 and over 10.

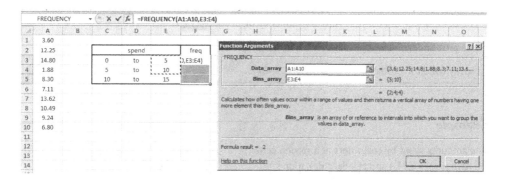

DO NOT CLICK ON OK.

With your left hand hold down the CTRL and SHIFT keys. Then, with your right hand, press the ENTER key.

Your table is complete.

If you have installed the *Data Analysis Toolpak* use the *Histogram* option to get the same result.

	A	B	C	D	E	F
1	3.60					
2	12.25			spend		freq
3	14.80		0	to	5	2
4	1.88		5	to	10	4
5	8.30		10	to	15	4
6	7.11					
7	13.62					
8	10.49					
9	9.24					
10	6.80					
11						

A4. Density functions

> A density function for a continuous variable defines a curve the vertical axis of which measures density.
>
> The **area** under the curve is relative frequency or probability {B2}
>
> The area under the whole curve is 1.0 or 100%.
>
> Mostly used for probability models {C3, C5–C7}.

Example

The amounts spent by customers at a garden centre have MEAN = £34.4 and standard deviation STDEV = £17.7 {A6, A7}.

The distribution of the spend is described by the curve at right {C6}.

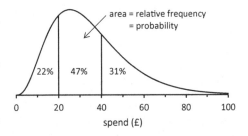

Proportions in each of three bands can be found easily once you have the EXCEL function (from{C6} in this case).

Rationale

The distribution of values of a continuous variable can be pictured in a histogram {A3}. The area of each rectangle of the histogram is frequency or, more usefully, relative frequency.

Imagine that you had an infinity of data so that you could make the classes as narrow as you wish while preserving the shape of the distribution. The bars of the histogram would merge to give a smooth curve, the density function:

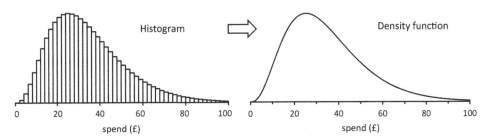

The same distributions that describe relative frequency are also, and more often, used to describe probability {B2}. In the Example say either that 22% of shoppers spend less than £20 or that the probability that the next shopper at the garden centre will spend less than £20 is 22%.

***

The shapes of different density functions {C3, C5–C7} are defined by formulae usually based on some assumptions about process or behaviour and so they provide a model for those behaviours. The model parameters can usually be found from MEAN {A6} and standard deviation, STDEV {A7}.

These models help in what-if testing for management decisions.

There usually is not any convenient formula for finding the area, which is what you want, but EXCEL functions do the job.

A5. No more than that: the cumulative distribution

To answer "how many equal to or less than?" or "what percentage equal to or less than?" use a cumulative distribution of frequency or relative frequency.

Example 1. From a relative frequency distribution {A2}.

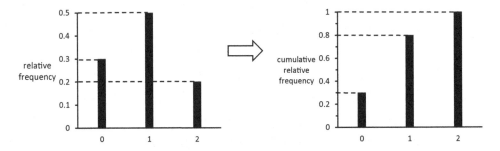

Example 2. From a histogram or table {A3}.

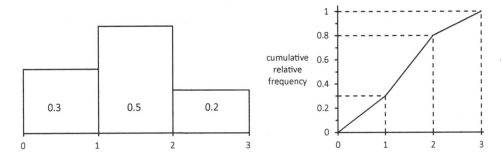

Example 3. From a density function {A4}. These are also **called distribution functions.**

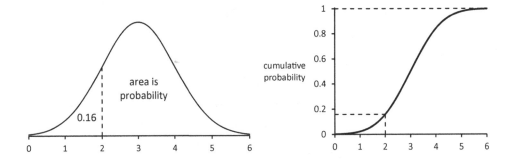

In EXCEL

Ten calls to a helpline were timed and are shown in cells A1:A10.

To get a cumulative distribution from data
(a) Sort the data.
    Select the cells and use *Sort & Filter* to *Sort Smallest to Largest.*
(b) To get cumulative frequency in percent number observations 10, 20, ..., 100.
    Use *Insert/Scatter* to get a chart.
(c) The result is correct but looks horrible, so
(d) Format the chart using the layout options.

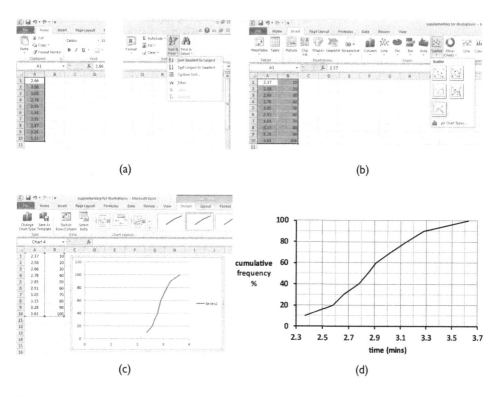

(a)   (b)

(c)   (d)

Note the gap at the start of the curve.

This may look odd but remember that the cumulative distribution shows the percentage of your data less than or equal to any value. Around 10% of your data (one observation) had a value less than *or equal to* the smallest value, 2.37. There will always be a gap like this when plotting data. The gap looks big here because you only had 10 values. If you had 100 the lowest value on the vertical axis would be 1%, not 10%, a smaller gap.

A6. Averages

> Use one of three measures:
>
> MODE — the most frequently occurring value
> · MEDIAN — splits ordered data into halves
> MEAN — the sum divided by the number of values

Example. Seven people give the number of flights they took last year: 2, 3, 3, 5, 7, 9, 12

MODE = 3. This occurs twice, all other values occur only once.

MEDIAN = 5. Three values are less than 5 and three higher.

If there were an even number of data, 2, 3, 3, 5, 7, 9 take the MEAN of the middle two: MEDIAN = $(3+5)/2 = 4$.

MEAN = $(2+3+3+5+7+9+12)/7 = 41/7 = 5.86$

Rationale

Perhaps the easiest idea of average is that it is the value in the middle of the data. But what does this mean? One interpretation of the middle is that it splits the data into two halves. This value is called the **MEDIAN**.

Because the MEDIAN only needs you to be able to order values it can be used with ordinal data {A1} as in attitude surveys {A13} when the responses are some version of agree, do not know, disagree.

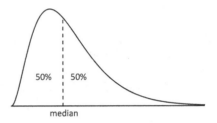

***

The average that most of us would find, without prompting, is just the sum divided by the number of values: this is called the **MEAN**. It represents another idea of being in the middle of the data. It is the balance point or centre of gravity. If weights were placed at points corresponding to the values then the MEAN would be the place where a balance is found. The mean of 2, 3 and 7 is $(2+3+7)/3 = 4$:

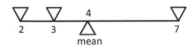

Unlike the other two measures the MEAN is affected by extreme values. If the highest value had been 17 then MEAN = 7.3. This can sometimes be important. For instance, the mean income in a country is likely to be very skewed {A10} to the extent that changes in the incomes of the highest earners result in an increase in mean income but the vast majority are no better off or may be worse off. Economists studying incomes therefore usually prefer to use the MEDIAN, which is unaffected by increases (or decreases) in the extremes. Deciding which average to use is important.

The MEAN can be used in calculation in way that the MEDIAN and MODE cannot. If the MEAN weight of components is 53.24g then a good estimate of the weight of a 100 components is 100×53.24 g = 5324g {B7}.

***

The third idea of average, of a typical value, is that value which is more frequently found than any other. This most popular value is called the **MODE**:

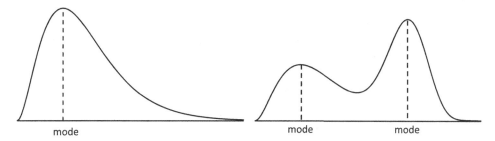

Unlike the MEAN and the MEDIAN, the MODE is not necessarily unique. This may be considered as an inconvenience or as a useful diagnostic aid: a production process may have two causes of failure and the two modes show this.

You can find the MODE for any type of variable: the most popular colour of shirt is pink.

***

When distributions are symmetric the three measures of average have the same value.

For asymmetric distributions the differences between the averages help you to assess the asymmetry or *skewness* {A10}.

***

Think before you choose which measure to use. Use more than one if that makes sense.

In making your decision you will have to take a view of what you think should be emphasised.

Here is a summary:

MODE   the most frequently occurring value
        not necessarily unique (which may help identify sub-populations)
        can be used with any variable, including nominal

MEDIAN splits ordered data into halves
        the middle value
        data must be at least ordinal, but not necessarily numeric
        unaffected by the value of all but the middle one or two data

MEAN   the centre of gravity of the distribution
        uses all data and so is affected by extremes
        can be used in calculations to give totals
        can only be used with ratio data

In EXCEL use functions

MEDIAN
MODE   If there is no mode (all values are unique) get the error message #N/A .
AVERAGE This calculates the MEAN.

A7. Spread

> Use one of the measures based on *range*:
>
> | | |
> |---|---|
> | RANGE | highest value − lowest value |
> | INTERQUARTILE RANGE | middle 50% of data |
> | INTERDECILE RANGE | middle 80% of data, |
>
> or one based on *deviation* from the MEAN:
>
> mean absolute deviation = MAD = MEAN[ABS(deviation)]
>
> variance = VAR = MEAN[(deviation)^2]
>
> standard deviation = STDEV = $\sqrt{\text{VAR}}$.

Example

The times (in minutes) taken by a machinist to sew ten items of clothing are given in the table. They have been ordered for convenience of presentation.

In a spreadsheet the times are in cells B2:B11.

	Time	deviation	ABS(deviation)	deviation^2
1	2.37	−0.554	0.554	0.307
2	2.58	−0.344	0.344	0.118
3	2.66	−0.264	0.264	0.070
4	2.78	−0.144	0.144	0.021
5	2.85	−0.074	0.074	0.005
6	2.91	−0.014	0.014	0.000
7	3.03	0.106	0.106	0.011
8	3.15	0.226	0.226	0.051
9	3.28	0.356	0.356	0.127
10	3.63	0.706	0.706	0.498
MEAN:		0.000	0.279	0.121

Spread based on range:

range = 2.37 to 3.63   for unordered data use functions MIN(B2:B11) and MAX(B2:B11)

then   lower quartile = QUARTILE.EXC(B2:B11, 1) = 2.64
upper quartile = QUARTILE.EXC(B2:B11, 3) = 3.18
the middle 50% of times are between 2.64 minutes and 3.18 minutes,

or   lower decile = PERCENTILE.EXC(B2:B11, 0.1) = 2.39
upper decile = PERCENTILE.EXC(B2:B11, 0.9) = 3.60
the middle 80% of times are between 2.39 minutes and 3.60 minutes.

Spread based on deviation:

MAD = 0.279

VAR = VAR.P(B2:B11) = 0.121   This is the variance of these 10 data.

VAR = VAR.S(B2:B11) = 0.134   But this is the best estimate of population variance from a sample: all this machinist's work not just these ten items. This is the most usual case {F6}.

STDEV = STDEV.S(B2:B11) = 0.366   = $\sqrt{0.134}$

Report the RANGE and INTERQUARTILE RANGE. This is easily understood.

Report the standard deviation if you are going to use the result for modelling {C3,C5–C6} or for inference {e.g. F3}.

Rationale

There are a two broad ideas about spread which can be summarised as:

"what are the highest and lowest values?"

and   "on average, how far away from the mean are the data?"

These two ideas give measures based on *range* and *deviation*:

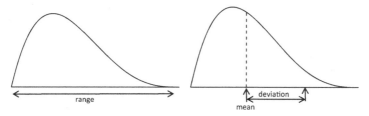

The RANGE is just the difference between the highest and lowest values. This is fine if the data we have are the whole population. If they are a sample from the population, which is more likely, then the range, being determined by only the two most extreme values, may be quite different from one sample to another. You want to use the range because it is so simple, anyone can understand it, but you see that a measure which is volatile is not of much use.

Therefore:

Disregard the most extreme values and report the trimmed range.

The two most popular of these reduced ranges are the INTERDECILE RANGE, which disregards the upper and lower 10% of the distribution, and the INTERQUARTILE RANGE, which disregards the upper and lower 25% of the distribution:

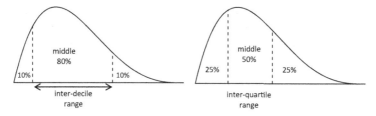

Think about how you want to report these ranges:

"the inter-quartile range is 0.54"

or "the middle 50% of times are between 2.64 mins and 3.16 mins, a range of 0.54 mins"

***

You have used some measure of average, probably the MEAN. It is natural to want a measure of the possible deviations from that average.

Taking the MEAN deviation seems a good idea but is useless because it will always be zero (as in the Example). This is because the MEAN is the centre of gravity of the data {A6} and so deviations, positive on one side and negative on the other, must always cancel. But you still want some measure of whether the deviations are, on average, large or small.

Therefore:

Avoid the cancelling effect by either by making all deviations positive or by squaring them.

The first method takes the absolute value (ABS in EXCEL) of each deviation to get the *mean absolute deviation*, MAD. This is an easily understood measure. It is used by forecasters in describing forecast errors but is not much used elsewhere.

The second method, squaring, gives variance, VAR. Variance is important when building statistical models. For example, it is the only measure of risk which can be summed when combining risky outcomes {E10}. But squaring deviations also squares the units in which they are measured: in the Example variance is measured in minutes^2. To have a measure in the original units take the square root to get standard deviation, STDEV, measured in minutes.

There is one change to make. Taking the mean squared deviation, 0.121 in the Example, certainly does give the variance of your data. But usually this is not what you want. Your data are a sample only and what you want is the best estimate you can get of the variance of the population from which the data are drawn. The simple correction factor {F6} is SAMPLESIZE/(SAMPLESIZE − 1): in the Example $0.121 \times 10/9 = 0.134$. This is the sum of squared deviations divided by (SAMPLESIZE − 1).

***

The spread of a distribution can be interpreted as error or uncertainty or risk. Which measure to use?

If your purpose is **reporting**, ranges are immediately understood and so are good for reporting spread to anyone. You may want to give a graphical summary using them; particularly good when comparing distributions {A11}.

If your purpose is **analysis** for **modelling** {C3, C5–C6} or **inference** {F2, F3} use standard deviation. It will be hard to describe to an audience with little or no statistical background just what a standard deviation is. Most people envision it in the context of Normally distributed variables {C3} — 95% of the distribution is within 2 standard deviations of the MEAN.

In **EXCEL**

The functions are given in the Example.

EXCEL gives two functions for evaluating quartiles (and percentiles too). Why?

Look at the Table in the Example. The lower quartile defines the lowest 10/4 = 2.5 values. This is somewhere between the second and third data, 2.58 and 2.66. There are many ways of interpolating an appropriate value (in a survey of methods Eric Langford found 15). The function QUARTILE.EXC uses one such method and gives quartiles which look about right: 2.64 is indeed between 2.58 and 2.66.

The function QUARTILE.INC uses another method and gives a lower quartile of 2.69. (This function is identical to the function QUARTILE in older versions of EXCEL.)

The differences between the results of the two functions (and the other thirteen!) get less as sample size increases.

Since quartiles are just particular percentiles these comments hold for the two forms of the PERCENTILE function too.

You have to choose. The .EXC functions look good.

A8. Calculation from tables

> Data have been grouped into classes. For each class find
>
> mid-point — m
> relative frequency as a proportion — p
>
> Then MEAN = SUM(p × m)
> variance = VAR = SUM[p × (m − MEAN)²].

Example

You are analysing the sizes of businesses in London. You have this table for 2012 (businesses are called workplaces in the census):

no. of employees	mid-point, m	number of workplaces number	number of workplaces proportion, p	p × m	p × (m − 333.827)²
1–9	5.0	282,310	0.755	3.774	81,620.989
10–49	29.5	34,090	0.091	2.689	8,442.065
50–249	149.5	13,225	0.035	5.287	1,201.475
250–499	374.5	4,130	0.011	4.136	18.268
500–2499	1499.5	10,955	0.029	43.924	39,802.073
2500 or more	3500.0	29,280	0.078	274.018	784,838.499
		373,990	1.000	333.827	915,923.368

Source: Office of National Statistics

MEAN = 338.83.
VAR = 915,923.368.
STDEV = √915,923.368 = 957.04

Rationale

You have a table from a report. You need to estimate the mean and variance but do not have the original data.

Therefore:

Make an approximation. Use the class mid-point for all data in each class.

You are not assuming that all businesses in each class have the same number of employees.

You are assuming that, in the first class in the Example, 5 × 282,310 = 1,411,550 is a good estimate of the number of people working in all the businesses with no more than 9 employees.

***

Sometimes, as here, the first or last class or both may be open-ended so you cannot take the mid-point. This needs you to make one of those sensible but arbitrary decisions. Fortunately, almost by definition, only a small proportion of your data will be in these classes so the effect of the arbitrariness is unlikely to be great.

A9. Coefficient of variation

> To assess if variability is likely to be a cause for concern use
>
> coefficient of variation = STDEV/MEAN.
>
> The higher the value the more important the variability is likely to be.
>
> This is an initial assessment only.

Example

Engineering components are made and have a mean weight of 2.5kg. The standard deviation of the weights is 0.1kg.

coefficient of variation = STDEV/MEAN = 0.1/2.5 = 0.04 or 4%

Rationale

Variation is important. It can result in costly sub-standard output.

Variation is most obviously measured by standard deviation, STDEV {A7}, and this is mostly what you need to measure process capability {J5, J6}. But sometimes you may want to compare variation for processes with different average output. For example, the same engineering company may also make a different model component with average weight MEAN = 1.5kg, so coefficient of variation = 6.7%. This level of variation might be more important.

***

This is no magic number but it may be useful in comparing different processes or performance levels.

You will need a context (it is your business after all) to interpret this ratio: how big is significant?

***

Versions of this coefficient are used in other sorts of business. For example, in measuring financial risk {K1}.

A10. Skew

To show the **shape** of a distribution make a chart {A2,A3}.

How symmetrical is the shape?

If you want a measure of the skewness of the distribution and you have the data use the EXCEL function SKEW.

If you do not have the data use

$$\text{SKEWP} = 3 \times (\text{MEAN} - \text{MEDIAN})/\text{STDEV}.$$

(The P is for Karl Pearson who proposed this formula.)

Do not mix these measures; be consistent.

Example 1

The table shows passengers (millions) at the 30 busiest airports in 2011.

ATL	92.4	DEN	52.8	SFO	40.9
PEK	78.7	CGK	51.5	PHK	40.6
LHR	69.4	DXB	51.0	LAS	40.6
ORD	66.7	AMS	49.8	IAH	40.1
HND	62.6	MAD	49.7	CLT	39.0
LAX	61.9	BKK	47.9	MIA	38.3
CDG	61.0	JFK	47.6	MUC	37.8
DFW	57.8	SIN	46.5	KUL	37.7
FRA	56.4	CAN	45.0	FCO	37.7
HKG	53.3	PVG	41.4	IST	37.4

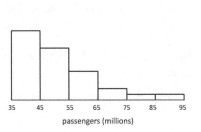

passengers (millions)

Source: Airports Council International

Using the EXCEL function SKEW = 1.34

Example 2

For the data above, if you only had the histogram and some summary measures:

MEAN   = 51.12
MEDIAN = 48.78
STDEV   = 13.30

so SKEWP   = $3 \times (51.12 - 48.78)/13.30 = 0.53$

Rationale

The main thing is to look at the distribution, this will probably be all you need to do:

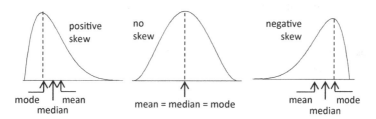

The descriptive names give you a language for talking about skew. In the Example there is a strong positive skew.

Note the order of the three measures of average {A6}.

***

You may sometimes also want a numeric measure of skew to help in comparing distributions or to make an inference {F1, F2} about the population skew.

Several measures have been proposed. Look at SKEWP. The value of (MEAN − MEDIAN)/STDEV measures the difference between MEAN and MEDIAN in standard deviations, which might help interpretation {C4}. If MEAN is greater than MEDIAN the skew is positive, if it is less skew is negative and if they are the same there is no skew.

The meaning of SKEWP is intuitively obvious

(MEAN − MEDIAN)/STDEV has values between −1 and +1 so SKEWP is bounded by −3 and +3, though these extremes are rarely found.

Values further from zero indicate greater skew.

***

The EXCEL function SKEW is not so easy to explain. It is generally considered to have better mathematical characteristics and so is almost universally used.

It has the same general properties — the further from 0 the greater the skew

As implemented in EXCEL there is a sampling correction built in. The assumption is that your data are a sample and you want the best estimate of the skew in the population from which the sample is drawn. This is what the function gives.

In the unlikely event that your data are not a sample but are the population multiply the function value by

$$(\text{SAMPLESIZE} - 2)/\sqrt{[\text{SAMPLESIZE} \times (\text{SAMPLESIZE} - 1)]}$$

In Example 1

$$1.34 \times 28/\surd(30 \times 29) = 1.34 \times 0.95 = 1.27$$

This correction does not apply to SKEWP.

***

Do not calculate these skew measures (or anything, of course) just because you can. A picture may be all you need to see the shape of the data.

A11. Picturing more than one distribution with boxplots

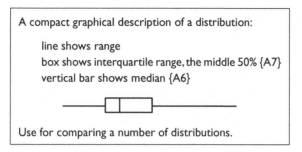

A compact graphical description of a distribution:

line shows range
box shows interquartile range, the middle 50% {A7}
vertical bar shows median {A6}

Use for comparing a number of distributions.

Example

An agricultural foodstuffs business sells a cattle feed supplement in 5kg sacks. The product is made at a central plant and transported in bulk to four regional depots, A–D, where it is put into sacks and sold to farmers. This is not a very precise process. The amount per sack seems about right: the MEDIAN weights of bags sampled are 4.95, 4.98, 4.95 and 5.08 at the depots. A plot of the distributions gives an idea of variation but is hard to read. Four box plots make an easier report.

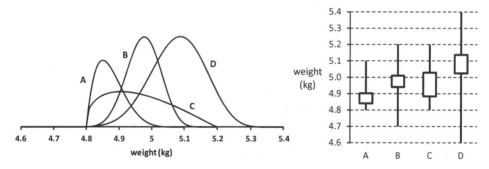

Rationale

You need a graphical comparison of a number of distributions. Just plotting a number of density functions {A4}, as shown above, or histograms {A3} can give a cluttered chart. It is hard to make a useful comparison.

Therefore:

Use an edited plot. You will lose some information but gain clarity. Use boxplots.

You will not be able to identify some features (multiple modes, for instance) but these are rare. If they are present decide if they are important. If they are important you may need either to abandon box-plots or make an annotation. This is unlikely to be a problem.

***

There are variations on the boxplot theme. For example, some statistical packages show data more than three standard deviations from the mean as outliers. If you are not using EXCEL check what your software shows.

You may choose to use the main line of the boxplot to show interdecile range {A7} rather than the range so as not to have a plot sensitive to extremes.

As with all editing you need to think what you want to say.

***

There are other ways of visually comparing distributions. In a piece in the *Financial Times* of 21 February 2015 headed *Walmart Raises the Bar for Low-Pay Employers*, the pay of different occupations in the US grocery sector were compared. The nine occupations were:

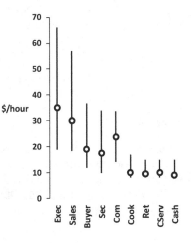

> Top executive, Sales manager, Buyer/purchasing agent, Security guard, Communications worker, Cook, Retail sales worker, Customer service representative, Cashier.

The comparison used a chart much like that at right.

The lines show the interdecile range {A7} covering the middle 80% of pay and the circles show the MEDIAN {A6}.

statsNote {G5} shows how to make these charts in EXCEL and also shows another use of them to show confidence intervals for estimates.

In EXCEL

EXCEL does not do boxplots. Using one of the financial stock options gives almost all you want. But not quite all, that is why the medians are not shown in the Example: just range and interquartile range.

Arrange the data as shown, with labels as the first row. Select these cells.

Choose *Insert/Other Charts/Stock* and the second chart type.

Click and you have the chart. Arrange the layout to suit your audience.

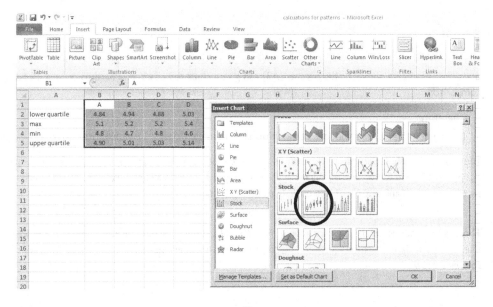

A12. Be kind to your audience and keep it simple

When presenting data make it as easy as possible for your audience to see what is going on. **Do not:**

> give results that you do not use
>
> give numbers with spurious precision and distracting strings of digits
>
> confuse the eye with silly graphics
>
> dump numbers in a table with no thought of how it looks

You will have gone to some trouble to collect and analyse the data. Make sure that your audience sees clearly what you are trying to tell them.

Example 1. Edit before using

You may have loaded the *Analysis Toolpak* into your copy of EXCEL.

If you have you may be tempted by the *Descriptive statistics* option. If you use that for the data in {A10} you will get the table at right.

This is very convenient. With just one click you have all these numbers.

Two questions:

1. Do you need them all? Clearly not the MODE, but what about Skewness and Kurtosis? Do you need Standard Error?
   Remove anything that **you** will not use in **your** report. Do not let your audience do your editing for you.
2. Do you need that level of precision?
   The mean is 51.1220557. Oh good.
   Probably 51.12 is good enough for your purpose. People will be able to comprehend 51.12 but will switch off when faced with 51.1220557.

Column1	
Mean	51.1220557
Standard Error	2.427896297
Median	48.7819795
Mode	#N/A
Standard Deviation	13.29813567
Sample Variance	176.8404124
Kurtosis	1.996665268
Skewness	1.344121983
Range	54.982998
Minimum	37.406025
Maximum	92.389023
Sum	1533.661671
Count	30

Example 2. It is not for a T-shirt

On the next page is another version of the chart in {A2}.

Why are the columns shown as rods or whatever they are?

Why those odd grid lines drawn on two sides of a shoe box? This is a simple two-dimensional picture. Adding extra dimensions looks fancy but is less clear because the third dimension is redundant.

Why the series key when you only have one series?

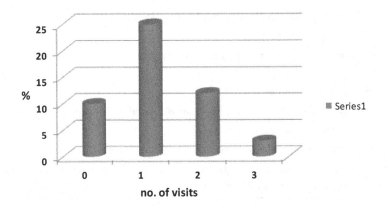

You may prefer a pie-chart. Ok, but remember that the eye reads **area** so make sure that the true area is shown as a circle (below right) and not distorted into an ellipse (left).

Again, why the third dimension?

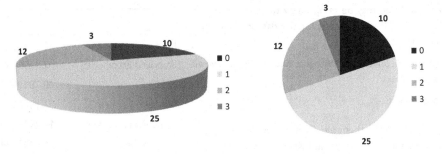

Example 3. Table

The table, Employment by Major Industries (2006), was published in the magazine *Barbados 2008* using data from the Labour Force Survey of the Barbados Statistical Service.

Employment by Major Industrial Division

Industry	2006
Sugar	400
Other Agriculture and Fishing	4,300
Construction/Quarrying	14,500
Manufacturing	5,500
Electricity/Gas/Water	2,300
Tourism	13,500
Wholesale and Retail Trade	16,700
Transport and Communication	4,400
Financial Services/Business Services	9,800
Government Services	27,100
General Services	32,000
Not Stated	200
Total	130,700

Why all those heavy grid lines?

Why that ordering?

All values seem to be in 100s.

Employment by Major Industries (2006)

Industry	Employment ('000)	%
General Services	32.0	24
Government Services	27.1	21
Wholesale and Retail Trade	16.7	13
Construction and Quarrying	14.5	11
Tourism	13.5	10
Financial and Business Services	9.8	7
Manufacturing	5.5	4
Transport and Communication	4.4	3
Other Agriculture and Fishing	4.3	3
Electricity, Gas and Water	2.3	2
Sugar	0.4	0
Not Stated	0.2	0
Total	130.7	100

This second table is better.

Giving the values in thousands cleans up the presentation and makes it easier to see the magnitude.

Giving percentages immediately helps the reader make sense of the structure of the economy.

Ordering according to size is another big help.

(In case you are wondering my guess is that sugar was put first because of an important cultural resonance for the island and its history of sugar and rum and the slavery that went with them.)

45

A13. Agree/disagree/neither

To present the results of a five-point (or seven-point or...) survey use:

Chart centred on mid-class

Median

Interquartile range

Example

A survey of job satisfaction[1] asked 512 employees to rate their satisfaction with five aspects of their job. Here are the results, in percentages:

	very dissatisfied	dissatisfied	neither	satisfied	very satisfied
Physical conditions	11.9	27.0	32.2	22.9	6.1
Recognition for good work	1.0	7.8	45.1	41.0	5.1
Rate of pay	37.7	35.2	22.1	4.5	0.6
Staff/management relations	1.2	2.3	33.8	52.5	10.2
Job security	2.5	8.4	54.7	32.0	2.3

Though only five classes are used it is not easy to read the table. Use a chart:

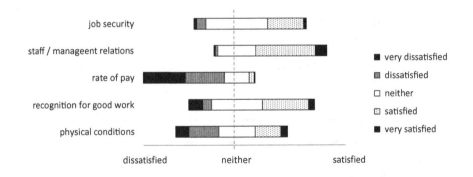

Notice that the horizontal bars are centred on the middle of the *neither* category. This makes it easy to see the strength of opinion in each direction. The intensity of the shading helps too (even better in colour).

If it is useful, supplement the chart with some measures of average and spread. Since the response is ordinal use MEDIAN or MODE {A6} for average and QUARTILES {A7} for spread:

46

	lower quartile	upper quartile	median	mode
Physical conditions	dissatisfied	satisfied	neither	neither
Recognition for good work	neither	satisfied	neither	neither
Rate of pay	very dissatisfied	neither	dissatisfied	very dissatisfied
Staff/management relations	neither	satisfied	satisfied	satisfied
Job security	neither	satisfied	neither	neither

Rationale

Opinion or attitude surveys are popular. You will have been asked to complete several, I am sure. But how to summarise?

The question asked in the survey requires an ordinal {A1} response: *very satisfied* expresses a greater degree of satisfaction than *satisfied*, but you can say no more.

Were you just itching to label the five responses 1, 2, 3, 4, 5?

Do not do it. The temptation is to believe that you have defined numbers on a ratio scale {A1} so that you can calculate the MEAN {A6} and other summaries. But this is an illusion. All you have done is to alter the labels. You could just as have easily used A, B, C, D, E.

You have ordinal survey data and need to show it.

> Therefore:
> Remember you have *ordinal* data. Use a diverging stacked bar chart (as in the Example), MEDIAN and QUARTILES.

Treating ordinal values as numbers rather than labels is, you will have seen, very common. Many people like the simplicity of ticking or circling one of five simple answers. It is quick and so encourages completion of the questionnaire. Unfortunately, many of these same people also like means and standard deviations because they can then use quite powerful methods (called *parametric* methods) to make inferences ({F15} for example). Other *non-parametric* methods are available for ordinal data: in these notes the chi-squared test {I1} would help you to judge if the responses to different questions were plausibly indicative of real differences in the population from which the respondents were drawn.

But assuming labels to be numbers is common. Psychologists and some others do this a lot. The five or more point scale is usually and wrongly called a Likert scale. A distinction is made between a Likert *item*, the responses to a single question, and a Likert *scale*. The Likert scale takes several (about eight is the minimum) Likert items which are believed all to measure the same attitude, assigns number values 1, 2, ... the responses and finds the mean score. The article from which the data described above are taken provides an example.

The argument, which is pragmatic rather than theoretical, is that this works in that calculations can be made and conclusions drawn. Other people do not buy this at all. Ordinal data are ordinal, whatever you do with them. Opinion is, to put it politely, divided. Much research in psychology, business, marketing and elsewhere relies on this numerical aggregation. The literature can get quite heated.

There seems agreement that responses to individual questions should be treated as ordinal. This does not stop abuse, but at least it will not be you.

Think about it:

$(4+5)/2 = 4.5$

(satisfied + very satisfied)/2 = ?

In EXCEL

[NOTE: Because this book is printed in black and white these charts are shown with patterns and borders rather than the colours EXCEL will give. This is to make the charts easier to read in this format.]

The table in the Example is in A1:F6.

Select those cells.

Select *Insert* and the stacked bar chart.

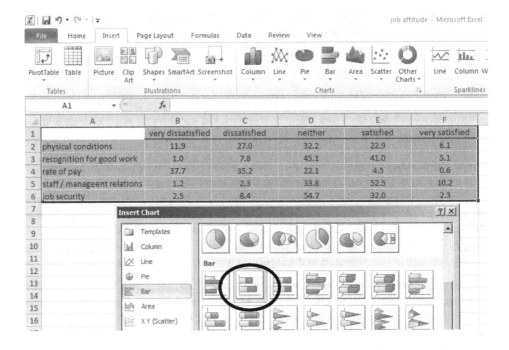

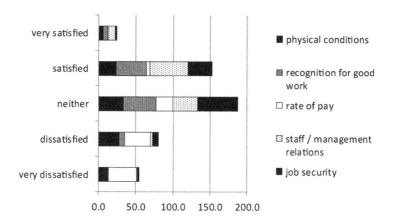

You have this chart.

The axes are the wrong way round.

Select *Design/Select Data/Switch*

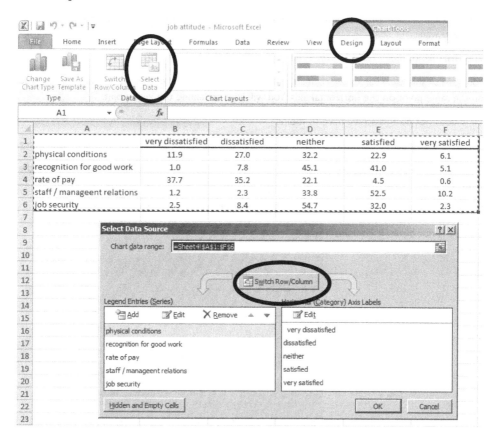

49

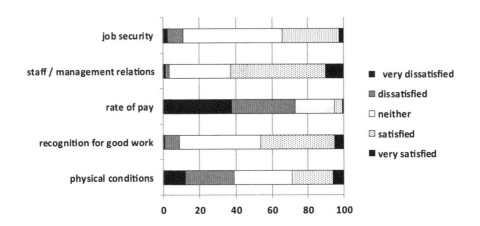

You can easily give axis titles and make other formatting changes to get the chart you prefer.

But

The bars all have the same fixed end points, 0 and 100. Your eye is drawn to the ends, which is not what you want.

The chart is not much easier to read than the table.

You need to shift each bar to the right so that the middle of the *neither* class for each item is centred on the same point on the horizontal axis. You will have redefined the zero point.

EXCEL does not do this so we have to fool it.

Put a blank class to the left of each bar so that each bar moves to be centred over the same point.

This means the sum of the percentages *very dissatisfied* and *dissatisfied* and half *neither* must have the same value.

Here is the adjusted spreadsheet. Column B is inserted and contains the new blank class.

Cell B1 is not blank. It contains a space.

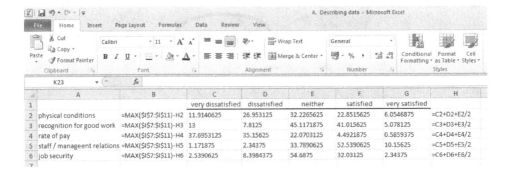

And the results are:

	A	B	C	D	E	F	G	H
1			very dissatisfied	dissatisfied	neither	satisfied	very satisfied	
2	physical conditions	28.91	11.9	27.0	32.2	22.9	6.1	55.0
3	recognition for good work	52.54	1.0	7.8	45.1	41.0	5.1	31.3
4	rate of pay	0.00	37.7	35.2	22.1	4.5	0.6	83.9
5	staff / manageent relations	63.48	1.2	2.3	33.8	52.5	10.2	20.4
6	job security	45.61	2.5	8.4	54.7	32.0	2.3	38.3

Get a Stacked Bar chart as before, making sure you highlight all columns A to G:

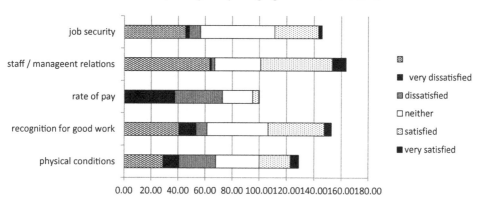

Make the leftmost class invisible by right clicking on the leftmost section of any bar and selecting *No fill.*

Make any formatting changes to get the chart you want.

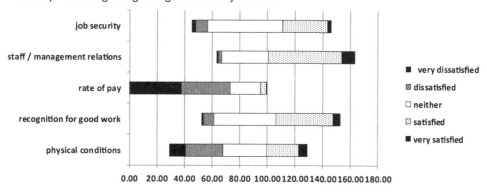

51

For the chart in the Example I clicked on the chart and used the *Insert/Shapes* option twice,

to insert the dashed vertical line above the central value, 83.9 (the maximum in column H);

to overlay a text box on the horizontal axis.

Clumsy, but it works if that is what you want.

Look at the chart in the Example. The eye is now attracted first to the central dashed line and you can read deviations from that.

Probability: the language of uncertainty

---

overview

Probability is the language of uncertainty.

We may not know exactly what is going to happen (will sales increase?) or exactly what state a system is in (just what is our market share?) but whatever the source of our uncertainty the result may be described using this common language {B1}.

Use a *probability distribution* {B2} to describe how uncertain you are about all possible values of a variable. This will help in finding the probabilities of a subset of those possible values (B3, B4).

The interaction (or lack of it) between two variables is of management concern for several reasons {B5}. A simple probability model {B6} describes the interaction.

Even though we are uncertain we still have to make decisions. The idea of expected value {B7} often gives a useful starting point.

Once you have probability values you need to tell others about them. To an audience unfamiliar with probability this is challenging. Using words to describe different levels of uncertainty offers a way to make an effective report, though you will need to be careful just what you say {B8, B10}.

Knowing a little probability is not just useful for making calculations. It can also give you a way of avoiding some common errors of judgement {B9}.

B1. Probability

> Probability measures uncertainty.
>
> It is a number between 0 and 1.
>
> PROB = 0 means we are **certain** that something **will not** happen or is **not true**.
>
> PROB = 1 means we are **certain** that something **will** happen or **is true.**
>
> Intermediate values represent degrees of uncertainty.
>
> Express probabilities as fractions, percentages or odds.

Example 1. Reason from basics

Use knowledge of the physical reality of a situation, though these situations are uncommon for managers. For a coin tossing experiment

$$\text{PROB}(\text{coin shows heads}) = \frac{1}{2}$$

Example 2. Use data: relative frequencies give probability values

If 60 in a group of 80 customers are satisfied with the service we provide then for a customer picked at random

$$\text{PROB}(\text{satisfied}) = 60/80 = \frac{3}{4}$$

Write as $\frac{3}{4}$ or 0.75 or 75%. Alternatively, say that the odds are 3:1.

Example 3. Use judgement

You have no relevant data or you do not have the time or money to collect it — what will be the market reception of a completely novel product? It may be that you feel unable to make any probability estimate at all and just go for it (think Masaru Ibuka and the Sony Walkman, Mark Zuckerberg and Facebook). But often you are able to use your judgement expressed as probability; subjective probability, of course {C10–C13}.

Rationale

As the Examples show, uncertainty can be the result of inherent variability — a manufacturing process, customer reaction — or it may arise because you have to make a judgement. Some combination of both is typical of the problems managers face.

Whatever the source some uncertainty is inevitable.

You need a language to describe your uncertainty.[1]

Probability is that language.

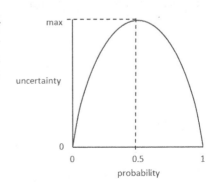

54

B2. Probability distribution

Make a distribution of probability to all possible outcomes in the same way that frequency is distributed.

For a **discrete** variable {A2} the sum of all probabilities must be 1. Make sure that the values are *mutually exclusive*: the variable *must* take one, *but only one*, of the values.

For a **continuous** variable use a density function {A4}. Area = probability. The area under the whole curve is 1 or 100%.

Example 1

About 60% of customers are female and so:

PROB(female) =	0.6	60
PROB(male) =	0.4	40
	1.0	100%

Example 2

The distribution of the value of online orders at an office stationery business is as shown.

The area under the whole curve is 100%: an order must have some value, however big or small.

83% of orders were for no more than £40.

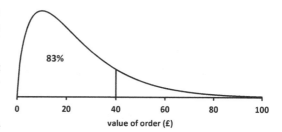

Rationale

However probabilities are arrived at {B1}, it is important that *all* possible outcomes are assessed and probability values given to each. In many cases this is straightforward and a standard probability distribution is often used {C1–C3, C5–C7}.

On the other hand, think of a doctor diagnosing an illness from symptoms. Based on symptoms and tests the doctor makes a judgement about which of the several illnesses the patient might have is the most likely. If the list is not complete and the actual illness is missing then no amount of testing will lead to a correct diagnosis. Perhaps it's an illness which the doctor has never seen before.

Therefore:

For discrete variables list **all** possible mutually exclusive (non-overlapping) values. Make sure probabilities sum to 1.

For continuous variables choose a model with an appropriate range. The area under the curve is 1.

B3. Probability of NOT that

> For some event or value, A, if you know PROB(A) then
>
> PROB(NOT A) = 1 − PROB(A).
>
> The events A and NOT A are *complementary*; they sum to 1 or 100%.

Example 1

The sales of UK national newspapers in January 2014 are shown in the table.

The probability that a newspaper reader reads a paper other than the *Daily Telegraph* is either

PROB(NOT *Daily Telegraph*) = 27.9 + 22.4 + 12.5 + 6.3 + 6.2
$$+ 3.8 + 2.9 + 2.9 + 2.6 + 0.8$$
$$= 93.1\%$$

or PROB(NOT *Daily Telegraph*) = 1 − PROB(*Daily Telegraph*)
$$= 100 − 6.9 = 93.1\%$$

The Sun	2,213,659	27.9
Daily Mail	1,780,565	22.4
Daily Mirror	992,256	12.5
Daily Telegraph	544,546	6.9
Daily Express	500,473	6.3
Daily Star	489,067	6.2
i	298,266	3.8
Financial Times	234,193	2.9
Daily Record	227,639	2.9
The Guardian	207,958	2.6
The Independent	66,576	0.8
	7,939,502	100%

Source: *The Guardian*, 14 February 2014

Example 2

The distribution of the value of online orders at an office stationery business is as shown.

The probability that the next order is greater than £40 is
PROB(more than £40)
$$= 100 − \text{PROB}(\text{NOT more than £40})$$
$$= 100 − 83 = 17\%$$

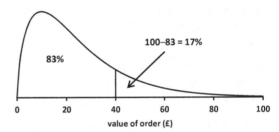

Rationale

You need the probability that a variable has some value or values which it would be difficult, or just tedious, to find. It would, however, be easier to find the probability that the variable does not have that value or values.

Therefore:

Find the easier probability and subtract from 1.

This relies on the events being *mutually exclusive*. This is usually the case:

> you can't both read the *Daily Telegraph* and not read the *Daily Telegraph*
> an order can't both be over £40 and not over £40.

There are ways of dealing with events which are not mutually exclusive {B4}. This will happen only infrequently.

B4. Probability of this OR that

> If two events or propositions, A and B, are mutually exclusive then
>
> $$\text{PROB}(A \text{ OR } B) = \text{PROB}(A) + \text{PROB}(B)$$
>
> otherwise $\quad \text{PROB}(A \text{ OR } B) = \text{PROB}(A) + \text{PROB}(B) - \text{PROB}(A \text{ AND } B)$

Example 1

The sales of UK national newspapers in January 2014 are shown in the table.

The probability that a reader who reads only one newspaper reads *either* the *Daily Telegraph or The Sun* is

PROB(*Daily Telegraph* OR *The Sun*)
   = PROB(*Daily Telegraph*) + PROB(*The Sun*)
   = 6.9 + 27.9 = 34.8%

The Sun	2,213,659	27.9
Daily Mail	1,780,565	22.4
Daily Mirror	992,256	12.5
Daily Telegraph	544,546	6.9
Daily Express	500,473	6.3
Daily Star	489,067	6.2
The Times	384,304	4.8
i	298,266	3.8
Financial Times	234,193	2.9
Daily Record	227,639	2.9
The Guardian	207,958	2.6
The Independent	66,576	0.8
	7,939,502	100%

Source: *The Guardian*, 14 February 2014

Example 2

On the 218 trading days on the London Stock Exchange in the first ten months of 2014 share prices in the supermarket company SAINSBURY rose 52% of the time. Shares in the technology group BAE rose 43% of the time. And 24% of the time both rose. On any one of those days the probability that just one of these shares rose is

PROB(BAE **up** OR SAINSBURY **up**)
     = PROB(BAE **up**) + PROB(SAINSBURY **up**) − PROB(BAE **up** AND SAINSBURY **up**)
     = 0.43 + 0.52 − 0.24 = 0.71

Rationale

For Example 2 the situation is:

		SAINSBURY		
		up	down	
BAE	up	0.24	0.19	0.43
	down	0.28	0.29	0.57
		0.52	0.48	

57

The share price movements are not mutually exclusive: the fact that BAE is up does not mean that SAINSBURY can't also be up. The probability that, on a given day, either will rise is shown by the three cells outlined

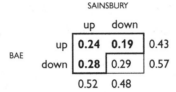

and so PROB(BAE **up** OR SAINSBURY **up**) = 0.24 + 0.19 + 0.28 = 0.71

Just be clear that "either" means either one or the other or both.

Think of this another way:

PROB(BAE **up** AND SAINSBURY **up**) = 0.24 has been counted twice.

Subtracting makes the necessary correction.

***

For Example 1 the situation is:

		reads *The Daily Telegraph?*		
		yes	no	
reads	yes	0	27.9	27.9
The Sun?	no	6.9	65.2	72.1
		6.9	93.1	100%

Because of the assumption that newspaper readers read only one national newspaper the two events, reading *The Sun* and reading *The Daily Telegraph*, are mutually exclusive:

PROB(*Daily Telegraph* AND *The Sun*) = 0

Politicians and media folk apart, this is a pretty fair assumption.

***

Be clear about the different probability distributions {B2} you are dealing with. There are three.

The **joint** distribution shows the probabilities of different combinations of events or outcomes:

SAINSBURY

	up	down
BAE up	0.24	0.19
BAE down	0.28	0.29

A **marginal** distribution shows the probabilities at the edge (margin) of the table. There are two marginal distributions: one showing the probabilities of BAE share movements disregarding what happens to SAINSBURY shares

SAINSBURY

	up	down	
BAE up			0.43
BAE down			0.57

and one showing the probabilities of SAINSBURY share movements disregarding what happens to BAE shares

SAINSBURY

	up	down
BAE up		
BAE down		
	0.52	0.48

Each of these three probability distributions sums to 1.

B5. Independence

> Two variables are independent if knowledge of one provides no information about the other.
>
> Sometimes independence is welcomed, sometimes not.

Example 1. Independence may or may not be welcomed

A pharmaceutical company is developing a new drug.

To establish whether the drug is any good some people are given the drug and some a placebo. Some recover, some don't. The results are tabulated — what was given and whether the patient recovered. Knowing that a patient had the drug should mean a higher chance of recovery. Independence is not what the company wants to see.

Testing for side effects is different. Independence is welcomed: the drug is as safe as the placebo.

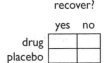

Example 2. Weighing the evidence

You are considering investing in a stock. You read that one bank has downgraded the status of this investment. You think twice. Then you read that a second bank has also issued a downgrade notice. Should you be even more wary?

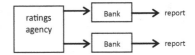

Not if both banks are using the same ratings agency and mostly just passing on what the agency says: you are just hearing the same message twice, not two independent assessments.

Example 3. Is there a pattern?

Cakes are made in standard batches. The number of faults found in each of forty-five batches is shown in the chart.

The manufacturer wants to know if there is any pattern to the faults. If there is it might diagnostically indicate the particular stage at which they occur. The first step is to decide whether the distribution in the chart is compatible with the assumption that rejects occur independently of each other.

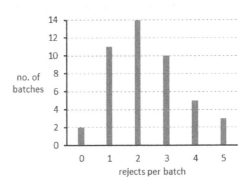

Building a model which assumes independence {C1} and comparing model predictions with data {C8} will help.

Rationale

An awareness of independence, or the lack of it, is one of the most useful ideas to have.

If two variables are not independent this means only that there is an observable correspondence between higher values of one variable and higher (or lower) values of the other. *There is no assumption of causation*, only a quantitative description of regular joint variation {I9}. Your interpretation will depend on causal theoretical frameworks (economics, pharmacology, engineering …). The statistical analysis just helps you identify that there is independence or not. It does not tell you why.

***

Building models is made simpler by assuming independence because then there is no need to account for the interactions between variables {B6}. Many theoretical models use this assumption {C1, C2}. You will need to decide if the assumption is justified.

***

Aggregating product sales forecasts for next year's budget {E11} or shares in an investment portfolio {K3} requires that you know whether the forecasts or returns are independent and, if not, by how much they are correlated {I2}.

Positive correlation increases risk, negative correlation reduces risk {E11}.

B6. Probability of this AND that

> If two events, A and B, are independent then
>
> PROB(A AND B) = PROB(A) × PROB(B)
>
> otherwise PROB(A AND B) = PROB(A GIVEN B) × PROB(B)

Example 1

Around 10% of staff are absent in any year due to domestic accident such as falling off a ladder or slipping on a path. There is no reason to believe that these accidents are related; if I fall that does not make you more or less likely to slip. Using this independence {B5} the probability that of two workers both are absent in this way is $0.1 \times 0.1 = 0.01$.

Example 2

At an Asda supermarket in Leicester an experiment was conducted. Different sorts of music, easily identified as either French or German, were played and the number of bottles of French and German wine bought was noted. During this period the probability that French music was playing was 0.59. When French music was playing the probability that French rather than German wine was bought was 0.83.

The probability that one of the wine buyers bought French wine and French music was playing is:

PROB(French wine AND French music)
= PROB(French wine GIVEN French music) × PROB(French music)
= $0.83 \times 0.59 = 0.49$

Rationale

The table at left shows the data for Example 2 as reported in the *Financial Times* of 13 November 1997. The table at right shows the **joint** and **marginal** probability distributions {B4}.

		Wine bought		
		French	German	
Music	French	40	8	48
played	German	12	22	34
		52	30	82

Frequencies

⇨

		Wine bought		
		French	German	
Music	French	0.49	0.10	0.59
played	German	0.14	0.27	0.41
		0.63	0.37	1.00

Probabilities

When French music was playing the probability that French wine was bought is

PROB(French wine GIVEN French music) = 40/48

also   PROB(French music) = 48/82

so   PROB (French wine AND French music)

= PROB(French wine GIVEN French music) × PROB(French music)

$$= \frac{40}{48} \times \frac{48}{82} = \frac{40}{82} = 0.49$$

The probability PROB(French wine GIVEN French music) is a **conditional** probability. There are four conditional probabilities for this problem:

		Wine bought		
		French	German	
Music	French	0.83	0.17	1.00
played	German	0.35	0.65	1.00

PROB(wine GIVEN music)

		Wine bought	
		French	German
Music	French	0.77	0.27
played	German	0.23	0.73
		1.00	1.00

PROB(music GIVEN wine)

You can use either conditional distribution to get the joint probability:

PROB(French wine AND French music)

= PROB(French music GIVEN French wine) × PROB(French wine)

= 0.77 × 0.63 = 0.49 as before.

***

You want to estimate the probability that one of the 82 purchases was of French wine. The probability estimate you make depends on what you know. If you do not know which music was playing use the marginal probability

PROB(French wine) = 0.63

but if you know which music was playing use the conditional probability, either

PROB(French wine GIVEN French music) = 0.83

or   PROB(French wine GIVEN German music) = 0.35

More information has improved your estimate: it is helpful to know which music was playing.

The different conditional probability distributions describe the strength of the relationship between the two variables. The three probabilities are not the same. These two variables are not independent.

***

In Example 1 there is no relationship. Marginal and conditional probabilities are equal

		worker A		
		accident	no accident	
worker B	accident	0.01	0.09	0.1
	no accident	0.09	0.81	0.9
		0.1	0.9	1.0

63

Your prediction of whether or not A will have an accident is the same whether you know nothing of B or you do. The variables are independent.

worker A

		accident	no accident	
	accident	0.1	0.9	1.0
worker B	no accident	0.1	0.81	1.0
		0.1	0.9	1.0

***

When variables are statistically independent there is no structural relationship to be captured in the conditional probabilities. This is a definition of independence {B5}. The joint probability is just the product of the marginal probabilities:

This forms the basis of a method of testing for independence given some sample data {I1}.

B7. Expected value

> You are uncertain what might happen. There are a number of possible outcomes. Each has a numeric VALUE and probability that it occurs, PROB. A useful summary is
>
> expected value = EV = SUM (PROB × VALUE)

Example 1

A company sells trucks. Based on records the number of trucks sold per week is

UNITS SOLD	PROB	SALES × PROB
0	0.1	0
1	0.3	0.3
2	0.3	0.6
3	0.2	0.6
4	0.1	0.4
	1.0	1.9

EV = 1.9. Expect to sell 1.9 trucks per week, on average; 19 trucks in the next ten weeks.

Example 2

You bid for a new contract to install an air conditioning system for a food producer. The cost of preparing the bid is £50,000. If successful the net profit will be £400,000. You estimate the chance of success at 60%. EV = £220,000

VALUE (£)	PROB	VALUE × PROB
−50,000	0.4	−20,000
400,000	0.6	240,000
		220,000

Rationale

Expected value is a summary with a dual character. In neither example will you get the expected value:

> the truck dealer will not sell 1.9 trucks next week but will sell 0 or 1 or 2 ...
> the contractor will not make £220,000 but will either make £400,000 or lose £50,000.

The difference is that the truck dealer will be selling trucks for a long time (if all goes well) and so can use EV to estimate total sales over a number of weeks.

The contractor cannot do this. The opportunity to bid is irregular and may be infrequent and, in any case, each bid is different with different costs and potential rewards and different chances of success. EV may be of help in comparing different bids {E6} if, for example, limited resources meant that only one bid could be made, though two or three possibilities exist.

If money is an issue (isn't it always?) avoiding the loss of £50,000 may be more important than the possibility of getting £50,000. This difference means that EV may not be a good guide, but it can be adapted {E7}.

B8. Words and numbers

> Communicating probabilities, especially to a general audience, is difficult.
>
> It is natural to use words to do this but be careful. You may think that you are communicating a difficult concept (number) in a more user-friendly way (word) but your audience may interpret your words to mean something other than you intended.

Example

You believe that the probability a sales target will be met is 70%.

You have to make a presentation to your colleagues and believe that they find numerical probabilities hard to understand, possibly they will switch off. To help them you decide to report that it is "quite likely" that the target will be met.

You hope this helps.

Rationale

Reporting probability is genuinely a hard problem.

If probability values are to be used for a calculation the problem doesn't arise. But when the probability value is to be reported, but not immediately used for calculation, the situation is more difficult. It may be that your audience is sufficiently familiar with probabilities that no words are needed. Otherwise it will be part of your responsibility to make a report which conveys your meaning in a way that engages the audience.

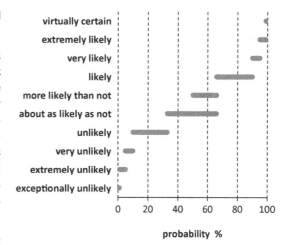

The Intergovernmental Panel on Climate Change (IPCC) certainly faced a communication problem: they had to tell the world's leaders about the risks and uncertainties of threats to the planet. Where outcomes could be estimated probabilistically the IPCC used one of ten phrases to communicate the likelihood of an event happening. The chart shows what they used.[2]

There are ten phrases (and one overlap). Perhaps using fewer alternatives would help the reader to follow the argument without having to refer back to the definitions. Some distinctions would be lost, but could the arguments still be made with satisfactory precision?

***

Some people (the IPCC, for example) also include analogies ("extremely unlikely" equivalent to rolling a die twice and getting six both times). These may be helpful but may also introduce an element of playfulness that might be seen as inappropriate for an important decision.

***

Whatever words you use will inevitably have meaning to the reader that may be different to your intention.

Some years before, the IPCC reported a small study[3] examined how doctors interpreted probability phrases. The range of values they gave is shown in the chart. (These are interquartile ranges {A7}, so more extreme interpretations were also given.) There is quite a wide variation.

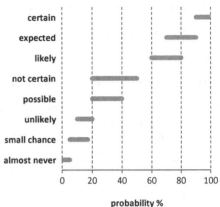

probability %

Doctors have to use these words in sometimes difficult situations.

The same is true for you. While much statistical reporting is not concerned with issues of life-and-death it can sometimes be a part of important business decisions.

***

Even with all these difficulties you have a job to do: you need to make a report, based in part on probability values, that is useful and retains the attention of the reader.

Therefore:

Think about your audience and the purpose of your report. If you decide that words are needed:

don't use too many

choose the words most likely to have meaning for your audience

think about using analogies

provide an explicit list (a lexicon) of your definitions

You will have formed a view on what is important for your business problem. Let your language reflect this while not giving needless spin or bias.

***

Some decisions are inherently probabilistic because they must deal with uncertainty but use no numbers at all. For example, a jury in England is asked to determine guilt "beyond reasonable doubt" in a criminal case but only to consider "the balance of probabilities" in a civil case. The jurors are not told what either means. It is doubtful if either jurors or judge could give a number. Yet trials proceed and verdicts are given.

B9. Beware rules of thumb

> When thinking about probability problems it is often the case that the "obviously common sense" result is wrong.
>
> Take time to recall (or find out) a little theory to check that you are on the right track.

Example 1

There is a lot of public debate about the wide variations in pay typical of many economies. For instance, this taken from the *This is Money* website: "Average total pay — including salaries, pensions and bonuses — for London's top-earning bankers surged 35% to €1.95m (£1.6m) in 2012, the European Banking Authority said."

What do you think is the average wage in the UK?

Example 2

Chris was chosen at random from the list of electors. Chris studied sociology at university and has retained an interest in all aspects of civil rights. Chris gives regularly to charities such as Oxfam and has firm views that there are not enough women on the staff of leading business schools. Rank the following according to how likely they are to be Chris's job:

    (a) a management consultant
    (b) a university professor
    (c) a management consultant who until recently worked in a business school
or (d) a National Health Service (NHS) manager

Example 3

There is increasing concern about the plight of the low-paid. For instance, in the UK the average income of the bottom 10% is just £8,600.

What do you think is the average wage in the UK?

Rationale

How did you get on?

In Example 2, how did you rank (a) compared to (c)? Many people would think Chris more likely to be (c) than (a) because the description is seen to be more representative of people holding Chris's view, for surely the business school experience is more likely to have provoked the opinion.

But this is wrong: (c) is a subset of (a) and so (a) must be the more likely. We often believe that because the extra information provides more of a match with the object (Chris in this case) the probability must be greater. This error is called the *conjunction fallacy*.

(By the way, did you think Chris was short for Christopher or Christine? Did it make a difference?)

***

Still with Example 2. What did you do with the information in the first sentence? In 2014, there were about 80,000 consultants, 36,000 NHS managers and about 20,000 professors. This is where you should start. The probabilities are (a) 59% (b) 15% (d) 26%. These are called *base rates*. With no other information, it is most likely that Chris, the person chosen at random, is a consultant.

The information about how Chris was selected looks dull compared to the more interesting biographical details. But they are the most important information you have. You have other data as well and can combine both if you know how they are related {D4}.

***

How about Examples 1 and 3? Were your answers the same? If they weren't it is likely that the first was the higher. This is because you would have a large figure in mind, £1.6m, and then moved down from this when estimating the average while in the second version you would be moving up from the much lower £8,600. This process is called *anchoring and adjustment*. The first value in your mind acts as an anchor and, for most people, the subsequent adjustment is never quite enough. This is a very common effect: how often have you seen a price of $19.99? You know that for all practical purposes this is really $20 and yet …

The average income in the UK in 2014 was £26,500.

***

When faced with problems for which we do not know or do not have time to compute the true answer we use rules of thumb, also called heuristics. We would not expect these rules to give exactly the correct computed answers but we would expect (hope?) that they would still be useful: there will be some error, we hope not much. But there may be another more troubling effect. Our rule of thumb may *consistently* give estimates which are too big or too small: there is bias. This is bad.

Therefore:

Don't jump straight to what seems an obvious answer for what seems like an obvious question. Check all the information you have and the assumptions you make.

The good news is that once you are aware of the possibility of bias you may be able to correct for it, or be on the lookout at least. The bad news is that bad behaviour traits are persistent, even when we know about them.

***

This awareness of possible bias is due in large part to the work of two psychologists, Amos Tversky and Daniel Kahneman. Their famous paper *Judgement Under Uncertainty: Heuristics and Biases* was published in the journal *Science* in 1974 and has resulted in much subsequent work. Have a look at Kahneman's 2011 book *Thinking Fast and Slow*.

In 2002 Kahneman (right) (Tversky died in 1996) shared the Nobel Prize not in psychology but in economics. The work on behavioural decision making was the basis for the new field of behavioural economics.

70

B10. Not sure? Give a range

> Report an estimate by giving a range. It is easily understood.
>
> Be aware of your audience.

Example 1

"How long will it take to drive to the airport?"

"Not sure. Depends on the traffic. Usually anywhere between an hour and an hour and a half."

Example 2

The *Financial Times* of 22 December 2000 carried a story with the headline "ECB ensures it is never proved wrong." The European Central Bank (ECB) had given range estimates for some of its forecasts. For example, that GDP would grow by 2.6%–3.6% the following year. Mark Cliffe, an economist at ING Barings Global Economics (now chief economist at ING Group), was quoted as saying "The ECB's forecasts for GDP and consumer price inflation may have rather limited use, given the projections are expressed as a wide range rather than a hard forecast."

Rationale

Every day we use imprecise estimates in what we say or what we hear. How useful they are depends in large part on what we want to do with them. What decision do we have to make that needs this information?

We don't want to miss our flight so allow an hour and a half, perhaps even a little more (a safety margin, we might say). Arriving early and killing time in the duty free shops is tedious (and expensive) but much less annoying than missing the flight.

Mark Cliffe's problem looks different. He wanted a "hard forecast" which presumably meant a single number, or a very narrow range. As an economist he may only have had models (mental or computational) which made arithmetic calculations based on single number inputs. They could not easily cope with uncertainty. The ECB were acting responsibly in giving a range to communicate in a straightforward way the uncertainty they felt about their forecast. It may have seemed to Mr. Cliffe a disappointingly imprecise estimate, but it was the ECB's judgement.

The difficulty is not just what you should say to convey uncertainty but what people may want to do with it and the mismatch between the two.

From the point of view of the receiver of a range estimate it is easy to either

> ignore uncertainty and take the mid-point as a best estimate

> take the optimistic or the pessimistic estimate depending on the consequences (as with the trip to the airport)

This works either as input to a calculation or just a number for your consideration. If the range is used as input to a formal model there are two more alternatives make a sensitivity test {E8} by taking the low, high and mid-point estimates as input and see what happens to the output; are different decisions made?

If the model can take probabilistic input {E6, E10}

fit a probability distribution to the range {C10, C13} and use as input.

This gives a lot of flexibility in interpretation — if the user knows how.

On the other hand, the user may not want to make the decision about how to deal with uncertainty and is happy to leave it to you — "just give me a number". But you will think that is irresponsible: whose decision is it anyway? What should you do? You must say something.

Therefore:

Give a range. You can have little control over your audience. If your estimate is very asymmetric give a most likely value too, to avoid a wrong interpretation of the mid-point.

You still have a decision to make. How wide should the range be? Too narrow and it is unlikely to contain the true value, though it looks nicely precise. Practice varies:

When describing variation of data interquartile or interdecile ranges are commonly used. The range contains the middle 50% or the middle 80% of the data {A7}.

Reporting an uncertain estimate it is customary (by habit rather than as the result of careful thought) to take a range that includes the middle 95% of the probability distribution {F19}. To avoid confusion say "I am 95% certain that …"

***

Consider giving full details of the probability distribution on which your estimate is based in a footnote or appendix. Those wanting to know more or who need to use this information as input to a probabilistic model can find it.

Probability models: the shapes of uncertainty

---

overview

Some types of process variability and outcome uncertainty are sufficiently common that it makes sense to have some standard models to describe them. Just which model to use from a particular family will depend on the values chosen for model parameters (typically one measure of average and one of spread).

The purpose of the model is usually to enable what-if tests to be made: what happens to the probability of an extreme event if the average increases by 20%? The average is increased and the model shows by how much the tail probability increase as a result.

Parameters for the models {C1–C3, C5–C7}, can be found either from data or from your judgement.

Data derived estimates are easily found and allow the model to be tested for adequacy {C8}.

Judgemental estimates are at one level easier (no data to collect) but correspondingly impossible to test (no data has been collected).

It is important that any judgements you make are those you feel comfortable making (easier to judge a range of possible outcomes that the standard deviation). This will influence the model you use {C13} and how you derive parameter values {C10–C12}.

C1. How many in this sample? The Binomial distribution

> The proportion of objects in a population has some property.
>
> To find the probability that in a sample a certain number have that property use the BINOMIAL distribution.
>
> To use this distribution three assumptions are made:
>
> each object in the population **must be** in one of **two states**
>
> the **probability** that any one object is in a particular state is **the same** for all objects
>
> the state of each object is **independent** of the states of other objects
>
> Check that these are plausible for your problem.

Example

As a venture capitalist you have invested in eight startup companies. These companies are in their first year of operation. Your target is to have at least three companies survive into the fourth year. Data from the Enterprise Research Centre[1] show that about 63% of startups survive the first three years.

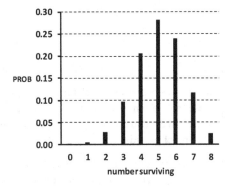

The probability that exactly three of the eight make it into a fourth year is

$$\text{PROB}(3 \text{ survive})$$
$$= \text{BINOM.DIST}(3, 8, 0.63, \text{FALSE}) = 0.097$$

There is a 10% chance that exactly three companies will survive the first three years.

The probability that at least three make it is {B3}

$$\text{PROB}(3 \text{ or more survive}) \quad = 1 - \text{PROB}(\text{no more than 2 survive})$$
$$= 1 - \text{BINOM.DIST}(2, 8, 0.63, \text{TRUE}) = 0.966$$

There is a 97% chance that three or more will survive until the fourth year.

Rationale

To see how the assumptions lead to the BINOMIAL distribution take a smaller problem, a sample of just two companies, A and B, still from a population in which 63% survive the first three years.

Assumption 1 each object in the population must be in one of two states.

given that PROB(survive) = 0.63

then {B3} PROB(fail) = 1 – PROB(survive) = 1 – 0.63 = 0.37

This assumption is a matter of definition: we have chosen not to identify degrees of failure.

Assumption 2 the probability that any one object is in a particular state is the same for all objects.

PROB(survive) = 0.63 and PROB(NOT survive) = 0.37 for *all* startups.

This assumption means that we make no differentiation between objects as more or less likely to survive; of the startups we back we do not believe that the differences between them make it either more or less likely they will fail.

Assumption 3 the state of each object is independent {B5} of the states of other objects.

The probability that one startup survives AND that another also survives is found by simple multiplication of probabilities {B6}

PROB(A survives AND B survives)
= PROB(A survives) × PROB(B survives)
= 0.63 × 0.63 = 0.40

This assumption is the one most likely to be violated.

If some of the companies are in the same sector — biotechnology, say — then their performances may be influenced by the fortunes of the sector as a whole as well as by the characteristics of the companies themselves. In this case the interdependencies will have to be modelled by specifying conditional probabilities {B6} and the BINOMIAL not used.

Bring these results together in a joint probability table {B4, B6}

		A		
		survive	fail	
B	survive	0.40	0.23	0.63
	fail	0.23	0.14	0.37
		0.63	0.37	

So   PROB(both survive) = 0.40

PROB(both fail)   = 0.14

and {B4} PROB(one survives) = PROB[(A fails AND B survives) OR (A survives AND B fails)]
= PROB(A fails AND B survives) + PROB(A survives AND B fails)
= 0.23 + 0.23 = 0.46

***

For more than two startups the calculation gets more complicated. The function BINOM.DIST does all the hard work, but uses just the same ideas and assumptions.

***

The BINOMIAL distribution for sample size n and population proportion p has MEAN and variance VAR {A6,A7}

$$\text{MEAN} = np$$
and $$\text{VAR} = np(1-p)$$

In the Example with $n = 8$ and $p = 0.63$

MEAN $= 8 \times 0.63 = 5.04$
VAR $= 8 \times 0.63 \times 0.37 = 1.86$
STDEV $= \sqrt{1.86} = 1.36$

C2. How many at this rate? The Poisson distribution

> The rate at which events occur is known (accidents per year, faults per batch).
>
> To find the probability that a particular number of events occur use a POISSON distribution. This is a special case of the BINOMIAL distribution {C1} when only the rate of occurrence is known.
>
> Check that the BINOMIAL assumptions are plausible for your problem.

Example

There are, on average, 2.6 accidents per month at a plant.

The probability that next month there will be exactly 4 accidents is

POISSON.DIST(4, 2.6, FALSE)
    = 0.141 or 14%

The probability of no more than 4 accidents is

POISSON.DIST(4, 2.6, TRUE)
    = 0.877 or 88%

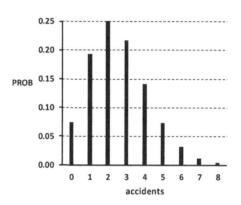

Rationale

Does the Example have the characteristics of a BINOMIAL problem {C1}?

    an accident will occur or not
    every worker is equally likely to have an accident
    accidents are unrelated

This is a pretty serviceable set of assumptions. Any may be wrong (a roof may collapse causing several casualties so invalidating the third assumption) but the model is likely to be good enough for many problems.

The BINOMIAL distribution needs a sample size and a proportion. This can be difficult. In the Example the sample consists of all the opportunities for an accident to occur. The number of seconds in a month is very large, about a quarter of a million. In each second, or fraction of a second, an accident might occur. But this division into seconds is arbitrary. All we can really say is that the sample size is extremely large. The probability of an accident occurring in any of these small time periods is correspondingly extremely small. So, in BINOMIAL terms,

    SAMPLESIZE (n) is unknown but very big

underlying proportion (p) is unknown but very small.

Though we cannot know n and p we can find, by experiment or survey, the rate $r = np$. In this case the mean accident rate is $r = 2.6$ accidents per month.

***

To demonstrate just how good the approximation becomes the table below shows that as sample size n increases the BINOMIAL and POISSON probabilities are the same. Only the first 11 probabilities are shown.

	Binomial probabilities			Poisson
accidents	$n = 10$ $p = 0.26$ $r = np = 2.6$	$n = 100$ $p = 0.026$ $r = np = 2.6$	$n = 1000$ $p = 0.0026$ $r = np = 2.6$	$r = 2.6$
0	0.049	0.072	0.074	0.074
1	0.173	0.192	0.193	0.193
2	0.274	0.253	0.251	0.251
3	0.256	0.221	0.218	0.218
4	0.158	0.143	0.142	0.141
5	0.066	0.073	0.074	0.074
6	0.019	0.031	0.032	0.032
7	0.004	0.011	0.012	0.012
8	0.001	0.003	0.004	0.004
9	0.000	0.001	0.001	0.001
10	0.000	0.000	0.000	0.000

In all cases the rate is the same, $r = 2.6$.

When $n = 100$ the BINOMIAL probabilities are well approximated by the POISSON. When $n = 1000$ the results are indistinguishable.

***

Problems like this are characterised by a known (or assumed) rate of occurrence:

the mean flow of cars on a road (vehicles per hour)
the mean number of defects in sheets of plastic (faults per sheet)
the mean number of calls to a telephone enquiry line (calls per hour)

From a modelling point of view the base is arbitrary (calls per hour or calls per day?). Decide what makes sense for your problem.

***

The POISSON distribution with rate of occurrence r has MEAN and variance VAR {A6,A7}

$$\text{MEAN} = \text{VAR} = r$$

C3. Normally like this: the Normal distribution

The NORMAL distribution is a symmetrical probability distribution for continuous variables. It is determined by the MEAN and standard deviation, STDEV. {A6, A7}

Many physical processes have this shape.

The NORMAL is a good approximation to some other distributions.

Example

The heights of sweets produced at a factory are Normally distributed with mean 7.4mm and standard deviation STDEV = 0.035mm. The proportion of sweets with heights not greater than 7.45mm is

NORM.DIST(7.45, 7.4, 0.035, TRUE) = 0.923 or 92%

The height below which 10% of the sweets are found (the lower decile {A7}) is

NORM.INV(0.1, 7.4, 0.035) = 7.355mm

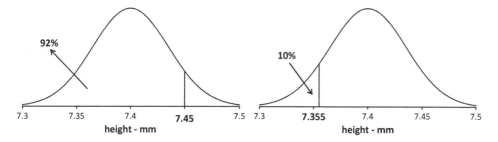

Rationale

The NORMAL distribution describes a lot of variables in which we may be interested (hence "Normal").

One justification for the NORMAL distribution rests on the *Central Limit Theorem* {F4}: the sum of or difference between a number of uncertain amounts is Normally distributed. This is useful when aggregating risk {E10} and making inferences from samples {F3}.

Many processes in the world are loosely aggregative:

the time taken to complete a task is the sum of the times to complete subtasks
the heights of sweets depends on the heights of the constituents, the temperature and pressure of the process and so on

***

Other probability distributions {C1, C2, C5, C6} are well approximated by the NORMAL distribution in some fairly common conditions, such as when sample size or MEAN is not small.

The chart shows a POISSON distribution {C2} with MEAN 12 and the approximating NORMAL distribution with MEAN = VAR = 12.

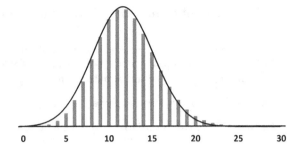

The approximation is good and gets better for bigger means.

***

The NORMAL distribution is a symmetric bell-shaped density. The area under the curve measures probability, so the area under the whole curve is 1.

The curve never quite touches the axis. Since there aren't many variables with values from minus infinity to plus infinity this may seem to make the NORMAL model useless. But most of the curve is within three standard deviations of the MEAN: the model is useful.

***

The NORMAL distribution is used a lot. In interpreting results it might help to remember the following,

range	probability (%)
MEAN ± ⅔ STDEV	50
MEAN ± 1 STDEV	68
MEAN ± 2 STDEV	95
MEAN ± 3 STDEV	99.8

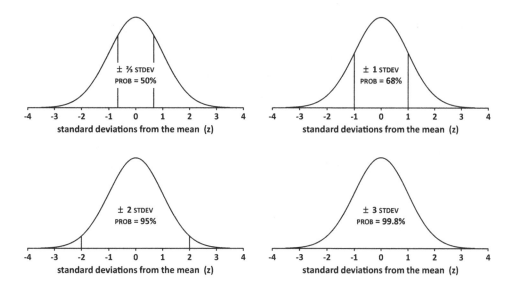

Rather than counting in milimetres of kilograms or £m or whatever count in "standard deviations from the mean" to have a common measure, called the z value {C4}.

These particular distributions are called *standard Normal distributions* and have MEAN = 0 and STDEV = 1. Use the EXCEL functions NORM.S.DIST and NORM.S.INV for dealing with them.

Do not forget what z means: the number of standard deviations from the MEAN.

∗∗∗

If you are making a judgemental estimate which is symmetric and only feel able to give values for MEAN and STDEV use the NORMAL distribution {D7}.

C4. z values

> To identify if a measurement or other value is unusual use
>
> $$z = [\text{value} - \text{MEAN}] / \text{STDEV}.$$
>
> The higher the absolute z value the more extreme the observation.
>
> | | |
> |---|---|
> | z = 3 or more | → only 0.2% of values are more extreme |
> | z = 2 or more | → only 5% of values are more extreme |
> | z = 1 or more | → ⅔ of values are more extreme |
> | z = 0.67 or more | → 50% of values are more extreme |
>
> These values assume a NORMAL distribution {C3}.

Example

The diameter of a component is 2.304cm. So what?

If the mean diameter of all components is 2.3cm and the distribution of diameters has a standard deviation STDEV = 0.002cm then

$$z = (2.304 - 2.3)/0.002 = 2$$

This diameter is 2 standard deviations from the mean, only 5% of components have diameters this far from the mean.

Rationale

You have to make a judgement about how unusual a value is:

> are these test results so unlikely that the process is malfunctioning?
> is this performance so unusual that standards are probably not being met?

You can find probabilities to see how unusual a result is but sometimes prefer a quick evaluation, a convenient mental yardstick you can use in different situations.

Therefore:

Look at the z value. If it is bigger than 2 you should pay attention.

z values are a very compact common language, a shorthand, for talking about variation, which do not depend on the particularities of the problem.

***

In identifying extremes the values z = 2 and z = 3 are usually used as indicators of what is unusual and extreme variation. These have become standard but, like all standards, are someone else's judgement {H4}. Use them for an initial appraisal but not slavishly. Your particular problem and the decision you must make may mean that different probabilities are more useful.

***

The use of the z value assumes that the variable is Normally distributed {C3}, or nearly so. For a manufacturing process, as in the Example, this is a good assumption. After initially identifying a variation which justifies your attention check this assumption of Normality if you haven't already done so.

***

Another quick indicator is the coefficient of variation {A9}. This makes no assumption of Normality, though it is hard to use it without having the Normal distribution in mind.

C5. Uncertainty about proportions: the Beta distribution

> To describe uncertainty about a proportion use a BETA distribution.
>
> This is a distribution for variables in the range 0 to 1 and has two parameters, ALPHA and BETA.
>
> You may be able to give values for ALPHA and BETA directly or you can find them if you know MEAN and standard deviation, STDEV:
>
> $$\text{ALPHA} = [(\text{MEAN/STDEV})^2 \times (1 - \text{MEAN})] - 1$$
> $$\text{BETA} = \text{ALPHA} \times [(1/\text{MEAN}) - 1]$$

Example

A radio station has a performance measure; the proportion of the population in its target area which listens at least once a week. Having been broadcasting for a short time this figure is not known precisely but is estimated to be "about 30%" which you take as the value of the MEAN. If you also judge that STDEV = 0.1 then

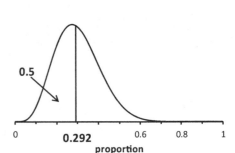

$$\text{ALPHA} = [(0.3/0.1)^2 \times 0.7] - 1 = 5.3$$
and $$\text{BETA} = 5.3 \times (1/0.3 - 1) = 12.37$$

The chance that the proportion who listened is less than the management's target of 20% is

$$\text{BETA.DIST}(0.2, 5.3, 12.37, \text{TRUE})$$
$$= 0.181 \text{ or } 18\%$$

There is a 50% chance that the proportion of listeners will be no more than

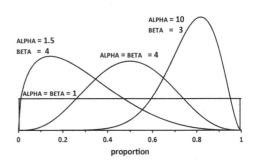

$$\text{BETA.INV}(0.5, 5.3, 12.37) = 0.292 \text{ or } 29\%$$

This is the MEDIAN {A6} estimate.

Rationale

The shape of the BETA distribution is fixed by the values of the parameters.

The *relative* values fix the shape. If ALPHA and BETA are equal the distribution is symmetrical

$$\text{MEAN} = \text{MODE} = 0.5 = \text{MEDIAN}$$

Larger values of the parameters give reduced variance.

The summary measures {A6, A7} are

$$\text{MEAN} = \text{ALPHA}/(\text{ALPHA} + \text{BETA}).$$
$$\text{MODE} = (\text{ALPHA} - 1)/(\text{ALPHA} + \text{BETA} - 2).$$
$$\text{VAR} = \text{ALPHA} \times \text{BETA}/[(\text{ALPHA} + \text{BETA})^2 \times (\text{ALPHA} + \text{BETA} + 1)].$$

***

If you know the MEAN and standard deviation, STDEV, either from data or as your judgement, the parameter values are easily found. But making a judgement about the standard deviation will not be easy. There are alternatives {C11, C12}.

***

The BETA distribution is defined for variables in the range 0 to 1, and so useful for proportions. We may sometimes want to model uncertainty about a variable that is bounded at both low and high limits but not by 0 and 1. The EXCEL BETA functions allow a lower limit other than zero but not a higher limit. There is an easy transformation.

For example, you may want to model the sales volume for a product. You have a guaranteed order for 5,000 units and a maximum production capacity of 30,000. A sales volume of 10,000 is transformed to a value in the range 0 to 1

$$(\text{value} - \text{low})/(\text{high} - \text{low}) = (10,000 - 5,000)/(30,000 - 5,000) = 0.2$$

which can be modelled by a BETA distribution.

***

See from the diagrams that the more symmetrical the distribution (the closer ALPHA is to BETA) or the smaller the standard deviation (bigger ALPHA and BETA) the more closely the BETA distribution resembles the NORMAL distribution {C3}.

For a large class of practical applications it is convenient to use a NORMAL approximation.

C6. No negatives: the Gamma distribution

To describe uncertainty about a non-negative variable use a GAMMA distribution. It has two parameters, ALPHA and BETA.

You may be able to give values for ALPHA and BETA directly or you can find them if you know MEAN and standard deviation, STDEV:

ALPHA $= (\text{MEAN/STDEV})^2$

BETA $=$ MEAN/ALPHA

Example

Research conducted by Nielsen (a research company) showed that in 2012 users of laptop and desktop computers in Australia spent an average of 6.5 hours per week streaming video online.

If we also know that the standard deviation of these data was 3 hours then

ALPHA $= (6.5/3)^2 = 4.69$

and   BETA $= 6.5/4.69 = 1.39$

The probability that a user spends no more than 3 hours online is

GAMMA.DIST(3, 4.69, 1.39, TRUE)
$= 0.092$ or 9%

There is a 20% chance that a user will be online for no more than

GAMMA.INV(0.2, 4.69, 1.39) = 3.95 hours

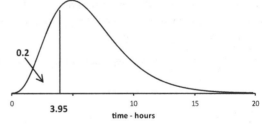

Rationale

GAMMA distributions are determined by the values of the two parameters:

ALPHA fixes the shape of the distribution.
BETA is a scaling parameter depending on the units used to measure the variable

The summary measures {A6, A7} are

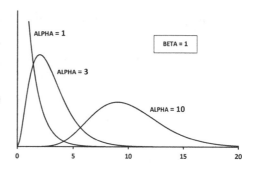

MEAN = ALPHA $\times$ BETA
MODE = (ALPHA $-$ 1) $\times$ BETA
VAR = ALPHA $\times$ BETA^2 = MEAN $\times$ BETA

***

If you know the MEAN and standard deviation, STDEV, either from data or as your judgement, the parameter values are easily found. But making a judgement about the standard deviation will not be easy. There are alternatives {C11, C12}.

***

These distributions are right or positively skewed {A10} but as ALPHA gets bigger they become more like a NORMAL distribution {C3}. A NORMAL approximation is sometimes convenient when ALPHA is large, which is when the MEAN is large compared to the standard deviation.

***

The GAMMA distribution with ALPHA = 1 is also called the Negative Exponential distribution {C7}.

C7. The negative exponential distribution

> To model a non-negative variable which is extremely skewed use a negative exponential distribution.
>
> The probability that a given value is exceeded is
>   EXP (–value/MEAN).

Example

You need to estimate the cost overrun for a project. All you know is that in similar projects the MEAN cost overrun was $2,000.

The probability of a cost overrun of at least $3,000 is

$$EXP(-3,000/2,000) = EXP(-1.5)$$
$$= 0.223 \text{ or } 22\%^2$$

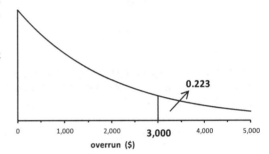

Rationale

You sometimes have to estimate values for an extremely skewed distribution and this is where the negative exponential distribution is what you need.

This is a special case of the GAMMA distribution {C6} with parameter ALPHA = 1.

***

Summary measures {A6, A7} are

        STDEV = MEAN
        MEDIAN = 0.693 × MEAN

***

For judgemental modelling the MEAN {A6} may be all you feel able to specify. Use the negative exponential distribution {D7}.

It may be easier to specify the MEDIAN because you can more easily think about this value which splits the variable into two equally likely ranges (think half-life). Make a judgement about the MEDIAN and then use MEAN = MEDIAN/0.693.

C8. Is the model good enough?

You want to use a probability model for the distribution of some system characteristic.

To test whether the model is an acceptably good model of the system:

1. Collect some data and form *observed* **frequencies**, O.
2. Find the frequencies you would *expect* if the model is correct, E.
3. Measure the dissimilarity between the distributions by

$$\chi^2 = \text{SUM } [(O - E)^2/E]$$

where the SUM is over all classes or values in the distribution.

4. Find how unlikely this value of χ^2 (CHI-SQUARED) is by finding the probability, p, that your sample, O, occurred by chance from a population which really is as modelled.

To find the probability p use the χ^2 (CHI-SQUARED) distribution with

degrees of freedom = no. of classes in the distribution
  - no. of values estimated from the data to get the expected frequencies.

The smaller the value of p the less likely your data if the model is correct.

Example 1. Uniform distribution

A new car is to be launched with four trim options A, B C and D and it is thought that each will be equally popular. In a small survey of 160 potential customers 38 preferred A, 33 preferred B, 36 preferred C and 53 preferred D. You want to know whether or not this is compatible with the assumption of equal shares in the population. The equal share model is

E = number preferring an option = SAMPLESIZE/4 = 160/4 = 40

Calculate the $(O - E)^2/E$ values for each category. For example, for A

$(O - E)^2/E = (38 - 40)^2/40 = 0.1$

trim	observed frequency O	expected frequency E	$(O - E)^2/E$
A	38	40	0.10
B	33	40	1.23
C	36	40	0.40
D	53	40	4.23
	160	160	5.95

And so $\chi^2 = 5.95$.

The model has **one** parameter found from the data, the SAMPLESIZE = 160.

The frequency distribution has **four** classes and so,

degrees of freedom = 4 - 1 = 3

The probability of a χ^2 value this big or bigger is

p = CHISQ.DIST.RT(5.95, 3) = 0.114

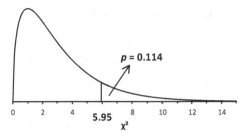

There is an 11% probability that sample frequencies at least as unequal as yours came from a population of equal shares.

You may think this not sufficiently unlikely to justify rejection of your model.

Example 2. Poisson distribution

A bank is reviewing the provision of in-branch advice. It is costly to employ dedicated advisors but relying on other branch staff (the numbers of which the bank is planning to reduce) may be to create unacceptable queues.

As a first stage in the review you need to establish if there is any pattern to this demand. If all enquiries are independent of each other the resulting number of enquiries per day will be POISSON distributed {C2}. This model will be useful because the chance of extreme demand can be linked to possible changes in aggregate average demand.

To test whether the model is plausible the number of enquiries, Q, on each of 115 days at a city-centre branch are analysed:

	DATA			MODEL	
enquiries Q	observed frequency, O	O × Q	Poisson probability	expected frequency, E	$(O - E)^2/E$
0	9	0	0.087	9.989	0.098
1	23	23	0.212	24.407	0.081
2	29	58	0.259	29.819	0.023
3	28	84	0.211	24.288	0.567
4	14	56	0.129	14.836	0.047
5	12	60	0.063	7.251	3.111
6+	0	0	0.038	4.410	4.410
	115	281	1	115	8.338

The mean number of enquiries per day is 281/115 = 2.443.

Now find POISSON probabilities. For example, the predicted proportion of days when there are 2 enquiries is POISSON.DIST(2, 2.443, FALSE) = 0.259.

(*NOTE:* The probability distribution must sum to 1. An open ended class, 6+ enquiries, contains the tail. We saw none but the model predicts that there is a probability of 0.038 that these levels will occur.)

Expected frequencies, E, are just scaled probabilities, each multiplied by 115, and so χ^2 = 8.338.

The model has **two** parameters found from the data, the SAMPLESIZE = 115, and the MEAN demand of 2.443 per day.

The frequency distribution has **seven** classes so,

degrees of freedom = 7 − 2 = 5

The probability of a χ^2 value this big or bigger is

$$p = \text{CHISQ.DIST.RT}(8.338, 5) = 0.139$$

There is a 14% probability that sample data this different from the expected frequencies came from a population in which daily demand is POISSON distributed.

You haven't seen anything particularly unusual. It looks safe to use the POISSON model.

Rationale

There are a number of reasons why you might find it useful to have a model of system behaviour, most likely because it will be a convenient way to test assumptions and make what-if predictions. In Example 2, forecast or speculation about changes in aggregate demand will change the MEAN of the POISSON distribution and this will enable you to see how the probabilities of different levels of demand change as a result. But to be useful the model must be credible.

Therefore:

Collect data and compare what you find with what the model predicts. Your data will not exactly match the predictions because of sampling error. Use the CHI-SQUARED distribution to see how unlikely the data are assuming the model is correct. If they are very unlikely you should reconsider adopting the model.

***

The value of χ^2, and therefore of p, depends on two things: shape and SAMPLESIZE.

The distributions of O and E may be very similar if you look at relative frequencies (percentages).

But the value of χ^2 is directly proportional to SAMPLESIZE. If you had twice as many data in Example 2 χ^2 would have doubled to 16.676, giving p = 0.005. Your data are now much less likely. This may lead you to seriously reconsider your model. The dissimilarity between the *shape* of the data and the shape of the model predictions has not changed but you now have more data and so more evidence.

This is typical of significance testing {H2}. The more data you have the more unlikely even small differences will be {H3}. The probability p is to *help* you make a judgement about the credibility of the model. Be careful to distinguish what is unusual and what is practically important {H3}.

***

Because the value of χ^2 depends on sample size **only use this test to compare frequencies, never use percentages or proportions.**

***

The χ^2 distribution is a theoretical distribution.

The sum of squared values from a number of independent NORMAL distributions with mean 0 and variance 1 (=z^2 {C4}) is distributed as χ^2. The number of distributions summed is the *degrees of freedom* {C9}.

The measure used here

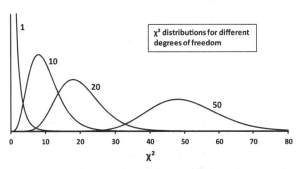

SUM $[(O - E)^2/E]$

is derived by an approximation to the Normality assumptions used to derive χ^2. Like all useful approximations it works well provided adjustments are made in certain cases. There are two rules of thumb for your guidance.

1. When there is only one degree of freedom it is suggested that the calculation be modified to

χ^2 = SUM $\{[\text{ABS}(O - E) - 0.5]^2 / E\}$

For example, if O = 12 and E = 13.6 use

$[\text{ABS}(12 - 13.6) - 0.5]^2/13.6 = [+1.6 - 0.5]^2/13.6 = 1.1^2/13.6 = 0.089$

rather than

$(12 - 13.6)^2/13.6 = (-1.6)^2/13.6 = 0.188$

The effect is to reduce the value of χ^2 and so increase p and make it less likely that you have enough evidence to reject the model.

2. Expected frequencies should not be too small. The most common recommendation is that none should be less than 5. Smaller values may be avoided by amalgamating classes, but this also reduces the number of *degrees of freedom* (not good). Be sensible about this. If you do not have many *degrees of freedom* to play with just try to avoid too many very low expected frequencies. This is, after all, a rule of thumb for your guidance.

***

This way of testing the adequacy of a model works when you need to model a frequency distribution, either for a single variable, as here, or for two variables when the frequencies are in the a table {11}.

There are other measures of model performance. Fitting a line to data (as on a graph) is quite common and has its own measure based on the reduction in estimation error which the model gives {15}.

C9. Degrees of freedom

> You fit a model to data then test how well it predicts those data. A measure of how severe a test this is given by
>
> *degrees of freedom* = df = no. of values to be compared
> – no. of model parameters estimated from the data

Example 1

You have two categories of customer according to where they live, Europe and Rest of World (RoW). You estimate that 40% of sales are in Europe. You do not have to make another estimate for RoW, just subtract from 100%.

This is a **one** degree of freedom problem:

df = 2 (categories of customer) – 1 (forecast for Europe) = 1

Flipping a coin is like this. If you see the coin shows heads you do not have to look at the underside to see what is there.

Example 2. Fitting a line

You want a model of how total cost varies with size of factory. You only have data for two factories so can just draw a straight line.

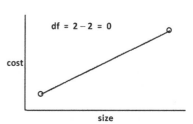

A perfect fit? But you have no idea how good this linear model is: you can fit a straight line to *any* two points and get a perfect fit.

A straight line has two parameters, SLOPE and INTERCEPT {14}, a and b,

cost = a + (b × size)

You are fitting to two points. So

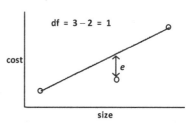

df = 2 (points) – 2 (parameters, a & b) = 0

You have used all the data to fit the model. There is nothing left over to test model performance.

No problem. You have data for a third factory. This shows that the two-point model is not a perfect predictor. The third point gives an error, e. You now have

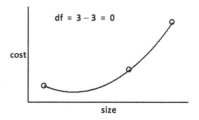

df = 3 (points) – 2 (parameters, a & b) = 1

This is better. You have a small idea of accuracy.

But you could fit a more complex model

$$\text{cost} = a + (b \times \text{size}) + (c \times \text{size}^2)$$

All error disappears again. But you have no *degrees of freedom* and so, again, no way to judge the model's performance:

$$\text{df} = 3 \text{ (points)} - 3 \text{ (parameters, a \& b \& c)} = 0$$

Needless to say, there is a bit more to fitting a line than this {I4} but the argument about *degrees of freedom* holds.

Rationale

A model is motivated by a plausible explanation of the mechanism which generates the data. You want to test if the data are consistent with the explanation. Your motivation may be either pragmatic (you need a model for what-if tests) or more theoretical (you want to know if the system behaves in the ways the model assumes). Whatever your motivation you want to know whether the model fits the data sufficiently well to justify its use.

Therefore:

Decide on a model. Collect data. From the data find values for model parameters.

The number of *degrees of freedom* measures the difference between the number of comparisons made to assess model performance and the number of parameters used to fit the model to the data. It shows how free the data are to differ from the model's predictions. If they do not, or not much, you may have some confidence in the model.

Model parameters are chosen to optimise the fit of the model to the data. You didn't draw just any line as a model for the two data points, that would be crazy. You chose values for the two parameters, INTERCEPT and SLOPE, which gave the best fit passing through both points. Because you use some (or all) of the data to optimise the fit you lose *degrees of freedom*.

Degrees of freedom do not measure something inherent in the data or inherent in the model but in the two taken together.

***

You would like a model which doesn't use too many parameters but still makes a lot of good predictions. This would be an efficient model (mathematicians say a parsimonious model). The more complex the model the better it will appear to fit the data but the less severe will be the test of that fit. This is much less of an issue with large data sets, of course.

***

The thinking behind degrees of freedom is quite general.

It is said that when faced with evidence which seemed to question his theory Sigmund Freud expanded and restated the theory to encompass the new evidence. You may think this is prudent learning. It certainly reduced the possibility of his theory being disproved.

It is much easier to keep track of degrees of freedom when the argument is quantitative but you should bear it in mind even (or especially) when the argument is in prose.

C10. Modelling your judgement with simple two and three point estimates

> Managers must sometimes make decisions based on imperfect information and so must use their judgement. A simple probability model can help describe your uncertainty.
>
> If you feel able to judge the **Low** and **High** values and nothing else use a **uniform** distribution and get probabilities
>
> $$\text{PROB(value less than x)} = (x - L) / (H - L)$$
>
> If you also judge the **Most** likely value you can use a **triangular** distribution and get probabilities
>
> $$\text{PROB(value less than x)} = (x - L)^2 / [(H - L) \times (M - L)] \quad \text{if x is less than M}$$
>
> $$= 1 - \{(H - x)^2 / [(H - L) \times (H - M)]\} \quad \text{otherwise}$$
>
> find MEAN and variance, VAR, if you need them.

Example 1

A marketing manager estimates the growth in demand for a product will be between 3m and 5m units next year.

Use a uniform distribution.

The probability that sales are no more than 3.5m is

sales (million)

$$\text{PROB(sales less than 3.5)} = (3.5 - 3)/(5 - 3) = 0.25$$

Example 2

The same as Example 1 but now the most likely value is judged to be 3.7m units.

Use a triangular distribution.

The probability that sales are no more than 3.5m is

$$\text{PROB(sales less than 3.5)} = (3.5 - 3)^2/[(5 - 3) \times (3.7 - 3)] \quad = 0.25/1.4 = 0.18$$

Rationale

We humans are not too good at thinking about probabilities but we are much better at thinking about shapes. It is not difficult to give estimates of the range of possible outcome values and, sometimes, the most likely as well.

Therefore:

Decide whether you only feel comfortable giving low and high limits or whether you can give an estimate of the most likely value too. Use a uniform or triangular distribution.

These simple shapes are a human-centred way of capturing your judgement of uncertainty. You can now find probabilities. Consider checking by calculating a few and see if they makes sense to you. If they do not, consider a different model {C13}.

***

In some types of risk analysis {E10} you need to give estimates of MEAN and variance, VAR {A6, A7}. If you have used the **uniform** distribution

$$\text{MEAN} = (L + H)/2$$
$$\text{VAR} = (H - L)^2/12$$

In Example 1 $\text{MEAN} = (3 + 5)/2 = 4$
$$\text{VAR} = (5 - 3)^2/12 = 0.33$$

If you have used the **triangular** distribution

$$\text{MEAN} = (L + M + H)/3$$
$$\text{VAR} = [(H - L)^2 - (M - L) \times (H - M)]/18$$

In Example 2 $\text{MEAN} = (3 + 3.7 + 5)/3 = 3.9$
$$\text{VAR} = [(5 - 3)^2 - (3.7 - 3) \times (5 - 3.7)]/18 = [4 - (0.7 \times 1.3)]/18 = 0.17$$

The triangular model greatly reduces variance and tail probabilities. Giving a most likely estimate has quite an effect.

***

Using these distributions certainly has the benefit of simplicity. But both mean and variance are fixed (you can't have a more pointy triangle); range is absolute, all values lower than L and higher than H have zero probability.

There are alternatives {C13}. For example, if you want a symmetric distribution and also want L and H to describe a most likely range rather than an absolute range consider the NORMAL distribution {C3} with L and H defining a range within which you think alternative values are most likely to fall. What does this mean? If you think "most likely" means 95% the range is MEAN ± 2STDEV and so

$$\text{MEAN} = (L + H)/2 = (3 + 5)/2 = 4$$
$$\text{STDEV} = (H - L)/4 = (5 - 3)/4 = 0.5$$

If you think "most likely" means at least 99% the range is MEAN ± 3STDEV and so

$$\text{STDEV} = (H - L)/6 = (5 - 3)/6 = 0.33$$

C11. Modelling your judgement with MODE

You make a judgement of the most likely value of a variable but don't feel able to make any other judgement. You want to say something about variability and spread but would prefer to do this interactively.

If the variable has natural limits (a proportion) use a BETA {C5} distribution. If the variable has no upper limit use a GAMMA distribution {C6}. Both have two parameters, ALPHA and BETA.

Judge the most likely value, the MODE.

Pick a value for the parameter ALPHA.

Because you have fixed the MODE the other parameter is also fixed

for a BETA distribution: $\text{BETA} = (2 - \text{ALPHA}) + (\text{ALPHA} - 1)/\text{MODE}$
for a GAMMA distribution: $\text{BETA} = \text{MODE}/(\text{ALPHA} - 1)$

Try different values of ALPHA until you are happy with the result.

Example

You need to estimate possible market share for a novel product about to be launched. Market share must be bounded between 0% and 100% so use a BETA distribution.

You think it most likely that the share will be about 10%.

The "most likely" value is the MODE {A6}, so

$$\text{MODE} = 0.1$$

But you aren't able to say what you meant by "about" 10%.

Try something and see how you feel about it. As a start set ALPHA = 4.

Make a spreadsheet that shows the shape of the distribution and also, equally important, shows the cumulative probabilities {A5} too.

See from the chart below that the probability of market share being no more than 0.2 is 90%. Does this reasonably reflect your judgement?

If you think it optimistic increase ALPHA. This will reduce the spread of your estimate. A lower ALPHA will increase the spread.

(EXCEL NOTE: To make the two charts put values between 0 and 1 in one column and in the next two columns use BETA.DIST with final parameter TRUE to get cumulative probabilities and FALSE to get the heights to draw the density function which shows shape.)

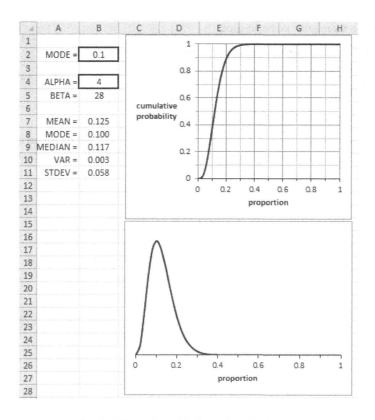

▲	A	B
1		
2	MODE =	0.1
3		
4	ALPHA =	4
5	BETA =	=(2-B4)+(B4-1)/B2
6		
7	MEAN =	=B4/(B4+B5)
8	MODE =	=(B4-1)/(B4+B5-2)
9	MEDIAN =	=BETA.INV(0.5,B4,B5)
10	VAR =	=B4*B5/((B4+B5)^2*(B4+B5+1))
11	STDEV =	=SQRT(B10)

Rationale

You need to specify a probability distribution to describe your judgement of some variable. You feel pretty confident about the *most likely* value and that the BETA (or GAMMA) distribution is the right shape. But you don't feel able to say much about the spread of the distribution, though you see that this is necessary.

Therefore:

Estimate the most likely value. This gives the MODE. This fixes the relation between the two parameters. You then only have to alter one parameter, ALPHA. Try different values and look at the resulting probabilities. Interactively find the value of ALPHA that best describes your judgement.

There are three assumption in this method:

> you are reasonably happy to give a "most likely" estimate

> you are not happy to give judgements about spread (high/low values or tail probabilities)

> but, you can react to results until you are satisfied

These seem reasonable. While you find it hard to give values of model parameters or standard deviations reacting to model probabilities shouldn't be impossible. Using ALPHA as a controller makes interaction easy.

C12. Modelling your judgement with percentiles

> You choose a probability distribution which is an appropriate model for your judgement but now need to estimate parameters. You don't feel comfortable in giving parameter values directly or in specifying an average.
>
> Give some percentiles. Then find the parameter values which best fit what you have specified.
>
> You can do this easily using the SOLVER option in EXCEL.

Example

You need an estimate of how long a project will take to complete. This is a non-negative variable so try a GAMMA distribution {C6}. You make four judgements:

    20% chance of finishing within 3 months
    50% chance of finishing within 5 months
    80% chance of finishing within 6 months
    95% chance of finishing within 9 months

Find the values of parameters ALPHA and BETA which minimise the sum of squared errors (a widely used measure {I4}). Set up a spreadsheet:

	A	B	C	D	E
1					
2		ALPHA =	1.000		
3		BETA =	1.000		
4					
5					
6		value	required	Gamma	error^2
7		3	0.2	0.950	0.563
8		5	0.5	0.993	0.243
9		6	0.8	0.998	0.039
10		9	0.95	1.000	0.002
11					0.848

	A	B	C	D	E
1					
2		ALPHA = 1			
3		BETA = 1			
4					
5					
6		value	required	Gamma	error^2
7		3	0.2	=GAMMA.DIST(B7,C2,C3,TRUE)	=(C7-D7)^2
8		5	0.5	=GAMMA.DIST(B8,C2,C3,TRUE)	=(C8-D8)^2
9		6	0.8	=GAMMA.DIST(B9,C2,C3,TRUE)	=(C9-D9)^2
10		9	0.95	=GAMMA.DIST(B10,C2,C3,TRUE)	=(C10-D10)^2
11					=SUM(E7:E10)

Click the *Data* tab and then use *Solver*.[3] The *Solver* window (below) shows the model.

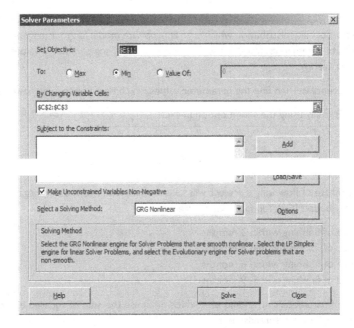

Click *Solve* to give:

	A	B	C	D	E
1					
2		ALPHA =	5.738		
3		BETA =	0.857		
4					
5					
6		value	required	Gamma	error²
7		3	0.2	0.171	0.001
8		5	0.5	0.571	0.005
9		6	0.8	0.735	0.004
10		9	0.95	0.959	0.000
11					0.010

The GAMMA distribution with parameters ALPHA = 5.738 and BETA = 0.857 is the optimal model.

The cumulative probability (below left) shows the model distribution and the four points you gave. A good fit.

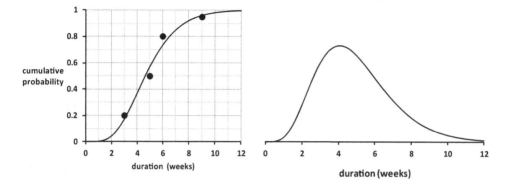

Rationale

You need to describe your judgement about the value of some variable. Giving percentiles is more natural for you than giving a MEAN or a MODE or a RANGE.

Therefore:

Choose a probability model which best fits the shape of your judgement. Give some percentiles and use *Solver* to give best-fit estimates of parameters ALPHA and BETA.

You have a model, a GAMMA distribution in the Example though other distributions, the BETA {C5} for instance, can also be fitted using this method.

∗∗∗

Think carefully about the order in which you specify percentiles. The anchoring and adjustment heuristic {B9} warns us that if we give the central value first (the anchor) then the subsequent adjustments for extreme percentiles might be inadequate. You may get a too optimistic model of your judgement. Starting at the extremes (20% and 95% in the Example) makes this less likely.

∗∗∗

Once you have the parameter values the MEAN {A6} and variance, VAR, {A7} are easily calculated, if you need them. For the GAMMA distribtion in the Example {C6}

$$\text{MEAN} = \text{ALPHA} \times \text{BETA} = 5.738 \times 0.857 = 4.917$$
$$\text{VAR} = \text{ALPHA} \times \text{BETA}^2 = 5.738 \times 0.857^2 = 4.214$$
$$\text{STDEV} = \sqrt{4.214} = 2.053$$

C13. Which model for your judgement?

> Using standard distributions to model your judgemental uncertainty gives you, for a little input, a way of finding probabilities and other useful information.
>
> Choose the judgemental inputs you best feel able to give.

Rationale

You need to make a judgemental estimate of an important variable (sales volume, market share …) but can only feel comfortable giving some value of average {A6} or spread {A7} or perhaps limits or percentiles.

Therefore:

Decide what you feel fairly comfortable in estimating. Choose an appropriate probability distribution and fit it to your inputs.

Probability models are defined by parameters, either MEAN and STDEV for a NORMAL model {C3}. For the BETA and GAMMA models {C5, C6} parameter values are easily found from MEAN and STDEV.

You can probably give a measure of average — MEAN, MODE or MEDIAN — but will find it more difficult to give a value for STDEV. In certain cases it might be possible (assume the same as last year) but generally it is just too hard to conceptualise. You are much more likely to be able to give a range or some percentiles.

The table suggests what distributions you might use depending on which measures of average and spread you feel able to give.

you judge average {A6}	you judge spread {A7}	assume	distribution	statsNote
	range	nothing	UNIFORM	{C10}
		symmetry	NORMAL	{C3}
MODE	range	shape	TRIANGULAR	{C10}
		symmetry	NORMAL	{C3}
MEAN	STDEV	symmetry	NORMAL	{C3}
		bounded	BETA	{C5}
		no upper bound	GAMMA	{C6}
MODE		bounded	BETA	{C5,C11}
		no upper bound	GAMMA	{C6,C11}
	two or more percentiles	bounded	BETA	{C5,C12}
		no upper bound	GAMMA	{C6,C12}
MEAN or MEDIAN		no upper bound	negative exponential	{C7}

Be careful not to choose distributions and inputs which are too optimistic {D7}; is the range you specify too narrow?

Evidence and judgement

---

overview

Managers make decisions based both on data and on their judgement. This is inevitable. But how should judgement be used? One approach is to analyse the data and then use judgement to interpret the results. This is often done. An alternative is to use judgement from the start of the analysis process so that initial judgemental belief is modified by evidence (data) to give a revised belief. This is usually described as the Bayesian approach and is the subject of this section.

The key to making sense of evidence is to describe the relation between the evidence and what might account for it {D1}. The more a possible cause accounts for the evidence the more you should believe it is the right explanation {D2, D3}.

A little probability theory enables you to combine evidence with your carefully considered judgement {D4–D6} and also to make sense of more evidence {D5}.

For some common problems standard probability models provide a simple way of revising judgement given data {D8–D10}.

It will come as no news to you that as more and more data are available the more people with initially different judgements will move to agreement. The Bayesian model shows how this happens {D11}.

The statsNotes in this section show how to use judgement and data in a common framework. In those cases where you have a large data set your initial judgement becomes irrelevant. Think of this as a special case. When you are not so fortunate use these models to make your judgement explicit and to revise it in light of the evidence available.

D1. Likelihood

Decide on the strength of the link between what you can see — **evidence** — and what might be responsible for it — possible **cause**.

Give the strength of the relation as the probability

PROB(evidence GIVEN cause)

This is called the **likelihood**.

Example

Applicants for a job are given an aptitude test. The test result reports the score as either *low*, *medium* or *high*. A candidate is tested. The result comes back as *low*.

From personnel records you find that 60% of people whose subsequent job performance was rated *poor* in annual appraisals had obtained this result. So

likelihood = PROB(score = *low* GIVEN performance = *poor*) = 0.6

Rationale

You collect evidence to help you make a decision. But the evidence is not a perfect indicator: test results are not infallible predictors of performance in the job. You need to know how much weight to give the evidence in the decision you have to take.

Therefore:

Calculate the likelihood to see the relation between cause and evidence. If you don't know how likely the evidence is you don't know what weight to give it.

There are two reasons to be careful:

there may be other possible causes

a likelihood may be low but still higher than the likelihoods for these other causes

Have you considered all causes? You will need to decide the relative strength of the evidence in favour of each {D2}.

Having a catch-all alternative cause — "none of the above" — is not good enough: how can you find likelihoods for non-specific causes?

***

Using single likelihoods can be useful if treated carefully. A poor level of a performance indicator *may* indicate management failure but it is not a proof. An unusually poor indicator signals that it is worth spending some time investigating further before deciding what to do {G1}.

Rejection of the assumed cause just because the evidence is unlikely is poor logic. Some analyses can be misused in this way by unthinking users {H2}: approach with caution.

***

The appreciation of what likelihood does and does not indicate is not limited to numerical problems. In his Foreword to Roberta Wohlsetter's 1962 book *Pearl Harbor: Warning and Decision*, Thomas Schelling wrote "There is a tendency in our planning to confuse the unfamiliar with the improbable".

D2. What caused it? Making an inference

You have evidence of some behaviour and want to decide what might be the cause.

list all possible causes

for each cause find the likelihood that it accounts for the evidence

Scale the likelihoods to sum to 1 to get a probability distribution which shows the degree of belief you should have in each possible cause:

belief *is proportional to* **likelihood**

Example

As {D1}. Applicants for a job are given an aptitude test. The test reports the score as either *low*, *medium* or *high*. A candidate is tested. The result comes back as *low*.

From personnel records you find that 60% of people whose subsequent job performance was rated *poor* in annual appraisals had obtained this result. Only 30% of those with *good* job performance had scored *low*. So the likelihoods {D1} are:

for *poor* performers: PROB(score=*low* GIVEN performance=*poor*) = 0.6
for *good* performers: PROB(score=*low* GIVEN performance=*good*) = 0.3

Based on the evidence of the test result believe with odds 2:1 that this applicant, if hired, will be a *poor* rather than a *good* performer:

PROB(performance=*poor* GIVEN score=*low*) = 0.6/(0.6+0.3) = 0.67
PROB(performance=*good* GIVEN score=*low*) = 0.3/(0.6+0.3) = 0.33

Rationale

Why would you do anything else?

Management decisions often need you to decide between a number of causes or explanations. Sometimes physical causes (a system malfunction) sometimes competing alternatives (who to hire) but in all cases you would like some evidence to help you decide. You need to use the evidence carefully so that your evidence-based belief is justified.

Therefore:

For each possible cause or explanation find how likely the evidence is. Then believe in the alternative causes in proportion to these likelihoods.

You will have a probability distribution. It may be that one probability is much higher than others and so you feel able to decide on that cause and act accordingly.

If this is not so you may collect some more evidence and further revise your belief {D5}, or you may have some prior information which you want to use {D4}.

***

Think of this use of evidence as switching between one set of conditional probabilities {B6}, the likelihoods PROB(evidence GIVEN cause), to another, the diagnostic probabilities PROB(cause GIVEN evidence).

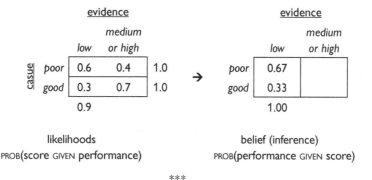

To see why this is a justified way of treating evidence use some simple ideas from probability theory:

1. Enter the likelihoods. These are the conditional distributions {B6}

    PROB(evidence GIVEN cause).

	low	medium or high	
poor	0.6	0.4	1.0
good	0.3	0.7	1.0

2. Start from scratch with no view about the candidate and so have marginal probabilities {B4, D6}

    PROB(*poor*) = PROB(*good*) = 0.5

    The table shows the joint probability distribution {B4}.

    There is a 45% chance of a *low* test result.

	low	medium or high	
poor	0.30	0.20	0.50
good	0.15	0.35	0.50
	0.45	0.55	1.00

3. If the test result is *low* there is a 67% chance of *poor* performance.

    If the test result is *medium or high* there is only a 36% chance of *poor* performance.

    These are the conditional probabilities

    PROB(cause GIVEN evidence)

	low	medium or high
poor	0.67	0.36
good	0.33	0.64
	1.00	1.00

***

Deciding what to believe about the alternative causes or explanations of some observed behaviour is often called making an **inference**. Doctors and other fault-finders speak of making a **diagnosis**.

***

This simple rule:

belief *is proportional to* **likelihood,**

is a form of **Bayes' Rule**, named for Thomas Bayes, an 18th century English priest, who first proposed it.

Thomas Bayes
1702–1761

D3. Not all evidence is helpful

> Evidence, data in some form, is informative only if it discriminates between possible causes.
>
> If the likelihoods are the same, or nearly the same, this evidence will be of little or no use in helping you decide what to do.

Example

As {D1}. Applicants for a job are given an aptitude test. The test result will report the score as either *low*, *medium* or *high*.

From personnel records you find that 60% of people whose subsequent job performance was rated *poor* in annual appraisals had obtained a *low* test result. Only 30% of those with *good* job performance had scored *low*. A *medium* test result was given to 40% of both *poor* and *good* performers.

The likelihoods and belief or inferential probability distributions {D2} are:

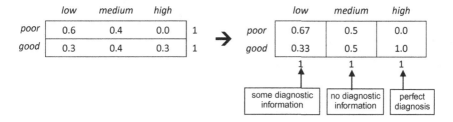

Based on available data:

test result *high*   is a perfect indicator of *good* performance in job

test result *low*   contains some information
odds are 2:1 that performance will be *poor*

test result *medium*   contains no information at all; it does not discriminate between performance levels.

Rationale

You want to collect evidence to help you decide which possible cause is the most likely. You want the evidence to be as useful as possible.

Therefore:

Find likelihoods for *all* possible causes. The usefulness of evidence decreases the more the likelihoods for that evidence are the same.

The Bayes framework clarifies just how useful evidence might be. The key is to consider all possible causes, certainly not just one. In the Example, if you had not considered more than one cause, you may have been led astray by concluding that because a test result *medium* was achieved by 40% of good workers the applicant would probably perform well if hired.

111

D4. Base rates: what we already know

When making an inference you may already have some view of the most likely explanation of your evidence. Express your view as **base rates**, the probabilities you give to alternative explanations *before* you look at the evidence . Then use

$$\textbf{belief} \textit{ is proportional to } \textbf{likelihood} \times \textbf{base rate}$$

to find what you should believe.

Example

A company makes components by a process of extruding plastic. The components may be misshapen if either the temperature or pressure controllers on the extruder are faulty. About 70% of the time it is a problem with temperature.

Engineers can make a test which indicates which of the two faults might be causing the problem. The test is not perfect: faulty temperature controllers are correctly identified 60% of the time; faulty pressure controllers are correctly identified 80% of the time.

The test indicates a faulty temperature controller.

Organise the calculation in a table {D2}:

1. Likelihoods
   Faulty temperature controllers are correctly diagnosed 60% of the time; faulty pressure controllers are correctly identified 80% of the time.

	test indicates		
cause		temperature	pressure	
temperature	0.6	0.4	1.0
pressure	0.2	0.8	1.0

2. Base Rates
   About 70% of the time it is a problem with temperature.

	test indicates		
cause	temperature	pressure	
temperature	0.42	0.28	0.7
pressure	0.06	0.24	0.3
	0.48	0.52	

3. Inference
   Test indicates *temperature*.
   There is an 83% chance that the temperature controller is faulty.

	test indicates	
cause	temperature	pressure
temperature	**0.83**	0.54
pressure	**0.17**	0.46
	1.00	1.00

Rationale

You have some contextual or other reason for believing that not all causes are equally likely and want to use that together with some new evidence to judge between the different possible causes.

Therefore:

Express your judgement as a probability distribution and use these *base rates* in Bayes' Rule.

Take care when giving base rates. In the Example you had some data on which to base your base rates. Previous experience provides a context for the diagnosis which it is legitimate, even necessary, to incorporate in your analysis.

If there are no such data you may still have a view. As a manager you are expected to use your judgement and this is a framework to help you. But be careful. Only use judgements that you are able to justify, in a narrative if not with data. If there is any doubt in your mind about this use equal or near-equal rates {D6, D7}.

***

Bases rates describe initial belief. This is revised by data.

In the Example start with belief PROB = 0.7 that temperature is the problem. This is revised to PROB = 0.83.

Something has been learned and belief revised accordingly.

Bayes' Rule emphasises this

revised belief *is proportional to* **likelihood** $\times$ **base rate.**

***

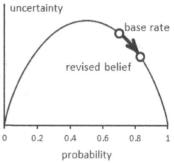

The framework is quite general enough to be of use even when numbers are not available. Suppose you read in one of those popular management books (probably written by a recently retired CEO) that "Of all the excellent business leaders I have known good communication skills have been vital to their success".

Assuming good leaders can be clearly identified your Bayes-inspired questions might be

what are the alternatives?	what about poor or average business leaders?
what are the likelihoods?	what proportion of excellent/average/poor leaders had those skills
what is the base rate?	what proportion of different types of leaders are there?

Even though you may not know the answers (and may never know) you have a good critical framework for evaluating the book you just bought at the airport.

D5. More evidence

When you have more than one source of evidence find the likelihood of each and multiply them:

revised belief *is proportional to* **likelihood** × **likelihood** × ⋯ × **base rate**

This works if the different sources of evidence are **independent**.

Example 1

Misshapen plastic extrusions have in the past been caused by a faulty temperature controller 70% of the time and by a faulty pressure controller 30% of the time. Tests by company engineers have indicated a faulty temperature controller. The test correctly identifies temperature faults 60% of the time and correctly identifies pressure faults 80% of the time.

The conclusion is that there is a fairly high chance, PROB = 83%, that the fault is with the temperature controller {D4}. Replacing the controller is expensive and so the manufacturer of the extrusion equipment is contacted and sends their own engineer (at a cost). The test used by the manufacturer works on a different principle from that used by company engineers and is more accurate: it correctly identifies either fault 90% of the time. This test also indicates that it is the temperature controller which is faulty. And so:

		base rate		likelihood test 1		likelihood test 2				result
fault	temperature	0.7	×	0.6	×	0.9	=	0.378	→	0.98
	pressure	0.3		0.2		0.1		0.006		0.02
		1.0						0.384		1.00

There is a 98% probability that it is the temperature controller which is faulty, enough to justify the decision to replace.

Example 2

A company sells in an overseas market using a local agent. In preparing a sales forecast for the coming year the sales manager has two forecasts: one from the local agent and one from consultants which the company has used for a number of years.

Previous forecasts are reviewed and compared with what actually happened. The results have been tabulated as likelihood distributions:

		consultants' forecast				agent's forecast			
		down	none	up		down	none	up	
actual sales change	down	0.6	0.3	0.1	1.0	0.5	0.3	0.2	1.0
	none	0.2	0.5	0.3	1.0	0.3	0.4	0.3	1.0
	up	0.1	0.1	0.8	1.0	0.1	0.2	0.7	1.0

For the coming year the consultant's forecast no change. The agent is more optimistic and believes sales will be up. The sales manager is new to the job and thinks it best not to express any strong views. So,

sales change		base rate		likelihood consultant		likelihood agent			result
	down	0.33		0.3		0.2	0.020		0.21
	none	0.33	×	0.5	×	0.3	= 0.050	→	0.54
	up	0.33		0.1		0.7	0.023		0.25
		1.00					0.093		1.00

It is most likely that there will be no change in sales.

The probability of no change is 54%.

Rationale

You have more than one piece of evidence to help you decide between a number of causes of some observed system behaviour. You want to use all the evidence.

Therefore:

Multiply the likelihoods and use this product in Bayes' Rule.

This is a simple application of the multiplication rule of probability {B6}. Instead of

likelihood = PROB(evidence)

you now have

likelihood = PROB(evidence1 AND evidence2 AND ⋯)

= PROB(evidence1) × PROB(evidence1) × ⋯

= likelihood1 × likelihood2 × ⋯ .

***

This works provided the evidence (data) sources are independent {B5}. But are they?

In Example 1, the two testing methods used different principles and so it seemed reasonable to assume independence.

In Example 2, it is not so clear. Suppose that both the consultant and the agent had just read in the *Wall Street Journal* about the prospects in this particular market and this has heavily influenced both. Their forecasts might not be exactly the same but they wouldn't be independent either.

Assuming independence is very convenient and makes life a lot simpler. But you need to be careful. In the majority of cases this is not a problem (Example 1). It is when dealing with opinions, as in Example 2, that you need to be vigilant.

***

Will you have likelihoods? Example 2 happily assumes that you have diligently kept a track record of forecast accuracy. How likely is that? But if you have no such record how can you evaluate the evidence?

115

D6. Be modest

Avoid improperly influencing the analysis of evidence by keeping your judgemental input, your base rates {D4}, as flat as possible consistent with what you feel is your well-justified belief.

Example

This is about how you think, so here is something for you to try.

Think about the prospects of some company. This is written in 2014 and I am going to think about the prospects for *General Motors*, you can choose something else.

See the equal probability distribution. Do you want to change this?

share price next year	equal probabilities	your estimate
up 3–10%	20	?
up not more than 3%	20	?
no change	20	?
down not more than 3%	20	?
down 3–10%	20	?
	100%	100%

Rationale

It is a natural human trait for us to think we are better judges than we are, and there is much research to show that we do. But, you may think, if I do this job I must have some expertise (that is what I get paid for, after all) and I should use it.

Therefore:
Start with equal probabilities. Write them down or enter in your spreadsheet. Only change them if you feel you have good reason.

Making judgements like this will force you to consider just how much you can justifiably alter the equal probabilities. This will reduce the possibility of your pretending to more knowledge than you have.

***

The act of writing the equal probabilities and then having to react to them is important. This process makes use of the anchoring and adjustment heuristic {B9}. The equal probability value, 20% in the Example, is the anchor. Its presence in your mind is likely to condition the probability you choose and in this way help you to be modest in your judgements.

***

Keeping your probabilities near-equal will also guard against charges of bias. There can be a concern that unscrupulous analysts (so not you) may deliberately choose base rates which ensure a result convenient for themselves. The technical word for this is cheating. The near-equal strategy helps you not to, even inadvertently.

The maxEnt methodology {D7} gives a formal mathematical expression to the near-equal rule.

***

The idea of focussing on equal probabilities can be traced back to Laplace and his Principle of Insufficient Reason. This addressed the issue of how we might have a quantitative definition of our ignorance. He argued that being ignorant means that we cannot say that one possibility is more likely than another and so, *voilà*, make all probabilities the same. An alternative view, of course, is that if we are ignorant we have no business even thinking about assigning probabilities {E5}.

But you still have a decision to make.

Pierre-Simon Laplace
1749–1827

D7. maxEnt

Avoid judgemental bias in base rate probability distributions by making them as flat as possible. The maxEnt criterion can help:

If you are able to specify only a MEAN use a negative exponential distribution.

If you are able to specify both MEAN and variance, VAR, use a NORMAL distribution.

Example

A health service manager wants to estimate the average number of visits patients make to their doctor each year.

No data are available but the manager's best judgement is that the MEAN might be 5.

The uncertain estimate is best described by a negative exponential distribution {C7} with MEAN=5.

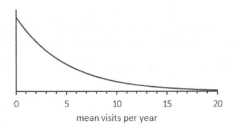

mean visits per year

Rationale

The maxEnt (for maximum entropy) method for specifying base rates uses the nearly-equal principle to avoid bias {D6}. That method was informal and relied on you to interpret the spirit of the recommendation as best you could.

Think of a simple two state problem. Maximum uncertainty is when both outcomes are equally likely (will the coin come down heads? Will the next customer be a man or a woman?). The less equal the probabilities the less uncertain the outcome (will the next CEO of Apple Inc. be a woman?), though the more surprising if the less likely happens.

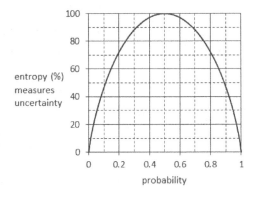

entropy (%) measures uncertainty

probability

118

The diagram shows this. The measure of uncertainty used is called entropy.

***

Maximising entropy is another way of keeping probabilities nearly equal.

The maxEnt methodology is due to ET Jaynes, a physicist, among other things, who was concerned that probabilities used in Bayesian revision of belief were, so far as possible, free from bias. This meant that base rates should be as flat as possible consistent with any prior knowledge you may have.

Edwin T Jaynes
1922–1998

Because entropy has a mathematical form[1] the principle can be expressed as a formal optimisation problem: maximise entropy (keep nearly-equal) given what you know as constraints. As what you know changes so does the result, but still with maximum entropy,

what you know → constraint(s) → maxEnt distribution.

Jaynes was strict about this: constraints should reflect only what you know and not what you *think* you know.

You may wish to use your well-founded judgments as well.

In the Example the MEAN is given as a judgement. The manager does not feel able to say more. You must decide for yourself whether the maxEnt principle should still be used. It provides such an elegant way of deriving probabilities from constraints — base rates from judgement — that both the general principle and some explicit results are hard to resist (I don't).

Three useful maxEnt distributions are:

(a) With no prior knowledge the maxEnt distribution is flat.

(b) If you specify a MEAN the maxEnt distribution is negative exponential.

(c) If you also specify the standard deviation, STDEV, the maxEnt distribution is NORMAL.

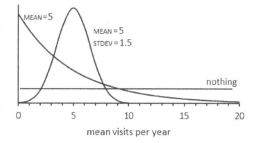

There is much more to maxEnt, of course, but these three results illustrate the method and give a justification for the distributions.

***

There are other ways of fitting a model to your judgement {C13}. If you use them remember maxEnt and choose a distribution as flat as possible subject only to what you can justify {D6}.

119

D8. Learning about proportions

You need to estimate the proportion of objects with some property.

In a sample of size n you find that x have that property.

Use a BETA distribution.

Before the sample your judgement (base rate {D4}) is described by a BETA distribution with parameters ALPHA and BETA.

After the survey your revised estimate of the proportion is BETA with

revised ALPHA = ALPHA + x

revised BETA = BETA + $(n - x)$

Example

You need to estimate the proportion of local small businesses which make use of a fairly new government scheme for export financing.

You initial judgement is described by a BETA distribution {C5, C13} with

ALPHA = 3

BETA = 10

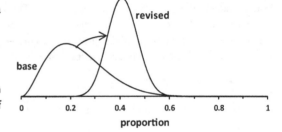

In a sample of 55 businesses 25 of them use the scheme and so your revised belief is

ALPHA = 3 + 25 = 28

BETA = 10 + (55 − 25) = 40

Rationale

You know something about the likely value of a proportion and then collect some data. You want to use both your prior knowledge and the data.

Therefore:

Fit a BETA distribution to your prior judgement. Update the BETA parameters from the data.

This is a case of learning from evidence. The mechanics and logic are the same as {D5}:

likelihood distribution is BINOMIAL {C1} which gives PROB (25 of 55 firms GIVEN proportion = p)

base rate is a BETA distribution {C5} which gives the prior probability of each value of p.

The mathematical forms of these two probability models are similar so that revision of your estimate is simply done by updating the parameters ALPHA and BETA.

***

Even with this moderate sized sample the revised BETA distribution looks very much like a NORMAL distribution {C3}.

This is quite common. Inferences about proportions {F10} often use this approximation together with the assumption that you have no prior judgement. This is good for big samples and sample proportions (25/55 = 0.45 in the Example) which are not extreme.

D9. Learning about rates

You need to estimate a rate of occurrence: how many per period.

In n periods you find x occurrences.

Use a GAMMA distribution.

Before the sample, your judgement (base rate {D4}) is described by a GAMMA distribution with parameters ALPHA and BETA.

After the survey your revised estimate of the proportion is GAMMA with

revised ALPHA = ALPHA + x

revised BETA = $1/(n + 1/\text{BETA})$

Example

You need to estimate defect rate; the number of faults per standard batch of manufactured components. You think that it might be "about 6" and so use a GAMMA distribution for your initial judgement {C6, C13} with

ALPHA = 8
BETA = 0.75

In 5 batches there are 15 defects and so your updated estimate is a GAMMA distribution with

ALPHA = 8 + 15 = 23

BETA = $1/(5 + 1/0.75) = 0.157$

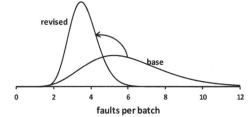

Rationale

You know something about the likely value of a rate and then collect some data. You want to use both your prior knowledge and the data.

Therefore:
Fit a GAMMA distribution to your prior judgement. Update the GAMMA parameters from the data.

This is a case of learning from evidence. The mechanics and logic are the same as {D5} with

likelihood distribution is POISSON {C2} which gives PROB(5 defects in 15 batches GIVEN rate = r).

base rate is a GAMMA distribution {C5} which gives the prior probability of each value of r.

The mathematical forms of these two probability models are similar so that revision of your estimate is simply done by updating the parameters ALPHA and BETA.

***

Even with this moderate sized sample the revised GAMMA distribution looks very much like a NORMAL distribution {C3}.

This is quite common. Inferences are often made using this approximation together with the assumption that you have no prior judgement. This is good for big samples.

D10. Learning Normally

> You need to make an estimate of a variable. The likelihood of the evidence is given by a NORMAL distribution with mean and variance MEAN(E) and VAR(E).
>
> Before you see the evidence express your judgement (base rate) as a NORMAL distribution with MEAN(B) and VAR(B).
>
> Combine base and evidence using weights
>
> $$w(B) = 1/\text{VAR}(B)$$
>
> and $\quad w(E) = 1/\text{VAR}(E)$
>
> So $\quad$ revised MEAN $= [w(B) \times \text{MEAN}(B) + w(E) \times \text{MEAN}(E)] / [w(B) + w(E)]$
>
> and $\quad$ revised VAR $= 1/[w(B) + w(E)]$

Example 1

As Singapore country manager for a large car importer your judgement is that new vehicle registrations will have a 50% chance of being between 45,500 and 46,300. Treat this as the middle 50% of a NORMAL distribution {C3}, 2/3 of a standard deviation either side of the MEAN, so

$$\text{MEAN} = (45,500 + 46,300)/2 = 45,900$$

and $\quad$ STDEV $= (46,300 - 45,500) \times 3/4 = 600$

You are then sent a forecast made by an econometric model which forecasts that new vehicle registrations will be 46,241. The forecast error is NORMAL with standard deviation 700.

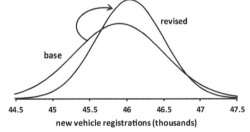

	MEAN	VAR	1/VAR	MEAN/VAR
base	45.9	$0.6^2 = 0.36$	2.78	127.50
forecast	46.241	$0.7^2 = 0.49$	2.04	94.37
			4.82	221.87

So $\quad$ updated MEAN $= 221.87/4.82 = 46.04$

and $\quad$ updated VAR $= 1/4.82 = 0.21$

Example 2. Learning about a MEAN

You are planning new production line. The process is novel and experimentation is expensive.

The Production Manager believes that the mean process time will be about 23 minutes plus or minus 2 minutes. Interpret this estimate as a 95% interval, 2 standard deviations either side of the MEAN, and so a NORMAL distribution with a mean of 23 and standard deviation of 1 {C3}.

In a small test of ten pieces the MEAN is 25 minutes and the variance is VAR = 5 minutes.

The likelihood distribution for means of these samples of 10 has variance VAR = 5/10 {F5, F8}.

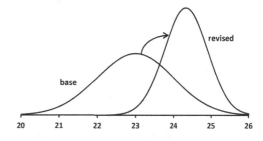

	MEAN	VAR	1/VAR	MEAN/VAR
base	23	1	1	23
data	25	5/10 = 0.5	2	50
			3	73

So   Updated MEAN = 73/3 = 24.33

and   updated VAR = 1/3 = 0.33

The evidence from data is more precise than the judgemental estimate so the updated MEAN is closer to the test value.

Rationale

You know something about the likely value of a variable and can specify the MEAN and variance, VAR, of a NORMAL distribution as your initial judgement.

You have evidence for which the likelihood distribution is also NORMAL and want to incorporate this in your revised estimate.

Therefore:
Find your revised estimate using the weights 1/variance to combine your initial judgement and your evidence.

This is a case of learning from evidence. The mechanics and logic are the same as {D5} with both likelihood and base rate distributions NORMAL. This means that the revised distribution is NORMAL too.

D11. Just how important is judgement?

> If you don't have many data your judgement is important.
>
> The more data you have the less important is your judgement.

Example

Two managers, A and B, have sharply different views about the brand recognition of their company (the proportion of people who, when asked, can identify the company from its name).

Their views are represented by BETA distributions {C5} with parameters ALPHA = 2, BETA = 3 for A and ALPHA = 7, BETA = 2 for B.

A quick lunchtime survey showed that 4 people of 10 asked recognised the brand. The initial (dashed lines) and revised (solid lines) beliefs {D8} are in the chart.

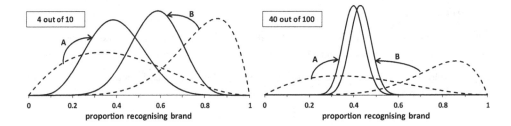

In a larger survey of 100 people, 40 recognised the brand. The revised beliefs of the two managers are now almost the same.

Rationale

This Example illustrates a quite general point: more data leads to a convergence of belief. Realistically large surveys, several hundred or more, will make the revised beliefs practically identical. It would be very odd if this did not happen.

At one extreme, if you have a large data set it does not matter what you believed to begin with, your initial belief will be swamped by data. At the other extreme, if you have no data (none exist or you haven't resources for a survey or test or whatever) then all you have is your judgement.

Therefore:

If you expect to have a large data set don't bother expressing a prior belief (base rate), just take the results of the data analysis {e.g. F8, F10}. If you aren't expecting to have many data carefully model your judgement {e.g. C3,C5 C5–C6, C13} and combine judgement and data {D8–D10}.

***

The common model of statistical inference from data {Section F} takes no account of prior judgement for two reasons.

First, because of a desire for objectivity which some see as undermined by the incorporation of judgement, which will be subjective. This is not a strong argument. You will only have given a judgement if you feel that it is justified and will have been careful how you made a probability distribution. If you have no such views give equal probabilities or a flat density {D6, D7}. For example, a flat NORMAL base distribution has infinite variance and so has no weight, $W(B) = 0$ in {D10}. The common method is just a special case of the more general Bayes model.

Second, because judgement is often overwhelmed by data anyway (as in the Example 2). This is a better and practical argument, but only if you have a large sample. You would have to have a very strongly held base view (very small variance) for this to have a significant impact when used with a large data set.

Risky decisions

---

overview

In this section you will get ideas for how to quantify risk and make risky decisions.

First identify and prioritise the risks facing the business {E1,E2}.

Then think about what action to take. You might at least be able to list the possibilities and give an evaluation of outcomes. This should enable you to simplify your decision by eliminating any obviously poor alternative actions {E3,E4}.

These decision situations with no probability assessments are called decisions under **uncertainty**. If you are able to give a probability assessment of what might happen you have a decision under conditions of **risk**. Be clear which you have {E5}.

For a risky decision {E6,E9} think about your attitude to risk {E7} and the precision with which you have been able to give probabilities {E8}.

If there are a number of sources of risk, let the assessment for each be made by those best able to do so then aggregate the results to give an overall risk assessment. If the aggregation is linear (just addition or subtraction) this is easy {E10–E12}. For more complicated models use an alternative method based on simulation {E13}.

To evaluate sequences of decisions and consequences use a decision tree {E14}.

These decisions will be group decisions. Your analysis and presentation of the results should make it easy for all members to participate in ways that are meaningful for them.

E1. Thinking about risk

There are two reasons you may need to think about risk.

First, a business is faced with a number of uncertainties. You need to compare and **prioritise** so that you can decide what to do.

Second, you must make a decision but do not have perfect information therefore there is a **risk** that the result of your decision will not be what you expected or hoped for.

Think about:

what external events might happen?
how likely are they?
what will be their effect if they happen?
are the different events related?
what is your attitude to risk?
what can you do?

Example

Think of a business you know or know about. What are the external threats to the business

resources, physical and human?
finance?
supply chain?
competitors?

What else?

Rationale

Most decisions are group decisions. Not only may there be several people involved but the decisions you make will have to be approved by others to whom you are accountable. You need to demonstrate the reasoning supporting your decision in a form which can be easily communicated.

You want the rigour which a quantitative model can bring but are aware that not everything is easily quantified. Some of your colleagues may be unhappy, even alienated, by a too mathematical approach they don't fully understand.

Therefore:

Keep it simple. Start by thinking about the points listed in the box above.

Rather than try for one big model a small number of simple models may be a much better way for you and others to develop a shared understanding of what best to do: What important assumptions need to be made? What information needs to be collected?

Developing a risk matrix {E2} can be a good place to start. You will be forced to think about both the probabilities that different things might happen and, if they do, the size of the impact on the business:

You will have a better understanding of the risky situation you face.

You are then well placed to decide whether further modelling will help.

E2. Prioritise risks with a risk matrix

> You think that your company (or country or whatever) is vulnerable to some external events and need to prioritise which are more important.
>
> Make a table: rows and columns showing
>
> > how likely an event is
> > and   the size of the impact.
>
> About five rows and five columns should be enough.
>
> Label rows and columns in as much details as possible. Just using an ordinal scale {A1} from low to high may be about all you feel competent to do. On the other hand, you may be able to give fuller descriptions or even quantify (probabilities, for example).
>
> Put each risk appropriately in the grid.
>
> Prioritise high impact and high probability risks.

Example 1

A European industrial company was concerned about the risk that key people would leave. The consultants McKinsey assessed each of the 460 employees according to how important their knowledge and skills were to the company and how likely they were to leave (based on market conditions, salary, family situation ...). Here is the table[1]:

High	Unique skills/knowledge, a pivotal person in the organisation	37	22	9	8	2
	Important resource whose specific skills/knowledge requires careful attention	69	50	39	15	19
Difficulty replacing this person	Important resource but person's competencies are shared and not at risk	74	28	21	14	14
	General competencies in own area	10	22	6	13	13
Low	No specific competencies, easy to find in the market	3	1	2	3	3
		0	25	50	75	100

Probability person leaving %

The numbers in the cells show the number of employees.

The twenty five cells have been grouped into three risk categories

High risk: the four shaded cells at top right
Low risk: the shaded cells at bottom left
Medium risk: the unshaded cells

The company now has an idea of the size of problem it faces.

Example 2

Here is a risk matrix used by the UK National Health Service[2]

			Impact/Consequences				
			negligible	minor	moderate	major	extreme
			1	2	3	4	5
	Almost certain	5	5	10	15	20	25
	Likely	4	4	8	12	16	20
Probability	Possible	3	3	6	9	12	15
	Unlikely	2	2	4	6	8	10
	Rare	1	1	2	3	4	5

Probability and impact are both described using words but then numbers as well. Multiplying the numbers for each row/column combination gives a score based on the same reasoning as expected value {B7}. These are shown in the table.

Using these numbers different levels of risk are defined and appropriate actions described:

Risk level	Score	Risk Level Description
Extreme	20–25	Unacceptable level of risk exposure that requires immediate corrective action to be taken, and monitoring at Board level.
Major	15–19	Unacceptable level of risk which requires measures to be put in place to reduce exposure, and monitoring at Executive and Board level.
	10–14	Unacceptable level of risk which requires measures to be put in place to reduce exposure, and monitoring at Executive level and potentially at Board level.
Moderate	4–9	Acceptable level of risk exposure subject to regular active monitoring measures by senior managers.
Minor or Negligible	1–3	Acceptable level of risk subject to regular passive monitoring measures at local management level.

What do the numbers add? Do they have meaning; is an impact of 4 twice as bad as an impact of 2? Do you feel reassured to have a system based on numbers, whatever their meaning?

Rationale

Bad things sometimes happen, but how bad and how unlikely?

You need to be aware of risks so that you can decide how they may be avoided or adverse effects reduced.

Don't try to be too ambitious to begin with. You are trying to prioritise the different sources of risk to facilitate discussion. To do this you need to capture the main points in an easily accessible form.

> Therefore:
> Make a simple probability / impact table (about 5×5) and mark on it each of the sources of risk you face.

You will now be able to see what you need to be most concerned about.

Some quantitative modelling will probably be helpful and you have established a context for it.

***

These tables go by a number of names. Risk matrix seems nicely descriptive though some call them heat maps.

***

When is quantification helpful and when is it not?

You might be able to give quantitative values — probability for likelihood and money value for impact — or you may only be able to give ordinal assessments (A to E). Do not rush to give ordinal variables number labels. This will tempt you to make calculations as if your ordinal variable was a ratio variable {A1,A13}. It makes no sense at all to multiply ordinal variables

$$2 \times 4 = 8$$
but $\quad B \times D = ?$

though you will need to think about what the co-occurrence of probability B and impact D means for your problem.

Avoid using numbers needlessly. There is a danger that you may fool yourself (and others) that you know more than you do {B8}.

In Example 1 it seems likely that the numerical probability values are there to ensure some consistency of categorisation but that in Example 2 the intent is clearly to multiply.

Giving number values may have a rhetorical purpose in convincing others (and yourself) that your evaluation is more "scientific" (the quote marks are deliberate) than it is. Don't do it unless you have established that you really do have ratio variables.

E3. Screening the alternatives

> To evaluate a number of alternative actions you need to know (at least)
>
> the alternatives
> what might happen in the business environment to affect your decision (the system states)
> what would be the result of each alternative/system state combination
>
> Show these in a table.

Example

A food processing company is concerned about the possible introduction of new regulations. If introduced these regulations would mean either that investment in new machinery will be needed or that existing products could be sold only in markets which are less profitable.

There is much uncertainty about what, if any, new regulation will be introduced. The feeling is that either none will be introduced or there will be some very tough regulations aimed at meeting all public concerns or some midway level of light touch regulation. The company can adopt a do nothing strategy and hope for no regulatory change or it can invest to meet either the maximum or the intermediate levels of regulatory change. A fourth alternative is to sell the company at the going rate, which is not high because of industry uncertainty.

Outcomes (also called payoffs) are rated A–E. The best outcome for the company is that the maximum upgrade is made and the maximum regulation change happens. The company will then be in an excellent position and may even be one of the industry leaders. At the other extreme, if this investment is made and there are no regulatory changes the investment must still be paid for but with no extra revenue. The full table of outcomes is

| | | regulation change | | |
		none	*light*	*tough*
	do nothing	B	C	D
possible	*small investment*	D	B	C
action	*big investment*	E	B	A
	sell the business	D	D	D

Rationale

You have a good understanding of the risks you face {E2} and must now decide what to do. At the early stage of a decision you need a simple way of engaging the decision group in discussion about external threats, what might be done and what would happen as a result. You need to get brains engaged in discussion.

Therefore:

Make a payoff table showing actions, system states and payoffs. At the start of discussion it may be easier to describe payoffs on an ordinal scale (A–E) rather than numerically.

You have displayed some of the main elements of your decision.

Enter the payoffs however is natural to the situation. In an initial meeting simple ordinal evaluations are likely to keep the discussion lively. Numerical values (money?) can follow once you have agreed a set of system states and possible actions.

***

Even ordinal evaluation can lead to decision:

If the company does not wish to be exposed to situations as poor as E then *big investment* can be eliminated.

In no circumstances is *sell the business* a better option that either *do nothing* or *small investment* so you may want to eliminate the *sell the business* option.

In this second case we say that *sell the business* is **weakly dominated** by *do nothing;* weakly because in one state their payoffs are the same. If *do nothing* had a superior score in all circumstances we can say that it **dominates** *sell the business.*

***

It is likely that during the discussion someone will say that they believe one system state is more likely than others. This will inevitably raise the question of whether it is reasonable to give probabilities {E5}.

***

In other statsNotes uncertainty has been measured by probability {B1}. In the kinds of problems in this section uncertainty has a different meaning.

If you have numerical values both for payoffs and probabilities you have a decision problem characterised by **risk**. You may calculate expected values {E6} and other measures {E9} as guides for your decision.

If you feel unable to give probabilities you have a problem characterised by **uncertainty**. A looser set of decision criteria can help {E4}.

This distinction between risk and uncertainty is important {E5}.

E4. Uncertainty and decision

> To choose between a number of alternatives list
>
> > the alternatives
> > what might happen in the business environment to affect your decision (the system states)
> > a number (e.g. revenue) for each alternative / system state combination
>
> Show these in a table.
>
> Decide your attitude to these outcomes and formulate a rule to help you choose the best alternative.

Example

A food processing company is concerned about the possible introduction of new regulations and has identified four possible actions in response {E3}. Money values (€m) have been found for the payoffs:

		regulation change		
		none	light	tough
	do nothing	1.4	1.0	0.7
possible action	small investment	0.5	1.7	0.8
	big investment	−1.5	1.6	2.0
	sell the business	0.6	0.6	0.6

The *sell the business* option is **dominated** {E3} by *do nothing*; which <u>always</u> gives a better payoff, whichever regulatory change, or none, is introduced. Consider dropping the *sell the business* option.

Of the remaining three alternatives

> choose *big investment* if you want the action which may give you the biggest payoff (2.0)
> choose *do nothing* if you want the action with the largest guaranteed payoff (0.7)
> choose *small investment* if you want the most robust action, that which is never far from the optimum.

Rationale

Which alternative you prefer depends on your attitude to payoffs and differences in payoffs. How important is it to get a big payoff? How important is it to avoid a poor payoff? and so on.

There is no correct answer, but there might be a criterion which is right for you.

Therefore:

Think carefully about your main criterion and try to use a simple rule that captures it. If you are ambivalent try two or more rules. Perhaps they give the same result, perhaps not. You will have learned something about your preferences.

***

There are a number of simple rules which have been suggested over the years. The basic idea is that if all the payoffs for an action can be reduced to a single number then you have a simple decision: pick the biggest (or smallest) number.

***

If you want to maximise payoff summarise each alternative by the biggest payoff in that row. Pick the row for which this is biggest, 2.0 in this case. For obvious reasons this is called the **maximax** rule.

		regulation change				
		none	*light*	*tough*	*max*	*min*
	do nothing	1.4	1.0	0.7	1.4	**_0.7_**
possible action	*small investment*	0.5	1.7	0.8	1.5	0.5
	big investment	−1.5	1.6	2.0	**_2.0_**	−1.5

Alternatively, you may be very cautious. Summarise each action by the worst payoff. For each row choose the smallest value. Picking the largest of these minimum values maximises the guaranteed payoff, which is 0.7 for this example. This is the **maximin** rule.

***

People often say they want a robust solution. What might this mean? Measure robustness by the amount by which an outcome is, with hindsight, suboptimal. Suppose the *tough* regulations are introduced (the third column of the table). If the company had chosen *big investment* they would have made the best decision; degree of suboptimality zero. Choosing *small investment* gives a payoff of 0.8 which is suboptimal by 2.0 − 0.8 = 1.2. These measures of robustness are called **regret**.

		regulation change			
		none	*light*	*tough*	*max*
	do nothing	0	0.7	1.3	1.3
possible action	*small investment*	0.9	0	1.2	**_1.2_**
	big investment	2.9	0.1	0	2.9

Choose the action with the smallest maximum regret. This is the **minimax regret** rule. Choosing *small investment* is the most robust solution because you will never be more than €1.2m below the optimum whatever happens. The *do nothing* option is not bad either.

***

It would be unusual if you or a colleague did not think that some states are more likely than others. So perhaps you can use probabilities. Perhaps so, but be careful {E5}.

138

E5. Risk or uncertainty?

> To choose between alternatives when outcomes are not known precisely it is natural to use probabilities to describe how likely are the alternative system states which condition those outcomes.
>
> Be careful.
>
> You may not have any good forecasts or you may feel uneasy about making any judgement about probability values. You can either
>
> > not use probabilities and so decide to use simple decision rules for an uncertain situation {E4}
> >
> > or make some cautious probability estimates but use sensitivity analysis {E8} to see what happens when the probabilities change within plausible bounds.

Example

A food processing company is concerned about the possible introduction of new regulations and has identified three possible actions in response {E3,E4}. Money values (€m) have been found for the payoffs:

		regulation change		
		none	*light*	*tough*
	do nothing	1.4	1.0	0.7
possible action	*small investment*	0.5	1.7	0.8
	big investment	–1.5	1.6	2.0

The politics influencing the government's decision are complex and seem to change daily.

Does it make sense to think you can give probability estimates for the government's decision?

Rationale

In 1921 the Chicago economist Frank Knight wrote this:

> It will appear that a *measurable* uncertainty, or "risk" proper, as we shall use the term, is so far different from an *unmeasurable* one that it is not in effect an uncertainty at all. We shall accordingly restrict the term "uncertainty" to cases of the non-quantitate type. It is this "true" uncertainty, and not risk, as has been argued, which forms the basis of a valid theory of profit and accounts for the divergence between actual and theoretical competition.[3]

One of his purposes was to distinguish between decisions which can be reduced to calculation (just like insurance) and those which cannot and so must require judgement. Knight's point was that only

139

those taking decisions of uncertainty are entitled to the high rewards which their success may bring. Those taking risky decisions are relying on calculations and so not entitled to high rewards.

Similar points were made by Keynes and, more recently, by Robert Skidelsky.[4] The most recent failures of the finance business may well have been due in part to the belief that uncertain events could be quantified (risk) when this was far too optimistic and a looser framework for judgement (uncertainty) should have been used. This would have forced a more open discussion of the judgements made. But risk models were (and are) necessary for financial engineering (interesting term) and to feed the algorithms.

***

The pressure to give probability estimates, not just in finance, is considerable. They enable calculation of single number values which summarises a complex situation. The danger is that the necessary assumptions have not been well understood and so bad decisions are made.

Therefore:

If you are comfortable with specifying probabilities and interpreting the result use a probability based risk model {E6,E9}.

But if you feel the situation is so fluid and opaque that you are unhappy even to consider probabilities use an uncertainty approach {E4}. This more transparent process should be helpful.

You need an appropriate support for your decision. How you treat the likelihood of different events is central. Using probabilities is just the thing, but only if you feel they are justified.

You may get reliable probabilities from data analysis or you may make judgemental estimates {C13,D6,D7}.

Just think carefully which modelling framework is a better fit for you and the problem you have.

E6. Risky decision

> You need to choose between alternatives but are not sure how likely are different possible outcomes.
>
> You feel able to make probability assessments for different system states.
>
> Use the expected payoff for each alternative as a guide for your decision.

Example

A food processing company is concerned about the possible introduction of new regulations and has identified three possible actions in response {E3,E4}. Money values (€m) have been found for the payoffs:

		regulation change			
		none	light	tough	EV
possible action	do nothing	1.4	1.0	0.7	1.06
	small investment	0.5	1.7	0.8	1.16
	big investment	−1.5	1.6	2.0	0.75
	PROB	0.3	0.5	0.2	

After some discussion {D6} about what the government might do you decide that

$$\text{PROB}(none) = 0.3$$
$$\text{PROB}(light) = 0.5$$
$$\text{PROB}(tough) = 0.2$$

For the *do nothing* option the expected value {B7} is

$$EV = (1.4 \times 0.3) + (1.0 \times 0.5) + (0.7 \times 0.2) = 1.06$$

The *small investment* option looks good.

Rationale

You need to assess which option is best, or to rank them. For each alternative you have a list of probability/payoff pairs. Simply comparing these lists to decide which alternative you prefer might just be possible for two alternatives and two payoffs. For realistically larger decision problems this easy comparison is likely to be beyond your cognitive ability. But you need some consistent way of evaluating alternatives.

Therefore:

Calculate the expected value for each option and use this as a basis for your decision.

You will have an evaluation based on two assumptions: that your probabilities are justified and that EV is a good summary.

Your probability estimates may be based on quantitative models {Section C} or judgement {D6,C13} or some mixture of both {D8–D10}. It is unlikely that you think these probability estimates are precise. Test the effects of imprecision by making some sensitivity analyses {E8}.

***

Using EV as your criterion implies that you are indifferent between, for the *do nothing* alternative, the three payoff/probability pairs, and a sure value of 1.06. For this to be true you must value a payoff increase of €100 equally whether it reduces loss or increases profit. This may well be what you do think but it makes sense to be aware of the assumption {E7}.

Expected value is an average. You may be concerned with how likely are high or low value outcomes or both and look at those {E9} as well as the average. Expected utility {E7} is another way of considering the full range of outcomes, but even if you use this it may still help your decision explicitly to consider those extremes.

***

Representing your problem in a table is good if you want to choose one of a number of actions based on the immediate outcomes. It is a static representation which is appropriate for many problems.

If your problem is more dynamic, and you need to think further ahead to subsequent actions the basic model can be extended to take account of a sequence of decisions {E14}.

E7. Are you risk averse?

In a risky decision problem you summarise a set of payoff/probability pairs by calculating expected value, EV.

This assumes that $100 has the same value to you whether it is reducing a loss or increasing a profit. But you may value reducing loss by $100 more highly than a $100 increases in profit.

Is this what you think?

Example

A hostile bid has been made for a company in which you own some shares. If the bid fails you will lose $200 but if it succeeds you will gain $500. You believe these outcomes are equally likely. A friend offers to buy your shares for $50. Should you accept?

The expected value {E6,B7} of your shares is EV = (-200 × 0.5) + (500 × 0.5) = $150.

Does this help?

Rationale

It is easy to think that people who are risk averse are those who wish above all to avoid bad outcomes. True enough, but in the context of a decision rule based on expected value there is a very particular interpretation which takes into account not just the magnitude of a loss or a profit but also how likely they are.

You are being offered less than the EV so why would you take it? Perhaps you do not like the possibility of losing $200. Perhaps you do not have $200 to lose. You would settle for less just because you get $50 for sure and avoid the possibility of losing $200. If you are that sort of person you are said to be **risk averse**, in this case paying a **risk premium** of $150 - $50 = $100 to avoid possible loss.

If your eyes are on the possibility of gaining $500 you would need more than $150 to compensate for forgoing that possibility. You would be **risk prone**.

If you thought that the EV of $150 would be about right you would be **risk neutral**.

In a risky situation what you decide depends on your attitude to risk. If you are risk neutral then use expected value, it's easy. But first you have to know if this is a good model of how you think.

Therefore:
For your problem pick the lowest and highest payoffs. Make a lottery with these payoffs and equal probabilities. Calculate the expected value. Would you be indifferent between the lottery and getting the expected value for sure? If you are then you are probably risk neutral.

This diagnostic test will let you know whether it makes sense to use expected value (of money or whatever payoffs are measured in) as a decision criterion. Otherwise you should weight payoffs to reflect your risk aversion or risk proneness. How can this be done?

These weighted values are called **utility**. For each payoff find the corresponding utility and use expected utility as your decision criterion: EU rather than EV.

Utility has no obvious units as does money. For convenience set the utility of the smallest payoff (–\$200) to 0 and the utility of the largest payoff (\$500) equal to 1:

$$u(-200) = 0 \text{ and } u(500) = 1.$$

Suppose you are indifferent between selling for \$50 and holding on to the shares. Your indifference implies that the utility to you of \$50 for sure is the same as the expected utility the risky outcome

$$\text{expected utility} = EU = (0.5 \times 0) + (0.5 \times 1) = 0.5$$

and this is *your* utility of \$50: $u(50) = 0.5$.

Plot this on a graph. Sketch in a curve.

If you had been risk neutral then this utility would have been at the value \$150,

$$u(150) = 0.5$$

You could change the probabilities and get some more points to sketch the curve. Be careful. We can all fairly easily imagine and understand a 50:50 lottery but might struggle for other values, so keep it simple.

If you had been risk prone the curve would have been below the risk neutral line, but the process the same.

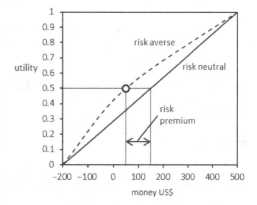

Once you have your utility curve transform all the payoff values into utilities and base your decision on EU rather than EV. This will take account of your attitude to risk.

***

This elegant scheme is due to the economist Oskar Morgenstern and the mathematician John von Neumann who developed it for their famous 1947 book *The Theory of Games and Economic Behavior*.

But could you do this in practice? Careful framing of the question as an insurance premium or investment in a project or a proposition for a venture capitalist will help. But while expected money value is quite easy to understand, expected utility may be harder because more abstract. This is the price of the elegant model.

***

John von Neumann
1903–1957

Do not lose sight of the purpose of all this: to help some people make a decision. If they do not understand what's going on they probably will not buy in to the solution the model gives. The simple diagnostic test helps in understanding what is meant by risk aversion. You may decide to use this as the basis for a discussion rather than trying for a utility-based model. But if those involved are happy to use utilities do that.

E8. Sensitivity test

> A model has a number of parameters and data as inputs. Values of some are known precisely but some not.
>
> Run the model a number of times with different plausible values to see the effect on output and decision.

Example

A food processing company is concerned about the possible introduction of new regulations and has identified three possible actions in response {E3,E4}. Money values (€m) have been found for the payoffs and expected values calculated {E6}:

		regulation change			EV
		none	light	tough	
	do nothing	1.4	1.0	0.7	1.06
possible action	small investment	0.5	1.7	0.8	1.16
	big investment	-1.5	1.6	2.0	0.75
	PROB	0.3	0.5	0.2	

The probability estimates are the best you could give but it is clear to all involved that they cannot be precise. It is agreed that there is a margin of error (imprecision) of about 0.1 for each probability estimate. Test what happens for different probability values. For example, increasing the probability of no regulatory change by 0.1 and maintaining the other probabilities in their same proportions to ensure they sum to 1:

PROB(none) = 0.3 + 0.1 = 0.4
PROB(light) = (1 - 0.4) × 0.5/(0.5 + 0.2) = 0.43
PROB(tough) = (1 - 0.4) × 0.2/(0.5 + 0.2) = 0.17

The results of all tests are:

		base	different probability estimates					
			none ± 0.1		light ± 0.1		tough ± 0.1	
PROBABILITY	one	0.3	0.2	0.4	0.36	0.24	0.34	0.26
	light	0.5	0.57	0.43	0.4	0.6	0.56	0.44
	tough	0.2	0.23	0.17	0.24	0.16	0.1	0.3
EV	do nothing	1.06	1.01	1.11	1.07	1.05	1.11	1.02
	small investment	1.16	1.25	1.07	1.05	1.27	1.21	1.12
	big investment	0.75	1.07	0.43	0.58	0.92	0.59	0.91
RANK	do nothing	2	3	1	1	2	2	2
	small investment	1	1	2	2	1	1	1
	big investment	3	2	3	3	3	3	3

Based on the EV values and rankings it is agreed that the *big investment* option could be dropped and that *do nothing* isn't quite as good as the *small investment* option. This confirms the initial finding and gives some reassurance that the recommendation is unaffected even by quite large swings in probability assessments.

Rationale

Most decisions have to be justified to third parties — your boss, the Board, the public — and they may well ask "whose judgement?" and "are these judgements skewing the decision?"

Judgements are necessarily imprecise. You (and those others) will want to know the effect of that imprecision on your recommendation. You want to show the effects in a way that is easily understood and that helps the decision.

> Therefore:
> Decide the ranges within which your estimates might lie and rerun the model changing one value at a time. Can you reasonably distinguish a single best recommendation or should two or more go forward for more discussion and analysis?

You will have gained some better understanding of how sensitive your model is to your imprecise judgements. In the Example one option could be eliminated and the better of the other two was pretty clear.

You will also see which source of imprecision has a particularly strong effect. In the Example the estimate for PROB(*none*) stands out while the different estimates for PROB(*tough*) do not alter your recommendation at all. Can you be more precise about this probability PROB(*none*)?

Although in the example the sensitivity ranges were the same for all probabilities this doesn't have to be the case. Think carefully about what you believe is plausible.

✳✳✳

This simple model is well suited to helping group discussion. Build a small spreadsheet and project it onto a screen so that everyone in the group can see. If, in the course of discussion, someone says "what happens if …" you can easily see just what does happen. The discussion is not interrupted, just the opposite.

✳✳✳

Rather than seeing the effects of one set of changes at a time you could consider describing your uncertainty about the probability values by giving probability estimates of your probabilities (called second-order probabilities). This has obvious appeal but may be more difficult to understand for most of us. File under "Try Later".

✳✳✳

In the Example the system state variable, the level of regulation, had three discreet values {A1}.

If you have system states described by a continuous variable (GDP or sales volume, for example) you will have used an appropriate probability model {C13}. Try making sensitivity tests for the parameter values.

E9. Two summaries: risk and value at risk

> For a risky decision it makes sense to think about the probability that something bad might happen.
>
> Either pick a target value of the outcome and find
>
> $$\text{risk} = \text{probability of missing target}$$
>
> or pick an acceptably small probability and find
>
> $$\text{value at risk} = \text{outcome defining acceptable risk}$$

Example

A sales estimate is described by a NORMAL distribution {C3} with mean £200,000 and standard deviation STDEV = £15,000.

The revenue target for next year for this product is £180,000. The *risk* of not meeting the target is 9%.

This is too big. A maximum risk of 2% is set. The corresponding *value at risk* is £169,200. This is a guide for a revised target or for a discussion of some action, if needed.

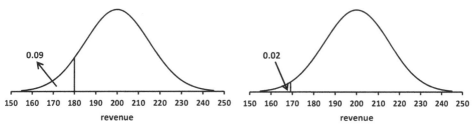

Risk	Value at risk
NORM.DIST(180,200,15,TRUE) = 0.0912 or 9%	NORM.INV(0.02,200,15) = 169.2

Rationale

Using the expected value {E6} or expected utility {E7} might seem an obvious decision criterion. In the Example the expected value is £200,000 which is above the target. All OK? You would be foolish to think so.

You often hear or read that a particular company is performing above (or below) expectations. If the expectation is just the expected value then there is a 50% chance that performance will be above expectations and also a 50% chance it will be below.

Other summaries combine measures of average and spread {A6,A7} of the distribution. For example, the coefficient of variation {A9} or, in finance, the risk/reward ratio {K1}. These are of some help in comparing options but they are not very decision oriented.

You want to describe the essentially risky aspect of the analysis in a way that can be easily understood.

Therefore:

Look at values which represent bad news (revenue too low, project duration too high) and set a target. The tail probability will show the risk of not meeting the target. Alternatively, set the level of risk and see what performance needs to be.

Whenever a summary measure is used information is lost. These two measures, because they focus on the tail of the distribution, preserve much of the information needed for discussion and decision.

Use a chart to give some extra appreciation of the tail probabilities. The distribution shown above easily gets the attention of your audience.

Also show the cumulative distribution {A5}, in this application called a *risk distribution* (right). It will help you read the relation between risk and outcome quite easily and so will help with the discussion.

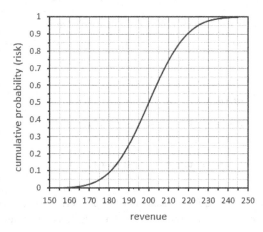

E10. Divide and conquer

Systems are made of subsystems. System performance is often the sum or difference of subsystem outputs:

project duration is the sum of task durations

contribution is the difference between revenue and variable cost.

To find the total risk find the MEAN and variance, VAR, of each constituent. Then combine the risks by:

adding or subtracting means as appropriate

summing the variances.

The distribution of these aggregated risks is NORMAL.

The simple addition works if the risks are independent. If risks aren't a slightly modified calculation is used {E11}.

Example

A company sells three products in different markets. Estimates of sales next year are

market	sales forecasts (millions of units sold)	
	MEAN	VAR
A	3.2	1.1
B	2.7	0.6
C	5.7	0.9
	11.6	2.6

The estimate of total sales is Normally distributed {C3} with

$$\text{MEAN} = 11.6$$
and $$\text{VAR} = 2.6$$
so $$\text{STDEV} = \sqrt{2.6} = 1.61$$

The risk {E9} of not hitting the global sales target of 9.5 million units is

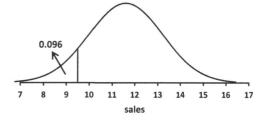

NORM.DIST(9.5,11.6,1.61,TRUE) = 0.096 or 10%

Rationale

Estimating total risk is difficult. The task has wide scope and so expertise is widely spread.

Therefore:

Disaggregate the problem into a number of constituents so that each has a scope which allows those with knowledge in that area to make meaningful estimates {e.g. C13,D8–D10}.

Re-aggregate these estimates to give the total you need.

In many cases of risk estimation it will be enough to add (or subtract) means and add (always) variances.

If risks are not independent variance will change, more if risks are positively correlated and less if they are negatively correlated {E11}.

This strategy of disaggregating a problem into a number of modules and re-aggregating the solutions is very common. It is sometimes called the strategy of *divide and conquer* to show its power. Engineering structures, computer programs and other objects are designed and made this way. So are many management decisions.

***

Probability estimates need to be re-aggregated. The *Central Limit Theorem* {F4} shows how to do this: add the variances. Variance is the *only* measure of risk that has this additive property. Always add variances even if you are subtracting means.

Using the simple rule — add or subtract the means and add the variances — works fine provided that:

1. Each constituent probability distribution is symmetrical or nearly symmetrical (ideally NORMAL) or if there are more than about 30 of them {F4}. This second condition is met in most applications.

2. If these conditions are not met use a simulation model {E13}.

3. The aggregation is linear: all you are doing is adding or subtracting individual risks. For other cases you may be able to use a different formula, but most often simulation does the job {E13}.

4. The risks are independent {B5,B6}. If they are correlated, as they may well be, the formula is easily extended to cope {E11}, provided you know the correlations {I2}.

***

There is a tendency among some analysts to reach for a simulation package in all circumstances. But a great many management problems are linear and so the simple rule is all you need.

E11. Correlated risks

> To find total risk divide the problem into parts and find the MEAN and variance, VAR, of each. Also estimate the correlation between the risks.
>
> For each pair of risks i and j the correlation effect is the product of their standard deviations, STDEV, and the correlation, CORREL, between them (called covariance)
>
> $$\text{STDEV}(i) \times \text{STDEV}(j) \times \text{CORREL}(i,j)$$
>
> The total risk is described by a NORMAL distribution with mean and variance
>
> $$\text{MEAN} = \text{sum (or difference) of means as appropriate}$$
> $$\text{VAR} = \text{sum of variances} + \{2 \times \text{SUM } [\text{STDEV}(i) \times \text{STDEV}(j) \times \text{CORREL}(i,j)]\}$$

Example

A company sells three products in different markets. Estimates of sales next year are

| | sales forecasts (millions of units sold) | |
market	MEAN	VAR
A	3.2	1.1
B	2.7	0.6
C	5.7	0.9
	11.6	2.6

Although the products are sold to different markets, sales fluctuations are related to some extent due to common global branding, economic conditions and so on. Records show the correlations {I2} between sales:

    CORREL$(A,B) = 0.7$

    CORREL$(A,C) = 0.6$

    CORREL$(B,C) = 0.4$

The increase in variance of total sales due to correlation effects is

$$2 \times [(\sqrt{1.1} \times \sqrt{0.6} \times 0.7) + (\sqrt{1.1} \times \sqrt{0.9} \times 0.6) + (\sqrt{0.6} \times \sqrt{0.9} \times 0.3)] = 2.77$$

(remember STDEV $= \sqrt{\text{VAR}}$ {A7}) so in total

    VAR $= 2.6 + 2.77 = 5.37$

and   STDEV $= \sqrt{5.37} = 2.32$

The risk of not hitting a global sales target of 9.5m units is

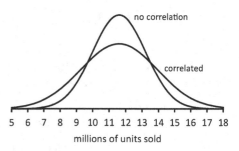

$$\text{NORM.DIST}(9.5, 11.6, 2.32, \text{TRUE})$$
$$= 0.183 \text{ or } 18\%$$

With no correlation the risk is 10% {E10}. Positive correlation has increased risk, the probability of low sales.

The probability of high sales has increased too, of course.

Rationale

Systems consist of connected elements so it is no surprise that when something changes something else changes too. For example,

returns from different shares are in some part determined by the individual companies but also by the general movements in the stock market {K2,K3}

the revenue estimates from several sales regions will depend both on the conditions particular to each region and also on common factors such as the general movement of the economy and the offerings of competitors.

You need to take account of these effects when estimating projected performance and how risky different options might be.

Therefore:

Think about the different sources of risk. For each pair decide whether they might be correlated to some degree. If you think they are find some data on past joint variation and calculate the correlation {I2}. Use these correlations when aggregating risks to give total risk.

You will have taken account of related risks. When correlation is positive variance, and so risk, is increased. So too is the probability in the other tail of the distribution, the one that represents very good outcomes such as high sales volumes. In adopting a strategy aimed at this high performance, investing in several firms in the same sector for example, you will increase both the chance of high returns but also the risk of very poor returns.

Negative correlations have the opposite effect of reducing risk and also the chance of high returns. There are times when this is a good thing.

A.P. Møller–Mærsk A/S is a Danish conglomerate probably best known for the shipping company Maersk Line which carries 15% of all seaborne freight. It has other businesses too one of which is Maersk Oil with interests in exploration and production. Based on comments by Nils Smedegaard Andersen, Group CEO, a story in the *Financial Times* on 12 November 2014, a time of falling oil price, reported

That means that while Maersk Line benefits from lower fuel costs, Maersk Oil suffers from the falling oil price with Mr Andersen saying the recent drop would cost the business $400m on an annualised basis. But he added that the recent drop in prices meant that it was cheaper to buy oilfields.

Whether as a matter of deliberate strategy or just good fortune this negative correlation has reduced risk in relation to overall group performance.

Correlation is not just a measure of relations in data: it is descriptive of aspects of what businesses do.

***

It may be possible easily to calculate CORREL values from data (of share prices or sales volumes, for instance). If this is not possible try making high and low estimates to get some idea of sensitivity {E8} to changes in the strength of the correlations. This may not be easy but you need to assess if it is important.

E12. Policy constants

> You have estimates of performance variables which are subject to uncertainty. They are sources of risk.
>
> You also have some decision variables which are set as a matter of policy. Their value is fixed. They are not sources of risk but do determine the value of results.
>
> Scale each risky variable by multiplying the MEAN and standard deviation, STDEV, by the policy constant.
>
> Now aggregate these scaled risks.

Example

A small regional airline flies four routes to feed the larger airport located at Bridgetown, Barbados. Estimates are made of traffic for the coming year from which MEAN and STDEV of each route forecast is available.

The airline wishes to test the revenue that would result from a particular proposed set of fares.

The calculations follow the form of {E10}: sum the means and variances

	source of risk		policy	result		
	passenger forecast		adult return	revenue forecast ($million)		
Feeder airport	MEAN	STDEV	fare ($)	MEAN	STDEV	VAR
Antigua	14,600	3500	380	5.548	1.330	1.769
Saint Lucia	16,400	2800	220	3.608	0.616	0.379
Grenada	21,800	2500	300	6.540	0.750	0.563
Dominica	23,000	4100	250	5.750	1.025	1.051
				21.446		3.761

For the Antigua traffic, for example, the revenue estimate is found from the volume forecast to have

$$\text{MEAN} = 14{,}600 \times 380 = 5{,}548{,}000$$
$$\text{STDEV} = 3{,}500 \times 380 = 1{,}330{,}000$$

The estimate of total revenue ($m) is Normally distributed with

$$\text{MEAN} = 21.446$$
and $$\text{STDEV} = \sqrt{3.761} = 1.939$$

The risk of not hitting a revenue target of $20m is

$$\text{NORM.DIST}(20, 21.446, 1.939, \text{TRUE}) = 0.228 \text{ or } 23\%$$

This assumes independent risks on the four routes. If this is unrealistic (and it probably is) estimate the correlations and use {E11}.

Rationale

You need to model the effect of adopting different policies: a price schedule, locations for new shops, specifications of a new product. Whatever the form of the proposal it will be defined precisely; no uncertainty because you have specified the values.

You cannot be certain of the effect (sales, for example) and so have an estimate described by a probability distribution.

The policy can be tested easily by simple multiplication:

> revenue = price × volume
> return = number of shares × return per share

You need to make policy decisions part of your risk estimate.

> Therefore:
> Multiply both mean and standard deviation of the risky outcome by the value of your policy variable. Aggregate the scaled risks assuming either independence {E10} or correlation {E11}.

This works because when a variable is scaled (from passengers to dollars) both mean and standard deviation are scaled by the same amount.

***

The assumption you need to think about is the independence between your policy and the system behaviour.

In some cases the independence is clear. Cost estimates for a hospital are a function of unit cost and patient numbers. Just because your catering costs increase will not alter the number of people needing an appendectomy.

Alternatively, there is a relation and it is accounted for in the risk estimate. The airline in the Example may have used a demand forecasting model which was price sensitive. The model gives an estimate of forecast error for each route. This is used in the calculation.

E13. Monte Carlo

You need to combine several sources of risk. Each is described by a probability distribution. The combination is not linear so simple analytic methods cannot be used.

Use Monte Carlo simulation to combine risks empirically using repeated sampling.

Example

A manufacturing company is considering relocating production to a lower cost location. The difficulty in evaluating this proposal is that demand for this new product is hard to predict. All that anyone is prepared to say is that it could be anywhere between 25,000 and 40,000 units in the first year. This will determine costs.

If demand is less than 30,000 unit cost will be 5, if less than 3,500 it will be 4.5 and if more it will be 3.5. All costs are in the local currency. Your bank needs estimates in US$. The local economy is subject to some instability. The exchange rate may be anywhere between 5 and 6 to the $.

All you have are low and high estimates so choose uniform distributions {C10} for both volume and exchange rate.

Here are the first two simulations:

	A	B	C	D	E
1	volume	unit cost (local)	total cost	exchange rate	$ cost
2	=25+RAND()*15	=IF(A2<30,5,IF(A2>35,3.5,4.5))	=A2*B2	=5+RAND()	=C2/D2
3	=25+RAND()*15	=IF(A3<30,5,IF(A3>35,3.5,4.5))	=A3*B3	=5+RAND()	=C3/D3

The EXCEL function RAND picks a value at random in the range 0 to 1. Use this and scale as appropriate.

The formula in column A uses RAND and scales the result to give values between 25 and 40. The formula in column D returns values between 5 and 6.

Column B gives unit costs dependent on volume.

The first two results are

	A	B	C	D	E
1	volume	unit cost (local)	total cost	exchange rate	$ cost
2	39.92	3.5	139.71	5.88	23.74
3	37.51	3.5	131.29	5.15	25.51

Copying row 2 down to row 1001 gives, in column E, a sample of a thousand estimates of cost. Group these values to show the distribution as a histogram {A3} and a risk function {E9}.

See from the risk function (below) that the probability that cost will not exceed $28,000 is 90%.

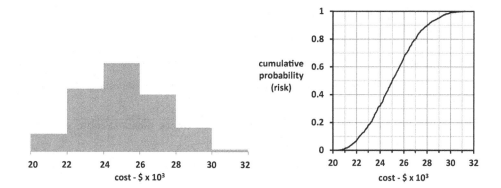

Rationale

This is sampling, usually called Monte Carlo simulation for obvious reasons.

The method is an empirical means of generating values randomly from known distributions and combining the results.

What makes this method so useful is that the model can be of any form. In the Example there were discontinuities in the cost function and division of one distribution by another (cost/exchange rate).

Although the example is just a small illustration the basic idea is clear:

1. Make a spreadsheet for your model in the normal way.
2. Wherever you are uncertain about the value of an input variable change that cell from a single value to a probability distribution.
3. Repeat the model and collect the results.

***

If you have a small model you could build your own simulation, as in the Example.

For the larger models which you are more likely to need there are readily available spreadsheet add-ins. These give you a wide range of probability distributions and output options. The repetitions are not done by copying rows, of course, but the principle is the same.

***

You will want to avoid results being subject to sampling variation so

1. choose a large sample (that is what computers are for)
2. repeat your analysis to check that the risk functions are just about the same

***

If your model is linear use an analytical method {E10–E12}: quicker and cheaper.

E14. Find risk through time with a decision tree

To decide what to do now you need a view of what will happen afterwards.

Draw a tree diagram showing the sequence of decisions and chance events.

Show decisions by a square and chance events by a circle.

At each chance event give your best estimate of the probability of each outcome.

At each end point of the tree write how much that outcome is worth; usually, though not necessarily, in money.

Work backwards from the most remote outcomes. For chance events calculate expected value. For decisions, decide.

Example

A small business develops ideas for new drugs which it sells to pharmaceutical companies. It can sell at different stages of development at prices which reflect how much work has been done at that point. Even a failed trial contains information. After the discovery stage there are two developmental stages. After a successful first stage the drug and all intellectual property rights could be sold for $2m. Even if the drug failed the test at the end of this stage it could still be sold for $0.7m to a company who could reformulate and re-test. After the second stage these figures are $6m and $0.2m.

Alternatively, the company could sell now for $1m.

At this time it is estimated that there is a 70% chance that stage 1 will be successful and an 80% chance for stage 2. Here is the tree.

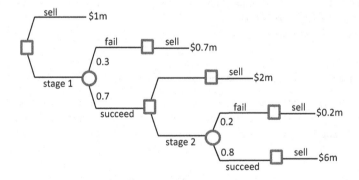

The expected value {E6,B7} of the chance result of stage 2 is $4.84m.

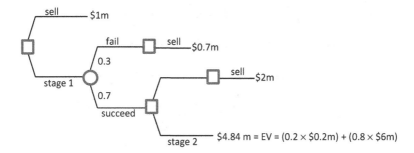

The decision at the end of stage 1 would be in favour of proceeding to stage 2 because $4.84m is bigger than $2m.

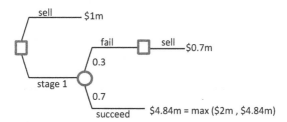

Finally, the expected value of stage 1 development is $3.598m which is greater than $1m.

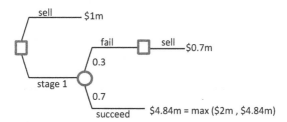

Recommendation: do not sell now but start stage 1 development. The expected value of doing so is $3.598m.

This recommendation is based on the sequence of events shown below in bold. But the company is not committed to that path and should re-analyse following the result of stage 1.

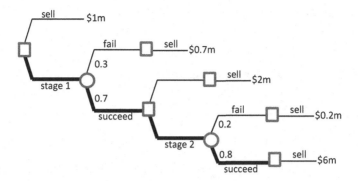

The purpose of this analysis was to decide what to do *now* given the current best estimates of probabilities and selling prices, all of which may change.

Rationale

Taking account of future events is necessary but not always easy.

Therefore:

Make a decision tree. This will clarify your thoughts about future decisions and outcomes.

Developing a tree showing the sequence of events (from left to right) is a useful exercise in its own right, especially if done in a group. Agreeing a picture of the future is a necessary first step and often generates much good discussion.

Collapsing the tree from right to left (sometimes called folding back) enables you to calculate the value of your decision. It does not imply any commitment to future decisions.

You may be uncertain about some of the values given, especially probabilities. Make a sensitivity test {E8}. This is easily done by making a spreadsheet for your problem or by using some readily available software.

Using information from samples

---

overview

You are interested in the value of some characteristic of a population but have only sample data on which to base an estimate. This problem occurs in many contexts: market research to find market share; opinion polls; measuring quality. There are many more, but in all cases it is the fact that you have only sample data and that is the difficulty {F1}.

The key idea is that when you take a sample to estimate a MEAN, for example, this sample mean will not be exactly the same as the mean of the population from which the sample is drawn. You can infer something about the population mean either by reporting what you find or testing against some target or assumed value {F2, F3, F8, F9, F19}.

The same general method is used for inferences about proportions {F10, F11}, variances {F12, F13} and about differences {F14–F17}.

Before any analysis you must have data. Either someone else will have collected the data or you will have to. Having a rational way of deciding how many data you should collect will help you plan your survey {F20}.

F1. Why sample?

> You need to measure a characteristic of a system: a key performance measure for an organisation, customer satisfaction.
>
> You cannot get data from everything or everyone, there are too many of them, and so take a sample.
>
> Decide sample size and how you will collect data to avoid a biased sample.
>
> Report what you find to include the precision of your estimate.

Example

Hodgson's, a long established UK company, was taken over by an overseas competitor with no history of trading outside its country of origin. Six months ago the product was rebranded from its old name, Hodgson's Biscuits, to the name of its new owner, Schultz Snax. Most people had heard of Hodgson's Biscuits. How many now recognize Schultz Snax? What do they think of the new brand?

It is obvious that the whole population of the UK cannot be asked but a sample can. How big a sample? How to pick them?

Rationale

You need to know how a system is behaving:

    is the proportion of rejects within tolerance?
    how many viewers watched this television show?
    how many people have heard of Schultz Snax?

All the members of the system constitute the **population** in which you are interested.

You may have access to all the population data. A supermarket will automatically store data describing who bought what so the average spend can be found exactly.

If your problem does not come with a convenient data logger you will not be able to find what you want exactly because it is just too difficult to count everyone or everything. You do not have the time or the money to ask or measure them all: you are not going to ask all 50 million adults in the UK what they watched on television last night. There may be a bigger problem. If you needed to test engineering components to destruction to find the stress at which they failed then testing them all would mean you had none to sell.

But you need to be able to say something about the population even though you cannot access each member.

    Therefore:
    Make a **sample** by selecting a number of objects from the population. Be careful to avoid bias in your selection. Think carefully what you are going to do with the sample. This will fix how big a sample you need.

You will now have some sample data about which you know everything you want, mean and variance, for example. So what are you justified in saying about the population, given what you know about the sample? There is a chance that whatever you say will be incorrect. Suppose your sample mean is 34. You are not justified in saying "the population mean is 34" but you can say "the population mean is 34-ish" or "the population mean is 34 plus or minus 2". Finding this imprecision and deciding what to report is the problem of **inference** {F2}.

The more data you have the more precise you can be. But more data means more time and money so thinking about how much precision you need will help you decide how much data to collect {F20}.

When you collect data, take care to avoid *bias*. Just buzzing out some emailed questions to your friends will not do. The ideal is to select at random from the population. These notes assume you did this or its equivalent.

F2. Inference: test or report?

You take a **sample** to find out about a **population**.

With the data you can either

> **test** if the data are compatible with a view you have of the population (is it likely that the target has been met?)

or **report** what you have calculated from the data with a margin of error.

Example

Your company makes consumer electronics. It takes customers' queries through its website. The level of service target is that the average time taken to answer these queries is 4 hours.

In a sample of 100 queries the MEAN time was 4.2 hours and the standard deviation STDEV = 1.56 hours {A6, A7}.

Test: If the helpdesk was hitting target the probability of a survey result this bad or worse is 10% {F9}

Report: There is 95% probability that the mean response time for all enquiries is between 3.9 hours and 4.5 hours {F8}

Which style do you prefer? Why? Are there grounds for management action? Is using both report and test helpful?

Rationale

Test Assume a target value in the population. This can be from a theory you want to test or from a performance level you want to impose.

If your assumption is true how unlikely is the value you calculate from the sample? Is it sufficiently unlikely that you are justified in believing that your assumption is probably wrong?

You need to specify a target and think about what "sufficiently unlikely" means.

Report Given your sampled value what might the population value be?

Report a range of values within which the population value might fall. The wider the range the higher the probability that it contains the true value.

You need to specify that probability.

Making a report is direct and therefore appealing. The natural way to talk about uncertainty is to give a range {B10}. On the other hand, some people think that the language of testing is more helpful because it seems more decisive.

> Therefore:
>
> Decide whether test or report better fits your management style and the culture of your organisation and audience.

Both methods require that you specify something as input: *test* requires a target and gives you a probability, *report* requires a probability and gives you a range.

***

166

The differences between *Test* and *Report* are to some extent a question of style.

There are some issues about which you need to think carefully.

To make a test you have to decide where to look for the unlikely evidence which may lead you to conclude that your target is not met. For most operational management problems you will only look at outcomes which are *either* more *or* less than your target *but not both*. For example, you will be worried that a response time target is not being met only if you find evidence of times greater than the target. You will look in only **one tail** of the appropriate probability distribution. But sometimes you will be concerned to see values greater or smaller than the target. For instance, a shelf in a flat pack bookcase is no good if it is either too long or too short. You will have to set a tolerance for this and will test for violations of the tolerance in **both tails** of the probability distribution.

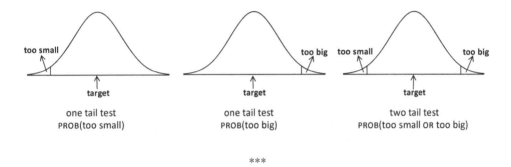

| one tail test | one tail test | two tail test |
| PROB(too small) | PROB(too big) | PROB(too small OR too big) |

***

The probability you get from a test tells you how unlikely is the sample result. Unlikely, but not impossible, just an extreme value in the tail or tails of a probability distribution. You cannot logically take it as evidence that your assumption is incorrect. Treat it as a flag, an indicator. If you are testing performance an unlikely test result means that it is probably worth trying to find out what is going on {G1}.

***

Knowing an interval within which a true value might lie is useful provided that you can interpret the value. In the example, the target value measures an operational variable, response time. You can conceptualise what different values mean in the context of your business.

But suppose you were interested in aptitude scores for new recruits. These scores were derived from theories in psychology and reported on a scale from one to ten. Can you conceptualise what different values might mean for your business decision? You have a score of 5.6 and I have a score of 5.9 — so what? In these circumstances some people prefer a test so that results are assessed by how unlikely they are rather than by their direct business impact.

You have a test result. Given your assumption or requirement the probability of your data is p. You need to interpret this result: is it unusual enough to justify action? Some context would help.

Therefore:
Don't just give the probability. Give the confidence interval {F19} too.

For example, write as: 95% confidence interval = 3.9 to 4.5; p = 10%

F3. Inference: Normal distribution for test and report

> You take a **sample** to find out about a **population**.
>
> To make either a test or report {F2} you can in many cases use the NORMAL distribution.

Rationale

The NORMAL distribution {C3} is useful for many problems of inference, particularly of means and proportions {F8–F11}.

The relation between the distributions used for *test* and *report* {F2} for a MEAN using a large sample {F8–F9} is shown in this diagram:

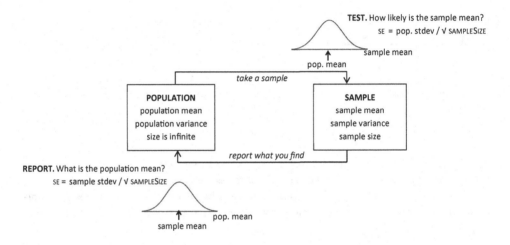

The standard deviations of the distributions for *test* or *report* are called standard errors, SE {F5}. They differ only in their use of either the population standard deviation or sample standard deviation. In many cases they are the same {F6}.

See the effect of SAMPLESIZE. However variable the system behaviour, however big the standard deviation, the standard error can, in principle, be made as small as you wish by collecting more data {F20}.

✳✳✳

This is a special case of Bayes' Rule {D10}.

We have no prior (base) rate so the *reporting* distribution is determined only by the data {D11}.

F4. Central Limit Theorem

You take a number of independent random samples of the same size from a population with known mean and variance {A6, A7}, MEANP and VARP.

The **sums** of these samples are Normally distributed with

           MEAN = SAMPLESIZE × MEANP

and   VAR = SAMPLESIZE × VARP

so   STDEV = STDEVP × √SAMPLESIZE

The **means** of the samples are Normally distributed with

           MEAN = MEANP

and   VAR = VARP/SAMPLESIZE

so   STDEV = STDEVP/√SAMPLESIZE

Example

Sheets of plastic may have a number of small blemishes (called nibs). The sheets produced at a factory have up to ten nibs per sheet.

The number of nibs per sheet, 0 to 10, are equally likely. The distribution of the nibs per sheet has a mean of 5 and variance of 10.

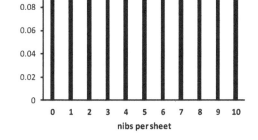

The **total** number of nibs in a sample of 100 sheets is Normally distributed with

           MEAN = 100 × 5 = 500

and   VAR = 100 × 10 = 1000

The **mean** number of nibs per sheet is Normally distributed with

           MEAN = 5

and   VAR = 10/100 = 0.1

Rationale

These results illustrate the Central Limit Theorem (CLT). Here is a demonstration of the process.

The number of nibs on a sheet was chosen randomly[1] from the distribution in the Example.

The sums of 500 samples of size 20 and 500 samples of size 50 are:

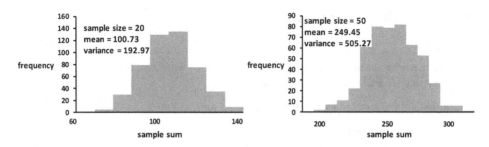

Sums of 500 simulated samples of size 20 and size 50

The population distribution was flat in the range 0–10. But the distribution of sums is symmetric and approaches NORMAL, as the theory predicts.

The means and variances are approximately twenty and fifty times the population values.

Now, dividing each sum by the sample size gives these two distributions of sample means:

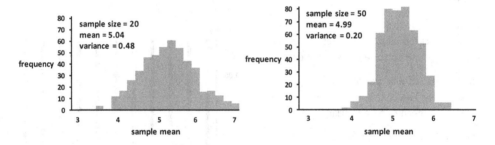

Means of 500 simulated samples of size 20 and size 50

The mean of the sample means is 5, the population mean.

The variance of the sample means is equal to the population variance, 10, divided by the sample size. The larger the sample the less the variability of the sample means.

F5. Standard error

Measure the variability of means of same-sized samples by

$$\text{standard error} = \text{SE} = \frac{\text{population standard deviation}}{\sqrt{\text{SAMPLESIZE}}}$$

This is also measures the precision with which you can estimate a population mean from a sample.

Example

Nibs are manufacturing blemishes on plastic sheets. For sheets produced in a factory the mean number of nibs/sheet is 5 and standard deviation 3.16 {F2}.

For a samples of size 100, SE = $3.16/\sqrt{100}$ = 0.316.

Because sample means are Normally distributed {F2} 95% of these sample means will be in the range $5 \pm (1.96 \times 0.316) = 5 \pm 0.62$ {F19, C3}.

Rationale

When you take a sample there is always the question of how much it can tell you about the population from which it is drawn. What would happen if you took another sample? Would the result be the same? Almost certainly not exactly the same, but how different? Suppose someone else took a different sample, would they reach different conclusions?

Two things determine just how imprecise is your estimate.

First, the variability of the behaviour you are investigating. Are you measuring the average of some characteristic which varies a lot from one member of the population to another or a characteristic which is almost constant? For example, the times taken by workers in a standard assembly task are not likely to vary much so neither will the means of a number of same-sized samples. On the other hand, the time spent exercising in the gym in a week would vary a lot from one person to another so the means of same-sized samples would vary a lot too. It will be harder to get a precise estimate of mean gym time than mean assembly time. You cannot change this. What you can do, and must do, is to measure this variability by finding the population standard deviation.

The second consideration is sample size. However hard the estimation might look because of high population standard deviation the estimate of the mean can, in theory, be as precise as you wish just by collecting more data. As you would expect, the more data you have the more reliable the result (why else spend all that money on a large survey?).

An estimate of a population mean {F8} or proportion {F10} from a sample must inevitably be imprecise. You don't have all the data, just a sample.

Therefore:

Calculate the standard error, SE = population standard deviation/$\sqrt{\text{SAMPLESIZE}}$

Larger SE means more variability and imprecision.

The name standard error does not mean error in the sense of a mistake but error because there will be a difference between the mean you know, the sample mean, and the mean you are interested in, the population mean. Error is perhaps not a good word to use; imprecision would be better. The possibility of error comes when you have to decide what to do with your estimate.

The standard errors for inferences of means and proportions are so often used they are given special names

STandard Error of Mean, STEM {F8}
STandard Error of Proportion, STEP {F10}

These are just particular applications of standard error. In general, standard error is the standard deviation of the estimate of any population value made from a sample.

***

Standard error depends on knowing the population standard deviation. But if your task is to estimate a population mean, because you don't know its value, then you certainly won't know the population standard deviation either. Fortunately there is an easy way of estimating it from sample data {F6} so this presents no problem. In EXCEL use the functions VAR.S and STDEV.S.

***

The effect of increasing sample size can be dramatic for small samples but less so for large samples (economists talk of decreasing returns to scale):

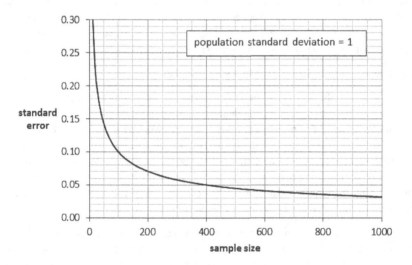

Standard error is inversely proportional to the square root of sample size so that, for example, to halve SE you need a sample four times as big; to reduce standard error by a factor of 2 increase your sample by a factor of $2^2 = 4$. For reduction by a factor of 10 you will need to increase the sample by a factor of 100.

Knowing how much precision you need will help you decide how much data you need and so how much time and money you need to budget for in planning your survey {F20}.

F6. But you don't know the population variance

> The best estimate of population variance based on a sample is
>
> SUM [(value – MEAN)^2 / (SAMPLESIZE – 1)]
>
> In EXCEL use VAR.S

Example

A sample consists of the five values 1, 2, 3, 4 and 5.

So   MEAN = 3

and   estimated population variance = $[(1-3)^2 + (2-3)^2 + (3-3)^2 + (4-3)^2 + (5-3)^2]/4 = 2.5$

Rationale

You have a sample. The best single number estimate of a population mean is the sample mean. But the best single number estimate of the population variance is not the variance of the sample data.

Variance is the average of squared deviations of each value from the MEAN {A7}. The MEAN of 1,2,3,4,5 in the Example is 3 and so the variance of the five numbers in the sample is

$$[(1-3)^2 + (2-3)^2 + (3-3)^2 + (4-3)^2 + (5-3)^2]/5 = 2$$

This would be fine if the population mean was really 3.

But you do not know the population mean.

The variance of any set of numbers is minimised by measuring deviations from **the mean of that set of numbers**. Measuring deviations from any other value will give a larger result.

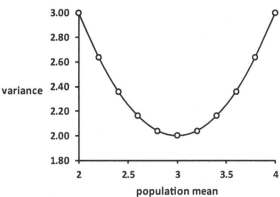

For example, if we knew that the population mean was 2 (not the sample mean 3) then the best estimate of population variance from the sample is

$$[(1 - 2)^2 + (2 - 2)^2 + (3 - 2)^2 + (4 - 2)^2 + (5 - 2)^2]/5 = 3$$

The chart shows what happens with other possible population means.

Because you do not know the population mean the sample variance, 2, will certainly be an under-estimate of the population variance.

The appropriate correction is to divide by (SAMPLESIZE – 1) rather than SAMPLESIZE when calculating variance.

This was first suggested by the German mathematician and astronomer Friedrich Bessel and is known as Bessel's correction.

In EXCEL use VAR.P to find the variance assuming your data are the population: VAR.P(1, 2, 3, 4, 5) = 2. This is likely to be of use only infrequently

Use VAR.S to find the best estimate of population variance using the sample: VAR.S(1, 2, 3, 4, 5) = 2.5. This is what you almost always need.

In these notes the results of these calculations of variance and standard deviation from data using VAR.S and STDEV.S will usually just be written STDEV and VAR unless otherwise stated.

Friedrich Bessel (1784–1846)

F7. t or Normal?

> To make an inference about a population mean you usually have to estimate the population variance from your sample.
>
> Use the t distribution with (SAMPLESIZE − 1) degrees of freedom.
>
> For large samples the NORMAL distribution gives practically the same results.

Example

You ask 20 managers how long they spent in meetings the previous day. The MEAN is 2.8 hours and the standard deviation is STDEV = 0.7 hours.

Standard error {F5} = STEM = $0.7/\sqrt{20}$ = 0.157

To report with a 95% confidence interval {F19} use t = T.INV.2T(0.05, 19) = 2.093

You can be 95% confident that the population mean is in the range

$$2.8 \pm (2.093 \times 0.157) = 2.8 \pm 0.328 = 2.47 \text{ to } 3.13 \text{ hours}$$

Alternatively, get the margin of error using CONFIDENCE.T(0.05, 0.7, 20) = 0.328

Rationale

If you are making an inference about a population mean and know the population variance use a NORMAL distribution {F3}.

But in most cases you will not know the population variance and so will estimate it too from the sample {F6}. Using sample estimates of both mean and variance complicates your problem so that the NORMAL distribution is no longer the right distribution to use. In its place use the t distribution. But this only works if the underlying population distribution is NORMAL, which seems quite a restriction but in practice is not.

✳✳✳

The t distribution is similar to the standard NORMAL {C3} but is fatter in the tails and lower at the peak. The magnitude of the difference between the two distributions depends on a parameter called *degrees of freedom*. This is a quite general idea {C9}. In this application

degrees of freedom = SAMPLESIZE − 1

The graph shows the two distributions. The t is for 9 degrees of freedom so a modest sample of 10. The difference is not great. For sample sizes greater than about 30 or 40 the differences are negligible unless you require a very high degree of accuracy.

But what if the population is not Normally distributed? In those cases where comparisons are possible the *t* distribution has been found to give a pretty good approximation.

Therefore:

Use the NORMAL distribution when the population variance is known. When it is not you should use a *t* distribution. But for samples of more than about 30 the NORMAL is a very good approximation to the *t* and can be used.

If you suspect that the population distribution is very non-Normal in shape, highly skewed for example, make sure you have a large sample.

In the example a NORMAL distribution would have given z = 1.96 rather then *t* = 2.09 and a 95% confidence interval of 2.37 to 3.23 hours. The interval would have been 3.6 minutes narrower.

In **EXCEL**

The value of *t* is the same as the value z for NORMAL distributions {C4}

$$t = (\text{value} - \text{MEAN}) / \text{STDEV}$$

For any value of a variable it measures how many standard deviations that value is from the MEAN (just like z).

If you know the value of *t* and want the corresponding probability, and with 19 degrees of freedom,

T.DIST (0.8, 19, TRUE) = 0.783   is the probability that *t* is less than 0.8
T.DIST.RT (0.8, 19) = 0.217   is the probability that *t* is greater than 0.8
T.DIST.2T (0.8, 19) = 0.434   is the probability that *t* is less than –0.8 OR greater than +0.8

If you know the tail probability and want the corresponding *t* value

T.INV(0.05, 19) = –1.729   for a tail probability of 0.05 use *t* = –1.729
T.INV.2T(0.05, 19) = 2.093   the sum of probabilities in both tails is 0.05; *t* less than –2.093 OR greater than +2.093

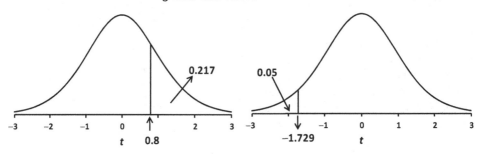

T.DIST.RT(0.8, 19) = 0.217   T.INV(0.05, 19) = –1.729

F8. Reporting a mean

You want to know the MEAN of a population.

Take a sample.

Estimate the population mean using a NORMAL distribution with

MEAN = sample mean

$$\text{standard deviation} = \text{STEM} = \frac{\text{standard deviation}}{\sqrt{\text{SAMPLESIZE}}}$$

Report using a confidence interval.

Example

Your company makes consumer electronics. It takes customers' queries through its website.

In a sample of 100 queries the mean response time was 4.2 hours and the standard deviation was STDEV.S = 1.56 hours.

The estimate of the population mean is a NORMAL distribution with

MEAN = 4.2
standard error {F5} = STEM = 1.56/√100 = 0.156

The 95% confidence interval {F19} is

4.2 ± (1.96 × 0.156) = 4.2 ± 0.3 = 3.9 to 4.5

Report that there is 95% probability that the population mean response time is between 3.9 hours and 4.5 hours.

Rationale

This is a particular example of inference {F3} and is the best way to **report** findings from a survey.

This method works for realistically large samples.

You may need to modify your calculation if your sample is small {F7} or if it is a large fraction of the population {F18}.

If you have a small sample and also a well-founded prior estimate of the population mean consider combining them {D10}. But only if your judgement really is well-founded, based on data from another place or time, for example.

F9. Testing a mean

You want to test if a population mean really has the value you assume or require.

Take a sample.

The probability that a sample with the mean you find came from a population with the mean you assume is found using a NORMAL distribution with

MEAN = sample mean

$$\text{standard deviation} = \text{STEM} = \frac{\text{standard deviation}}{\sqrt{\text{SAMPLESIZE}}}$$

Find how unlikely your sample mean is if your assumed mean is true.

If it is sufficiently unlikely your assumption *may* be wrong.

Example

Your company makes consumer electronics. It takes customers' queries through its website.

The level of service target is that the average time taken to answer these queries is no more than 4 hours.

In a sample of 100 queries the mean response time was 4.2 hours and the standard deviation was STDEV.S = 1.56 hours.

To find how unlikely is your sample mean use a NORMAL distribution with

MEAN = required mean = 4.0
standard error {F5} = STEM = 1.56/√100 = 0.156

The probability that a sample mean of 4.2 or higher came from a population with mean 4.0 is

1 − NORM.DIST(4.2, 4, 0.156, TRUE) = 0.1

There is a 10% chance of this result. You must now decide whether this is sufficiently unlikely that you should believe some management action is needed.

Rationale

This is a particular example of inference {F3} and is the best way to **test** an assumption about a population mean using findings from a survey.

The analysis gives you a measure of how unlikely is your sample mean. The probability is from the tail (sometimes from both tails {F2}) of a NORMAL distribution showing all possible sample means so yours can never be ruled out, it may just be unlikely and no more. What you do, if anything, is a matter of judgement — your judgement. This problem is common in all monitoring {G1}.

This method works for realistically large samples.

You may need to modify your calculation of if your sample is small {F7} or is a large fraction of the population {F18}.

178

F10. Reporting a proportion

> You want to know the proportion of a population with some property.
>
> Take a sample.
>
> Make an inference of the population proportion using a NORMAL distribution with
>
> > MEAN = sample proportion = p
> > VAR = $p(1 - p)$ / SAMPLESIZE
> > standard deviation = STEP = $\sqrt{[p(1 - p) / \text{SAMPLESIZE}]}$
>
> Report using a confidence interval.

Example

A market research company asks a sample of 200 people which brand of breakfast cereal they most prefer. 80 say they most prefer *Wheaties*.

The estimate of the population proportion is a NORMAL distribution with

> MEAN = sample proportion = p = 80/200 = 0.4
> standard error {F5} = STEP = $\sqrt{(\,0.4 \times 0.6\,/\,200)}$ = 0.035

The 95% confidence interval {F19} is

> $0.4 \pm (1.96 \times 0.035) = 0.4 \pm 0.07 = 0.33$ to 0.47

Report that there is 95% probability that 33% to 47% of the whole population like *Wheaties* the best.

Rationale

This is a particular example of inference {F3} and is the best way to **report** findings from a survey.

The proportion p is just the mean of a sample where all those preferring *Wheaties* are given a score of 1 and others a score of 0. The variance of these data is $p(1 - p)$. As with other means use a NORMAL distribution {F8}.

This method works for realistically large samples.

If the sample is small or the proportion extreme (close to 0 or 1) your confidence interval may go outside the range 0 to 1. Use a BETA distribution rather than a NORMAL {C5}. Otherwise the NORMAL distribution is a good large sample approximation of the BETA distribution.

Using a BETA distribution makes it easy to incorporate a well-founded prior estimate of the population proportion {D8}. Think about doing this only if your sample is small and your judgement really is well-founded, based on data from another place or time, for example.

F11. Testing a proportion

> You want to test if the proportion of a population with some property really has the value you assume or require.
>
> Take a sample.
>
> The probability that the sample came from a population with the assumed proportion is found using a NORMAL distribution with
>
> > MEAN = assumed proportion = P
> > VAR = P(1 − P) / SAMPLESIZE
> > standard deviation = STEP = √[P(1 − P)/SAMPLESIZE]
>
> Find how unlikely your sample proportion is if your assumed proportion is true.
>
> If it is sufficiently unlikely your assumption *may be* wrong.

Example

A food company makes a breakfast cereal, *Wheaties*. After a reformulation and product re-launch the aim was to get at least 45% of consumers nominating *Wheaties* as their preferred cereal.

A market research company asks a sample of 200 people which of four brands of breakfast cereal they most prefer. 80 say they most prefer *Wheaties*.

To find how unlikely is your sample proportion use a NORMAL distribution {C3} with

> MEAN = required proportion = P = 0.45
> STEP = √(0.45 × 0.55/200) = 0.035

The probability that a sample mean of 80/200 = 0.4 or lower came from a population with mean 0.45 is

> NORM.DIST(0.4, 0.45, 0.035, TRUE) = 0.08

There is an 8% chance of this result. You must now decide whether this is sufficiently unlikely that some management action is justified.

Rationale

This is a particular example of inference {F3} and is the best way to **test** an assumption about a population proportion using findings from a survey.

The analysis gives you a measure of how unlikely your sample proportion is. The probability is from the tail (sometimes from both tails {F2}) of a NORMAL distribution showing all possible sample proportions so yours can never be ruled out, it may just be unlikely and no more. What you do, if anything, is a matter of judgement — your judgement. This problem is common in all monitoring {G1}.

The proportion P is just the mean of a population in which all those preferring *Wheaties* are given a score of 1 and others a score of 0. The variance is P(1 – P). As with other means use a Normal distribution {F8}.

This method works for realistically large samples.

If the sample is small or the proportion extreme (close to 0 or 1) use a Beta distribution rather than a Normal {C5}.

F12. Reporting a variance

You want to know the variance of a population.

Take a sample.

Report using a confidence interval. Do this by using the chi-squared (χ^2) distribution with

  degrees of freedom = (SAMPLESIZE − 1)

Find the confidence interval limits for χ^2 and then use

  POPULATIONVARIANCE = (SAMPLESIZE − 1) × SAMPLEVARIANCE/χ^2

to get the confidence interval for population variance.

Example

A small food company sells organic muesli in 1kg bags. 25 bags were weighed. The mean weight was 1.02kg and the standard deviation 15g.

degrees of freedom = 25 − 1 = 24

The 95% confidence interval {F19} limits for χ^2 are

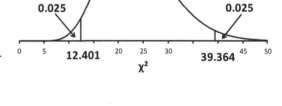

  χ^2 = CHISQ.INV(0.025, 24)
    = 12.401
and χ^2 = CHISQ.INV.RT(0.025, 24)
    = 39.364

The 95% confidence interval limits for population variance are

  24 × 15^2/39.364 = 137.18
and 24 × 15^2/12.401 = 435.44

The 95% confidence interval limits for population standard deviation are $\sqrt{137.181}$ and $\sqrt{435.44}$ so report that there is a 95% chance that the population standard deviation is between 11.7g and 20.9g.

Rationale

This is an inference problem of the same form as for means and proportions {F8, F10} but with the complication that there is no convenient probability model for variance. Fortunately the standard chi-squared distribution can be used with the transformation

  χ^2 = (SAMPLESIZE − 1) × SAMPLEVARIANCE/POPULATIONVARIANCE

Because χ^2 is inversely related to POPULATIONVARIANCE the low and high interval limits for χ^2 are reversed to get the high and low limits for variance.

***

182

The χ^2 distribution varies according to the number of *degrees of freedom* {C8}.

For this application just treat it as a parameter equal to (SAMPLESIZE − 1).

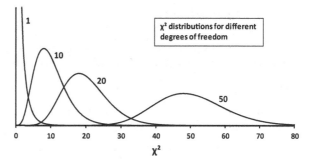

χ^2 distributions for different degrees of freedom

F13. Testing a variance

You want to test if the variance of a population has the value you assume or require.

Take a sample.

The probability that the sample came from a population with the assumed variance is found using a chi-squared (χ^2) distribution with

$$\chi^2 = (\text{SAMPLESIZE} - 1) \times \text{SAMPLEVARIANCE}/\text{POPULATIONVARIANCE}$$

and   degrees of freedom = (SAMPLESIZE – 1)

Find how unlikely your sample variance is if your assumed variance is true.

If it is sufficiently unlikely your assumption *may be* wrong.

Example

A small food company sells organic muesli in 1kg bags. 25 bags were weighed. The mean weight was 1.02kg and the standard deviation 15g.

The target is for the bag filling process to have a standard deviation of 13g.

degrees of freedom = 25 – 1 = 24

and $\chi^2 = 24 \times 15^2/13^2 = 31.953$

The probability that the sample standard deviation of 15g or higher came from a population with the required standard deviation of 13g is

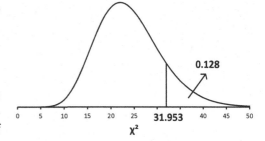

CHISQ.DIST.RT(31.953, 24) = 0.128

There is a 13% chance that your data, came from a population with the assumed variance. This is probably high enough to be considered not exceptional. No intervention needed. But your decision.

Rationale

This is a particular example of inference {F3} and is the best way to **test** an assumption about a population variance using findings from a survey.

The analysis gives you a measure of how unlikely is your sample variance. The probability is from the tail (sometimes from both tails) of a distribution showing all possible sample variances. Yours can never be ruled out, it may just be unlikely and no more. What you do, if anything, is a matter of judgement — your judgement. This problem is common in all monitoring {G1}.

184

F14. Testing and reporting differences in means and proportions

You have two samples from different populations, A and B, and want to know about the difference in means.

Subtract means and add variances

The estimated difference between two sample means is NORMAL with

MEAN(difference) = MEAN(A) – MEAN(B)

VAR(difference) = VAR(A)/SAMPLESIZE(A) + VAR(B)/SAMPLESIZE(B)

It may be more convenient to use standard error SE {F5}

SE(difference) = √[SE(A)² + SE(B)²]

Use the same method for differences between proportions.

Example 1. Difference in means

Surveys were made in two towns to investigate the mean number of magazines read per head of population per month. Here are the results for both towns {F8, F9} and the difference

	town A	town B	difference: B – A
MEAN	3.8	4.4	0.6
SAMPLESIZE	50	40	
Sample variance	1.6	1.9	
SE {F5}	0.179	0.218	0.282

Report. The 95% confidence interval {F19} for the difference in means is

0.6 ± (1.96 x 0.282) = 0.05 to 1.15

The interval is wholly positive so you can be pretty sure that there is a difference between the two populations but you can't be precise about how big a difference.

Test. If the two populations had the same reading patterns the difference in population means would be zero.

Use a two-tailed test {F2} to find the probability of an absolute difference this big if there is no difference in population means

2 × NORM.DIST(–0.6, 0, 0.282, TRUE) = 3.3%

If there is no difference in the population means there is only a 3% chance of an absolute difference in sample means bigger than 0.6. This may be low enough for you to conclude that there probably is a difference in the populations.

Example 2. Difference in proportions

In a survey of 110 shoppers 76 were in favour of clearer labelling of ingredients on food packaging. Last year, 46 out of 80 were in favour. Has there been a shift of opinion? Here are the results for both periods {F10, F11} and the difference

	now	last year	difference
SAMPLESIZE	110	80	
no. in favour	76	46	
p %	69.09	57.50	11.59
SE {F5}	4.41	5.53	7.07

Report.   The 95% confidence interval {F19} for the difference in proportions is:

$$11.59 \pm (1.96 \times 7.07) = -2.3\% \text{ to } 24.4\%$$

The interval is mostly positive indicating that the average for town B is probably the larger. The value zero, indicating no difference between populations, is within the interval. It would not be in a 90% interval.

You cannot be sure there has been an effect, though it looks likely.

Test.   If there has been no change the difference in population proportions would be zero.

Use a two-tailed test {F2} to find the probability of an absolute difference between sample proportions of 11.59 percentage points if there is no difference in population proportions

$$2 \times \text{NORM.DIST}(-11.59, 0, 7.07, \text{TRUE}) = 10\%$$

There is a 10% chance of an absolute difference this big in sample proportions if there is no difference in the population proportions. You may think this not unlikely enough to justify rejecting the idea that there is no difference in population proportions. But your decision.

Rationale

Managers often need to make comparisons:

Have new work practices improved performance?
Is staff turnover at one of your two stores higher than at the other?
Do men and women have different responses to your new product?

These important management problems require evidence about the possible differences in two populations:

before and after the introduction of new work practices
turnover rates at two stores
preferences of men and women

Most commonly you will be interested in differences between averages or proportions.

You want to find out about the differences but cannot question or measure all members of the populations.

Therefore:

Take sample data from each population. Either report the difference or both test the difference against some target or other important value {F2}.

Combine the standard errors from the two samples to get the standard error of the difference in means or proportions {F4}.

For small samples use a *t* distribution {F7, F15}.

***

Usually the members of the two samples are different, men and women or workers at two different stores. If you can arrange to use the same members for both surveys this will increase the precision of your inference {F17}. This is most likely to be possible in before and after studies; measure the performance of the same workers when assessing improvements from new work practices.

F15. Testing and reporting differences with small samples

You have two **small** samples from different populations, A and B, and want to know about the **difference** in means. From each sample you know the MEAN, the sample variance, VAR, and standard error, SE {F5}.

Use a t distribution with

$$\text{MEAN(A–B)} = \text{MEAN(A)} - \text{MEAN(B)}$$

Case 1. If the two population variances are **not the same** use

$$\text{SE(A–B)} = \sqrt{[\text{SE(A)}^2 + \text{SE(B)}^2]}$$

$$\text{degrees of freedom} = \frac{\left[\text{SE}(A)^2 + \text{SE}(B)^2\right]^2}{\dfrac{\text{SE}(A)^4}{\text{SAMPLE SIZE}(A) - 1} + \dfrac{\text{SE}(B)^4}{\text{SAMPLE SIZE}(B) - 1}}$$

Case 2. If the population variances are **the same** the best estimate of that common variance is

$$\text{VAR}(A \& B) = \frac{\left[(\text{SAMPLE SIZE}(A) - 1) \times \text{VAR}(A)\right] + \left[(\text{SAMPLE SIZE}(B) - 1) \times \text{VAR}(B)\right]}{\text{SAMPLE SIZE}(A) + \text{SAMPLE SIZE}(B) - 2}$$

and $\quad \text{SE(A-B)} = \sqrt{[\text{VAR(A\&B)}\times(\,1/\text{SAMPLESIZE(A)} + 1/\text{SAMPLESIZE(B)}\,)]}$

$$\text{degrees of freedom} = \text{SAMPLESIZE(A)} + \text{SAMPLESIZE(B)} - 2$$

Use the same method for differences between proportions.

Example 1. Unequal population variances

A steel making plant has developed two possible improvements to its processes. Testing is expensive. 10 steel plates were manufactured by each process. The tensile strength (N/mm²) of each was found. The results are shown in the table at right and the summaries below.

	A	B	difference
SAMPLESIZE	10	10	
MEAN	253.67	255.40	1.73
VAR	0.26	1.32	
SE	0.16	0.36	0.40

A	B
253.55	255.72
253.05	254.11
254.34	254.25
254.12	256.40
253.54	253.86
253.23	256.14
254.50	256.70
253.09	254.61
253.51	256.99
253.76	255.21

You have no reason to believe that the two processes give results with the same variance and these data seem not to contradict that assumption so

$$\text{degrees of freedom} = (0.16^2 + 0.36^2)^2/(0.16^4/9 + 0.36^4/9) = 12.4$$

188

To make a 95% confidence interval {F19} estimate of the difference in means of the two processes find the appropriate *t* value {F7}

T.INV.2T (0.05, 12.4) = 2.18

and so the 95% interval is

1.73 ± (2.18 × 0.40) = 0.86 to 2.60

You can be pretty sure that process B gives a higher tensile strength by somewhere between 0.86 N/mm^2 and 2.60 N/mm^2.

Example 2. Equal population variances

The table shows two steel samples with the same means as in Example 1 but now the variances are not that different. If you assume that the population variances are the same the best estimate of that common variance is

	A	B	difference
SAMPLESIZE	10	10	
MEAN	253.67	255.40	1.73
VAR	0.96	1.32	1.14
SE			0.48

(9×0.96 + 9×1.32)/18 = 1.14

The standard error of the difference in means is

SE = √[1.14 × (1/10 + 1/10)] = 0.48

and   degrees of freedom = 10 + 10 − 2 = 18

To make a 95% confidence interval {F19} estimate of the difference in means of the two processes find the appropriate *t* value {F7}

T.INV.2T(0.05,18) = 2.10

and so the 95% interval is

1.73 ± (2.10 × 0.48) = 0.73 to 2.73

You can be pretty sure that process B gives a higher tensile strength by somewhere between 0.73 N/mm^2 and 2.73 N/mm^2.

Rationale

This is a particular problem of inference {F2} when you do not have many data and so use a *t* distribution rather than a NORMAL {F7}.

You must decide whether the two population variances are the same. If you believe they are, combine both data sets for an estimate of this common variance. Because of the small samples data are scarce. Combining them will give a much better estimate of the common variance, VAR(A&B), called the *pooled sample variance*.

The benefit of reducing variance by pooling can be substantial. Use the variance ratio test {F16} to test this assumption of equal population variances.

***

The examples show how to report confidence intervals for the difference. To test the difference against some target value use the same process as with a large sample {F14} but using the appropriate *t* distribution, as in the Examples.

If, as a special case, you want to test against a target difference of zero (there is no difference in population means) you can use the EXCEL function T.TEST. For example, if the data are in rows 1 to 10 of the first two columns of your spreadsheet the function will look like this

$$\text{T.TEST(A1:A10, B1:B10, 2, 3)}$$

= 1 to test if one population mean is greater than the other = 2 to test if the population means are equal	= 1 for paired samples {F17} = 2 for same population variances = 3 for unequal population variances

For Example 1 this returns 0.0009. The probability of a difference in these sample means of 1.73 if the populations have equal means is just 0.09%. There are very strong grounds for suspecting that population means are different.

In the Examples both samples are the same size. This is not necessary for the analysis.

F16. Testing and reporting differences in variances

You have two samples from different populations and want to know about the difference in population variances.

Use the *ratio* of the variances, not the numerical difference, then the F distribution where

   F = ratio of sample variances / ratio of population variances.

The degrees of freedom for the F distribution are (SAMPLESIZE – 1) for each sample.

Example

Shelves are cut from standard width coated chipboard for inclusion in flat pack furniture kits.

An unacceptably high proportion are scrapped because they have been cut too long or too short to be used. A total of 120 shelves were measured. The lengths seemed to be Normally distributed with a standard deviation of 0.98 mm. Some new machinery was installed. A sample of 200 shelves was measured and found to have a reduced standard deviation of 0.85 mm. You want to decide whether there has been a real improvement and, if so, how big.

Report.   Use the relation: ratio of population variances = ratio of sample variances / F

The ratio of sample variances is
   $0.98^2/0.85^2 = 1.329$
degrees of freedom are

   $120 - 1 = 119$
for the numerator
and $200 - 1 = 199$
for the denominator

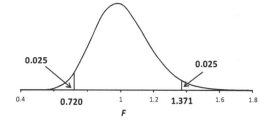

The 95% confidence interval {F19} limits for F are

   $F = F.INV(0.025, 119, 199) = 0.720$
and $F = F.INV.RT(0.025, 119, 199) = 1.371$

The 95% confidence interval limits for the ratio of population variances are

   $1.329/1.371 = 0.969$
and $1.329/0.720 = 1.847$

Report that the population variance ratio is between 0.969 and 1.847

The ratio looks likely to be at least 1 so there probably has been an improvement.

Test. Use the relation: F = ratio of sample variances / ratio of population variances.

You want to test whether there has been any *reduction* {F2} in variance and so test that the proposition of no change; ratio of population variances = 1

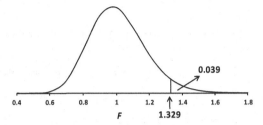

so $F = 1.329/1 = 1.329$

The probability of a value that extreme or more is

  $F.DIST.RT(1.329, 119, 199) = 0.039$ or 4%

You may think this sufficiently unlikely that you conclude there has probably been an improvement. Your decision.

Rationale

Variance (and standard deviation) is a measure of process variability {A7}. Reducing this is important, most obviously in manufacturing and other engineering applications. It is useful in other areas too; providing a consistent customer service level, for example.

You will want to monitor process variability and try to make improvements if needed {J5}. You will need information about variance at different places (performance comparison) and at different times (performance improvement). But you cannot question or measure all members of the populations.

Therefore:

Take sample data from each population and either report the difference or test the difference against some target or other important value, or both {F2}.

Comparing variances is also needed for other problems:

when comparing means of small samples you need to decide whether to pool sample variances to get the best estimate of the common variance {F15}

when assessing the usefulness of a regression model you may want to know if errors of estimation, measured as variances, have been reduced by use of the model {I6}.

***

There is no convenient distribution for the *difference* in sample variances in the way there is for means and proportions {F14}. Fortunately, the *ratio* of variances can be modelled

  F = ratio of sample variances / ratio of population variances

Use this as shown in the Example.

***

The F distribution describes the distribution of the ratio of variances of two Normally distributed populations.

192

There is not just one *F* distribution but a whole family depending on the degrees of freedom of the two variances. In the Example these were 119 and 199, given in that order in the function.

You will get the same result if you made the variance ratio the other way

$$0.85^2/0.98^2 = 0.752$$

provided that you reversed the degrees of freedom too, using

F.INV(0.025, 199, 119)

***

The ideas behind the concept of degrees of freedom are general and important {C9} but for this method you can just think of them as parameters of the *F* distribution.

F17. Before and after in pairs (if you can)

> You need to assess the effect of some management intervention.
>
> Measure the relevant performance variable before the intervention and again afterwards.
>
> If at all possible use the same sample for both and measure the difference in performance of each individual.

Example

An engineering manufacturer thinks that by introducing a new procedure the time taken for a particular assembly task can be reduced.

The ten workers performing that task are timed making one assembly each.

The new procedure is explained and some training given.

After a week working with the new system a single assembly is again timed for each of the same ten workers.

The table shows the times in minutes.

Use the differences in the rightmost column and report what you have found using a t distribution {F7} for this small sample.

worker	before	after	difference
1	5.7	5.3	0.4
2	6.8	5.8	1.0
3	6.0	5.8	0.2
4	5.8	5.2	0.6
5	6.2	5.8	0.4
6	5.0	5.3	−0.3
7	5.5	5.0	0.5
8	5.1	5.1	0.0
9	5.9	6.0	−0.1
10	6.0	5.4	0.6
SAMPLESIZE	10	10	10
MEAN	5.80	5.47	0.33
VAR	0.28	0.12	0.15
SE			0.12

Find standard error {F5}

$$\text{SE} = \sqrt{(0.15/10)} = 0.12$$

For a 95% confidence interval {F19} use

$$t = \text{T.INV.2T}(0.05, 9) = 2.26$$

The 95% interval is $0.33 \pm (2.26 \times 0.12) = 0.05$ to 0.61

You can be pretty certain that there has been a reduction in mean task time of between 0.05 mins and 0.61 mins.

Rationale

You need to infer the difference in task times for the two populations — before and after — of all tasks by all workers. You have two samples to help you do this.

There are three reasons why task times vary:

some workers are quicker

no worker takes exactly the same time for each task completed

there has (you hope) been an improvement due to the new way of doing things

You might be able to improve the process by redeploying or replacing slow workers but for now you just want as good a measure as you can get of the effect of this new procedure.

Therefore:

Eliminate variability due to differences between workers by measuring only task improvement. Do this by using the difference in performance for each worker and finding the mean difference.

If the times had been taken for different workers before and after you would have had to measure the difference in means {F15} rather than the mean difference. The standard error would have been 0.2 and the confidence interval would have been from –0.09 to +0.75. This is wider and includes the value zero. This is much weaker evidence for an improvement.

***

The example shows how to report the difference. To **test** whether there has been any improvement at all use the function T.TEST {F15}. With the data in columns A and B of your spreadsheet test for an improvement by using

T.TEST(A1:A10, B1:B10, 1, 1) = 0.012

The chance of you seeing an improvement this large if there was no difference in population mean task times is only 1.2%. This is quite strong evidence that there probably has been an improvement.

It is not always possible to make paired tests, of course, but you will benefit if you can.

F18. Sample is large part of population

You want to estimate a population mean and have collected data which represent a large fraction of the population.

Adjust the variance found from the sample by the factor

(POPULATIONSIZE – SAMPLESIZE) / (POPULATIONSIZE – 1)

Example

There are 99 video games developers in Scotland listed by the Scottish Games Network (September 2014).

You contact 25 of them. The mean number of employees is 15.3 and the sample variance is 8.4.

The variance of the estimate of the mean {F5} is

$(8.4/25) \times (99 – 25)/(99 – 1) = 0.254$

and {F5} STEM = $\sqrt{0.254}$ = 0.50

Rationale

Calculations for reporting and testing means and proportions depend on SAMPLESIZE {F3} but take no account of how large the sample is compared to the population. Surely, if you have surveyed a large part of the population, it has some effect in reducing uncertainty and error?

It does.

The graph shows how the correction factor varies as SAMPLE SIZE increases for a small population of 100. It is a straight line because with very little loss of accuracy the factor is

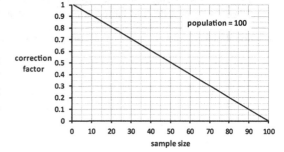

1 – (SAMPLESIZE/POPULATIONSIZE)

As the fraction sampled gets smaller the factor, called the *finite population correction*, approaches 1.

***

Most sampling theory assumes an infinite population. What that means is that the population is so big that the sample is only a trivially small fraction of it and so the correction factor is practically 1. No correction is needed.

***

It is unlikely you will have to use this correction and certainly not often. Think carefully about the population. In the Example are you *really* interested *only* in Scottish games developers or are they just convenient and it is a far wider community which is your concern? Just this year?

196

F19. Confidence interval

> To report your estimate of mean or proportion use a *confidence interval*.
>
> First calculate the standard error, SE {F5}.
>
> Second, set a *confidence level* which is the probability acceptable to you that the interval will contain the true value. Find the corresponding interval.
>
> You may find it useful to use a z value {C4}. For example
>
> | confidence level | % | 90 | 95 | 99 |
> |---|---|---|---|---|
> | | z | 1.64 | 1.96 | 2.58 |
>
> Then,   confidence interval = MEAN ± (z x SE)
>
> The half width of the interval (z x SE) is called the *margin of error*.

Example

The average lifespan of 85 small businesses was 2.8 years from startup. The standard deviation of lifespans was 1.6 years. The standard error for the estimate of mean life {F8} is

$$\text{STEM} = 1.6 / \sqrt{85} = 0.174$$

You want a 90% confidence interval so z = 1.64 and

$$90\% \text{ confidence interval} = 2.8 \pm (1.64 \times 0.174) = 2.8 \pm 0.29 = 2.51 \text{ to } 3.09$$

There is a 90% probability that mean lifespan is between 2.5 and 3.1 years.

Other EXCEL options are given below.

Rationale

Sample data are collected to provide evidence about what is going on in the population {F1}. Because the estimate is based *only* on *partial* information it can only be approximate: it is imprecise. What you must do is to give a good indication of that imprecision.

The most natural way to report an approximation is to give your best guess "plus or minus a bit" {B10}, and that is just what you ought do. Statistical theory helps you to get a grip on how big that bit ought to be, and why.

The smaller the interval the more useful it looks but the less likely it is to contain the true value. Reporting that the mean life is *exactly* 2.8 years is foolish; the probability under a NORMAL distribution of 2.8 ± 0 is zero.

A larger interval is more likely to contain the true value but is also likely to be less useful. The probability that the true mean lifespan is somewhere between 1 year and 50 years is almost certain to be true, but so what?

You must strike a balance between an interval so narrow as to be certainly untrue and one so wide that while it is true it may be useless.

Therefore:

Decide how confident you want to be that your interval contains the true value.

Report the confidence interval.

The tension is between the width of the interval and the probability that that interval contains the true value — the *confidence level* of the estimate. The more confident you wish to be that the interval contains the true value the wider (less precise) will be the interval. It is up to you to decide where to strike the balance. If you set a confidence level then you can calculate the corresponding precision and *vice versa*.

***

You may find it easier to think of the *risk* that your report is wrong: there is a 10% risk that the true value lies outside a 90% interval.

***

This is all fine except that we (any of us) are likely to find it hard to decide the confidence level because we find it hard to think about probability {H4}. A number of values have become accepted as a sort of common language among users: the 95% interval is one of them. This gets you out of the hole of having a nice method but no way of using it.

But remember that you are free to choose a different confidence level if it better suits your purpose.

***

How should you report your confidence interval? The whole point of the calculation is to find the effect of incomplete information (the sample) on your report. Do not throw that away. If you write or say "2.8 ± 0.29" it is natural that your audience will focus on the 2.8 and ignore, or not give full weight to, the "plus or minus 0.29". If you write or say "the mean life is between 2.5 and 3.1 years" your audience has no choice but to recognise the imprecision. So do that.

In EXCEL

To find the margin of error use CONFIDENCE.NORM.

As well as standard deviation and sample size give (1 – confidence level). For a 90% confidence interval give 1 – 0.9 = 0.1:

CONFIDENCE.NORM(0.1, 1.6, 85) = 0.29

For small samples use the function CONFIDENCE.T {F7}.

If you just want to find a z value set the last two parameters to 1:

CONFIDENCE.NORM(0.1, 1, 1) = 1.64

F20. How big a sample?

Decide how many data you should collect to estimate a population mean or proportion by thinking of the confidence interval report that you wish to make {F19}.

Chose a *confidence level* and find the corresponding z value.

Decide how wide you want the confidence interval to be: MEAN ± w.

Make an estimate the standard deviation, STDEV. Then

$$\text{SAMPLESIZE} = (z \times \text{STDEV} / w)^2$$

To estimate a proportion make your best guess at its value, p. Then

$$\text{SAMPLESIZE} = p \times (1 - p) \times (z/w)^2$$

Example 1

You want to estimate the mean number of hours per day that people spend watching television.

You would like the resulting report to be a 95% confidence interval of ±10 minutes.

A similar study carried out a couple of years ago had a standard deviation of 1.4 hours. There seems no reason to believe that this has changed much.

So, $z = 1.96$
        $w = 10/60 = 0.17$ hours
        $\text{STDEV} = 1.4$ hours
and $\text{SAMPLESIZE} = (1.96 \times 1.4 / 0.17)^2 = 260$

Example 2

A polling company is commissioned to make a survey of voting intentions. The client, a national newspaper, wants the result to have a margin of error of 2 percentage points. There are just two parties in the election and it is expected to be a close race. It is a usual practice for polling organisations to use 95% confidence intervals.

So, $z = 1.96$
        $w = 0.02$
        $p = 0.5$

and $\text{SAMPLESIZE} = 0.5 \times (1 - 0.5) \times (1.96/0.02)^2 = 2401$

Allowing for about 50% refusal budget for 5,000 interviews.

Rationale

Collecting data is usually expensive in time or money or both and so you would like a small sample. On the other hand, if your sample is too small the result will be too imprecise to be of much use and so you would like a large sample. You must make the familiar trade-off between quality and cost.

Therefore:

Simplify the problem by, in the first instance, ignoring the constraints of cost and time and concentrating just on finding a sample size based on the quality of the result. If the sample needed is within your budget, fine. If it isn't then collect as much data as can be afforded, provided that the result is still worth having. If it isn't then either increase the budget or accept that you will be uncomfortable with what you get.

This recommendation for sample size assumes that the output of the survey and analysis is a confidence interval and that you are able to specify in advance what you would like the margin of error to be

$$w = z \times \text{STDEV}/\sqrt{\text{SAMPLESIZE}}$$

from which the equation for SAMPLESIZE is found.

***

There are three variables over which you have control:

the confidence level (and so z) sets how **certain** you want to be of the result
the half-width, w, sets how **precise** you want the result
the SAMPLESIZE sets the time and money **cost**

Fixing any two determines the third. Here we fix the quality, z and w, to find the cost.

***

To plan for your sample size you need need an estimate of the standard deviation, STDEV. Get a figure by:

making a pilot survey
looking at some other survey carried out for a similar problem
making a guess

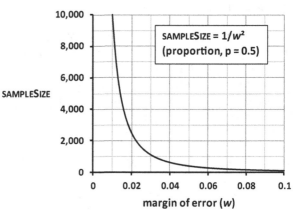

It will be better to err on overestimation of the standard deviation and so of SAMPLESIZE.

If you are estimating a proportion this caution means putting $p = 0.5$. This maximises the standard deviation = $\sqrt{p(1 - p)}$ {F10} and so gives a conservative estimate of the data requirement. Assuming a 95% confidence interval gives $z = 2$ (close enough to 1.96) the recommendation is

$$\text{SAMPLESIZE} = 0.5 \times (1 - 0.5) \times (2/w)^2 = 1/w^2$$

For a margin of error of 2 percentage points

$$\text{SAMPLESIZE} = 1/(0.02)^2 = 2500$$

This is what the pollsters got in Example 2.

***

For all problems SAMPLESIZE increases as the *square* of the reduction in the margin of error. To halve the width you will need four times as many data; to reduce the width by a factor of ten needs one hundred times as many data. Diminishing returns set in. A poor result can be improved pretty cheaply but improving an already fairly good estimate will be costly.

***

The other consideration is to make sure the sample is big enough to justify using the NORMAL distribution for you report or test {F4, F7}. This will typically need many fewer data than the recommendations here, so all should be well.

***

Do not forget that what you will have as a result of this analysis is a *recommendation* for SAMPLE-SIZE. For instance, your survey data may have a different standard deviation then you estimated so you may get a better result than you expected or not so good. A recommendation is not a guarantee.

Monitoring

---

overview

Finding out how well a business unit or a person or a process is performing is a common part of a manger's job. If the performance is not satisfactory some intervention may be needed.

To keep the task within manageable limits a strategy of managing by exception is useful {G1} in drawing attention only to the unexpected.

There are many aspects of performance that could be monitored so it is important to think what you want to measure and why {G2} rather than just measuring everything you can and hoping to make sense of it all.

A statistical interpretation of what you find {G3, G4} will help you to distinguish between performance and chance. This is always a good thing to do, of course. As a first step take a view about the performance of the system as a whole, all the people or teams or business units taken together {G7}. If there are grounds for believing that the system is not behaving as expected then look at individual performance measures. Take a statistical approach to distinguish the effects of good and poor management performance from good and poor luck {G5, G6}.

G1. Management by exception

> Look only at outcomes which are exceptional (of course).
>
> Count as exceptional anything which is so unusual that the chances of it occurring just by chance are small.

Example

The *Financial Times* of 20–21 August 2011 carried a piece about UK hospitals with the headline

> Care record of flagship hospitals in spotlight
> Post-surgery scores well below average

The key phrase is "well below". The scores measure the health gain of patients after surgery. Identifying scores which are simply below average is fairly pointless; assuming a NORMAL distribution (roughly symmetrical, anyway) half of all hospitals have below average scores and half above. The piece continues

> In total, 15 NHS hospitals are identified as having patient outcomes so far below the national average that the health department has given them "alarm" labels. This indicates there is only a one-in-1,000 chance that the hospital's poor score can purely be because of bad luck.

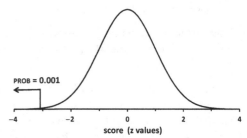

The health department has defined an exceptional event as one with a less than 0.001 probability of happening by chance. As a trigger for management intervention this is reasonable: any event that unlikely ought to be investigated.

Rationale

As a manager you do not want to look at everything, you would have no time for anything else.

On the other hand, you have responsibilities; operations and policies for which you are accountable. If you do not look at everything you may miss an important malfunction. This is always a risk.

> Therefore:
> Choose a level of risk which makes sense to you. Use this to define how exceptional an event has to be for you to use your time and skills to investigate further.

You should choose a probability after thinking about what happens if you intervene and what happens if you do not. What would the intervention be? Who would be affected?

In the Example the health department was conservative. There can be no argument that a one in a thousand event is sufficiently unusual to merit attention. The intervention might just be publication of the list showing performance indicators or it may also mean more direct intervention; drafting in a new management team, financial penalties. While these *may* be beneficial they will certainly have an impact on morale. On the other hand, things must improve.

***

The probability which defines the exceptional is also the risk that the person or business unit is in fact not exceptional at all. A performance has been produced which is unusual, certainly, but it is only that. In the Example there is a risk of one in a thousand that the hospitals are functioning normally and that identifying them as underperforming is a mistake. This is a very small risk.

***

Your problem may be more straightforward, or just less political. A performance appraisal for one of your team, perhaps.

The contribution of statistical thinking is to shift your attention away from just looking at a performance indicator numbers to thinking about how unusual — how exceptional — such numbers might be.

***

It is natural to want to compare individuals with each other or with a system average or standard. But variation is inevitable. Comparisons of individual performance should recognise this {G3,G5}.

The idea that exceptional means that which is very unusual makes sense only if the proportion of individuals showing unusual performance is not what you expect. In the Example, if the system was one thousand hospitals you should not be surprised to find one hospital with a one in a thousand score. The hospital *system* would be behaving as expected. If, on the other hand, ten hospitals — 1% of the system — showed one in a thousand performance levels you may have cause for concern {G7}.

Looking at the performance of the system as a whole provides a context for identifying the exceptional.

G2. What to monitor?

When thinking about how well or badly individuals or organisations are performing, don't just look at the average performance. Good and bad performance is found at the extremes of a distribution.

Example 1

In *Our Service Pledge for 2013* the service standard for the Hong Kong Metro was that

99.5% of passenger journeys will be completed within 5 minutes of the timetabled journey time.

Example 2

The UK inshore rescue is run by a charity, The Royal National Lifeboat Institution, RNLI. Their target is to reach 90% of those incidents no more than 10 miles from shore within 30 minutes.

Example 3

A team of surgeons work in a hospital. The surgeon agreed by all to be the most competent is given the most difficult cases, those where the patient has a high risk of not surviving the operation. The mortality rate for this surgeon's operations is above average.

Rationale

System outputs are variable:

    not every train is delayed by the same amount
    not every project has the same duration
    not every sales representative achieves the same sales volume

Outputs will be described by a probability distribution, most likely a NORMAL distribution {C3}.

You have to decide what to measure.

Averages are important because they measure capacity or throughput. Call centre monitoring will evaluate, among other things, the average speed of answer for each operator. This is important because quicker average response increases capacity and so reduces wage costs.

Standard deviation is a good measure of process variability, though you may prefer ranges for report {A7}.

Exceptions are those that bring sorrow and joy. Users and customers are unlikely to be unhappy because they get average service but rather when they experience unusually poor service. They will be delighted by unusually good

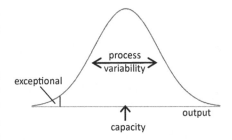

service. What is unusually good or poor depends in part on how different the service or product is from what is expected. Exceptions are found in the tails of the distribution. In Examples 1 and 2 performance standards have been set to control exceptionally poor performance.

You need to make sure that the process produces acceptable outputs.

Therefore:

Identify those aspects of output which you need to monitor. Start by identifying your customers (internal and external) and what they want.

Set a target and monitor performance against that target.

Even when you have all the data for a whole period, you need to think carefully about how well the data represent the underlying performance {G3}.

***

Monitoring requires comparing what you see with what you expect to see.

The simplest idea is that the process you are monitoring takes a set of cases as input and processes them. You monitor the output (the mean task time, say). The cases (clients, contracts, assembly tasks, hospital patients) vary in their qualities. Measuring performance against a group mean or percentage assumes that cases monitored have characteristics representative of the whole population of cases. The same assumption as random sampling.

If the sampling is biased in some way (the surgeon in Example 3) it would be unrealistic of you to monitor against group average performance. Or you may decide that the process is such that the biases should be compensated by performance and so the output should not vary that much from group average. This might be the strategy you, as manager, adopt to maintain good aggregate performance.

But to avoid demotivation you may need to consider differences in the characteristics of the different tasks each operator or operating unit has to process.

Therefore:

If you wish to manage aggregate performance by setting a common performance target whatever the input characteristics use the same target for all.

But if you wish to take account of inputs which are biased either by design (the best surgeon gets the trickiest operations) or by environment (some markets are just harder than others), set targets which account for this.

In some cases you might be able to monitor output against input in the same way you would make a before and after study {F14–F17}. Monitor improvement rather than absolute performance.

G3. Manager view vs. stats view

> Interpret performance data carefully.
>
> A single reported measure describes what has happened.
>
> A confidence interval is a better basis for diagnosing system performance.

Example

A company has a policy of increasing the proportion of women in senior positions to 40%. A year ago it adopted new practices aimed at achieving that target.

In the last year, twenty senior positions were filled, 5 by women. The Board is concerned and calls for a report from the human resource (HR) manager.

The HR manager reports that while only a quarter of new senior appointments went to women there were only twenty such appointments in the year and that it is too soon to judge the implementation of the new policy. Taking these twenty appointments as a sample of what the newly implemented selection practices will deliver gives a 95% confidence interval {F10} of between 4% and 45% for the proportion of women that will be appointed in the longer run. While the performance was a little disappointing it provides no strong evidence that the new practices are inadequate. Let's review again in six months.

Convinced?

Rationale

Targets are set and are expected to be met. In any year that target will either be met or not. That much is clear. This clarity is useful in focussing effort, ratcheting performance and all those other good things.

On the other hand, all this management activity is aimed at improving the underlying performance of the organisation. If a different twenty positions had become available perhaps the result would have been different. You need to try to distinguish between effective management action and random effects {G4}. Treating the data as a sample of underlying system performance does this.

You want to be able to monitor performance against target and to take action to improve poor performance when this is necessary. But you do not want to make changes without good justification (you recall the old saying "out of the frying pan, into the fire").

> Therefore:
>
> Treat performance data as a sample. Make an inference by reporting a confidence interval or testing against the target or both {F2}.
>
> How you use this careful evidence in motivating others is up to you, but at least you'll know how strong the evidence is.

This is all about a culture clash: the careful statistician and the performance focussed manager. The persuasion and rhetoric needed to motivate improved performance is an important skill. But if you act too quickly there is a danger that you will create volatility, churn, without necessarily improving performance. Performance may get worse. Many sports teams have behaved like this (the managerial merry-go-round).

The statisticians' view ensures a degree of caution. The evidence has to be strong enough so that you can be pretty sure of what the data are telling you.

G4. When you win it's skill. When you lose it's bad luck

When identifying good and poor performers do not rely on the single headline performance measure.

Think about reporting confidence intervals {G3,F19}.

Think about performance averaged over a number of periods.

Example

One of your sales staff happens to have a customer who lands a very big contract and so places a correspondingly big order with you for necessary components. Nothing to do with your sales staff, though the lucky individual will easily top the sales table for that year. The following year the very big contract collapses due to political instability in the client country. The same sales person is bottom of that year's ranking. Has the salesperson suddenly become incompetent?

Rationale

This poster was part of an advertising campaign by Ladbrokes, a UK-based betting and gaming company. It makes you smile. The self-serving nature of the proposition is obvious. But winning may just be good luck too. Skill may have nothing to do with it, or not much.

These ideas are used every day, often as a form of criticism. The analogy is often made between Wall Street or the City of London and a casino, for instance. The clear implication is that high rewards are undeserved. The bankers and fund managers just got lucky.

But the man on the poster would argue that he uses his knowledge and skill when choosing which team or horse will win. And he does. But how important is that effect compared to just purely chance outcomes?

In investment management there is a running argument about whether managed funds (for which their managers charge handsomely) are any better that tracker funds which just follow the market. Do the managers effectively deploy any skill?

***

This theme runs through all discussions about performance assessment and is a good reason for adopting a cautious statistical approach {G3}.

An organisation may manage performance by each year rewarding those with high levels of performance and doing just the opposite to those with low levels. Even Ladbrokes' poster boy would think this unfair: when you lose it is only bad luck, after all.

This carrot and stick approach will get people's attention but are the rewards and punishments justified?

***

Suppose all is luck. The Example shows what might happen. If performance is a random variable conditioned to some degree by the skill of the salesperson an exceptionally high value will be of low probability, by definition of exceptional. It is very likely that the next value chosen from the distribution (next year's sales) will be lower. Similarly, poor performance in one year is likely to be followed by improved performance the following year. (Another triumph for the HR department's training programme? Perhaps not.)

This behaviour where extreme values (good or poor) are likely to be followed by values closer to average performance is an example of a process called *regression to the mean*.

You want to identify truly good and poor performance, not just the lucky and unlucky.

Therefore:

If you have performance data for only one period use statistical reasoning by at least finding how likely extreme performances are {G1} or making a confidence interval {G3,G5}. An average of performance over several periods will give a better indication of ability.

Aggregating results gives more information. Think of sports leagues and knockout cup competitions. A league performance is the aggregation of a number of match results whereas your favourite team (or tennis player or whatever) can be eliminated from a knockout competition by just one below par performance. Perhaps something not controllable in that match or race determined the result. Knockout competitions can be more exciting but performance in a league is a better measure of ability.

The statistical analysis does not absolve you from the responsibility to develop the staff or organisations for which you are responsible. But it will help you avoid drawing unjustified conclusions from limited data.

***

Some think of business strategy as revealed, not wholly planned; a combination of what was intended, what was not realized and what emerged. Modifying the diagrammatic representation of this model of strategy[1] provides another way of thinking about performance:

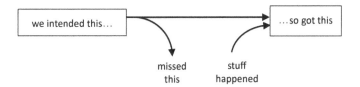

How much of what was missed and what was unintended but happened anyway can be attributed to luck, skill or incompetence? This is not likely to be easy to decide and so you may want to monitor different parts of the process and not just the final outcome. For example, monitoring the performance of a smoking cessation clinic by the percentage of those setting a date to quit who did quit {G5} is a better idea than monitoring the proportion of all those attending who quit. The conversion of smokers to smokers setting a date to quit is a different issue.

There is scope for deploying the bad luck argument which you will need to think about carefully.

Because of these complications a final result which is unlikely (low probability) is an invitation for you to examine what is happening, not a certain indicator of poor performance, though that may be what you conclude after your investigation.

G5. League tables

> To identify meaningful performance differences between business units or people treat the data for each as a sample.
>
> Find and plot confidence intervals.

Example

You want to compare the performance of smoking cessation programmes run by local authorities in the North East of England. The performance measure used is the proportion of those smokers who set a date by which they would stop and who did then stop.

The table shows data for the year ending March 2014.[2]

Local Authority	set a date	quit	% quit
Darlington	1088	562	51.7
North Tyneside	1328	667	50.2
Newcastle-Upon-Tyne	1841	907	49.3
County Durham	5690	2766	48.6
South Tyneside	2403	1157	48.1
Gateshead	2443	1123	46.0
Sunderland	3854	1682	43.6
Stockton-On-Tees	2878	1175	40.8
Northumberland	3086	1215	39.4
Hartlepool	1970	734	37.3
Redcar & Cleveland	1551	532	34.3
Middlesbrough	1836	532	29.0
Total	29968	13052	43.6

For each authority confidence intervals are calculated {F10}. For example, for Darlington

$$\text{STEP} = \sqrt{(51.7 \times 48.3 / 1088)} = 1.52$$

and the 95% confidence interval is

$$51.7 \pm (1.96 \times 1.52) = 48.7 \text{ to } 54.6$$

These intervals are shown in the chart. It is hard to justify differentiating the top five. Middlesborough is unambiguously the least successful.

Rationale

When comparing the performance of different units or individuals, you want to take account of the uncertainty implicit in inferring underlying performance {G3, G4}. When you feel confident that there are meaningful differences it makes sense to identify and understand why they exist: is it a failure of local management, a particularly difficult operating environment, or something else? On the other hand, deciding that meaningful differences exist when they may not, can lead to wasted management effort {G1}.

Therefore:

Make a chart showing confidence interval estimates. Higher confidence levels will give larger intervals and so less discrimination. Use higher levels for a more cautious approach. Choose a level which suits your style. This may be hard so make a start with 95% {F19} but be prepared to experiment.

Once you have a chart you must decide where action is justified. This will depend on the comparisons you make.

Compare units with each other, as in the Example. This works if your purpose is to differentiate between units or people. You will find some pairs which you feel justified in believing have different performance, but not all. Look for overlapping confidence intervals to see where differentiation may not be justified. If this is important and the overlap is not great make a more precise pairwise comparison {G6}.

Compare against the average performance. This appeals because people find it natural to identify values above and below the average. Taking a statistical approach will identify units which can be classed as neither above nor below (Sunderland and Gateshead in the Example). But remember that you expect about half of units will have a performance indicator above and half below, so perhaps not a useful way to look for exceptions {G1}.

Compare against a standard or target. If you want to drive improvements in performance you will probably have a target. For example, if your target value was 50% the top three authorities are likely to be satisfactory and the next two may be. The rest not.

***

The more data you have the more precise you can be in interpreting the result. In the Example, County Durham had 5,690 cases and so quite a small confidence interval. North Tyneside had only 1,328 cases and so a much wider interval. You probably won't be able to do much about this. Some authorities or business units are smaller than others. But the statistical approach gives you a way of acknowledging the effects.

***

A league table shows the performance of individual units or people. You may also find it helpful to look at the performance of all individuals *taken together as a system* for service delivery {G7} to give a useful context when you have to decide what, if anything, you ought to do.

In EXCEL

Use a chart designed to show the variability of stock prices in order to show intervals.

Arrange the data in three columns (G to I below) in the order of upper limit of interval, lower limit, followed by MEAN.

Highlight these cells.

Then use the *Insert/Other Charts* options to find the *Stock* chart as shown:

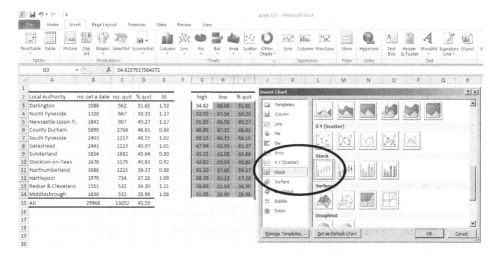

Click OK to get this

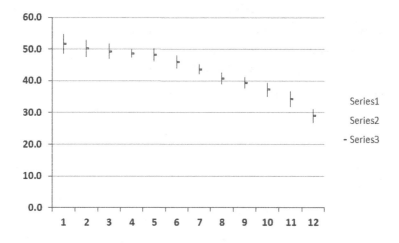

You want the names of the local authorities as labels not 1, 2, 3 …

Click on the chart and the *Design/Select Data* option at the top of your spreadsheet.

In the window (below) choose the *Edit* option for *Horizontal (Category) Axis Labels* and highlight the cells with the authorities' names (A3:A14).

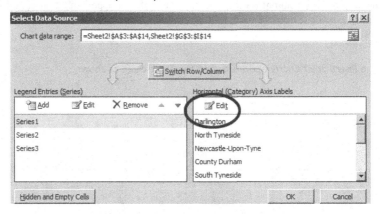

From here it is for you to decide what you want to show.

To get the chart shown in the example:

> delete the series legends at right of the chart
>
> click on the markers for average values and format (e.g. circles)
>
> click on vertical bars to choose line style

and if you want the chart to have local authority names on the vertical axis

> give vertical axis labels in reverse order
>
> rotate labels on both axes 270° in the *Alignment* option
>
> copy and paste to a Word document
>
> click on the image and then use *Picture Tools* to rotate through 90°

All this is a matter of taste and what you believe will best work for your audience. These are suggestions only.

G6. Comparing intervals is conservative

> Use confidence intervals for performance assessment. For any pair, if the confidence intervals do not overlap decide there is a difference in performance.
>
> If there is overlap a pairwise comparison will give a more precise estimate of the difference in performance.

Example

The performance of smoking cessation programmes run by local authorities in the North East of England is compared by measuring the proportion of smokers who set a date by which they would stop, and did stop {G5}.

	Sunderland	Stockton	difference
no. set a date	3854	2878	
no. quit	1682	1175	
% quit	43.64	40.83	2.82
STEP	0.80	0.92	1.22
95% confidence interval			
from	42.08	39.03	0.43
to	45.21	42.62	5.20

The confidence intervals for Sunderland and Stockton overlap and so you might decide that there is no performance difference.

But looking at the confidence interval for the difference in proportions {F14} you should decide that the quit rate in Sunderland is greater than that in Stockton by between 0.43 and 5.20 percentage points.

Rationale

There are two units A and B (Sunderland and Stockton in the Example), the confidence intervals for which overlap. The widths of the intervals, and so the extent of the overlap, is determined by the standard errors {F5}, STEP(A) and STEP(B), in particular by the sum STEP(A) + STEP(B).

The standard error of the difference {F14} is less than the sum of the two STEP values because *it is the variances which add* and so:

$$\text{STEP(A}-\text{B)} = \sqrt{[\text{STEP(A)}^2 + \text{STEP(B)}^2]}.$$

The situation is just like the Pythagoras you may remember from school.

Because STEP(A−B) is less than STEP(A)+STEP(B) the pairwise analysis will always be more discriminating than looking at overlapping confidence intervals.

***

A statistically literate league table {G5} presents performance information on all units in an easily understood chart.

You are comparing the performance of two units. Their confidence intervals overlap, perhaps not by much. Your decision as to whether their performances can justifiably be differentiated is organisationally (politically?) important.

> Therefore:
>
> Find the confidence interval of the difference in performance indicators and use that to support your decision.

The Example is for proportions but the same argument holds for differences between means using STEM rather than STEP {F14}.

G7. Cause for concern? The funnel plot

Each member of a system (each person, team or business unit) produces a number of measurable outputs in a period of time.

To find if the system as whole is behaving as expected compare the performance of each member against the mean performance. Use a chart with

> *performance* on the vertical axis
> *number of outputs* on the horizontal axis

Show *control limits* to identify unusually high or low performance levels.

Compare how many observations are outside the limits with how many you would expect: about 1 in 20 should be outside a 95% control limit.

Example

The results of thirty-three surgeons in the UK carrying out procedures (operations) on patients suffering from an abdominal aortic aneurysm (AAA) are shown below. The performance measure is the percentage of patients who did not survive.

procedures	mortality %	procedures	mortality %	procedures	mortality %
7	0.0	33	3.0	24	0.0
15	0.0	53	0.0	39	7.7
11	0.0	55	3.6	22	4.5
19	0.0	26	7.7	12	8.3
59	0.0	64	3.1	23	8.7
81	1.2	104	1.0	46	2.2
32	3.1	47	2.1	7	0.0
19	0.0	17	11.8	134	0.0
47	2.1	26	7.7	90	0.0
20	0.0	16	12.5	55	1.8
34	2.9	7	0.0	71	0.0

Source: The National Vascular Registry[3]

This is a safe procedure. In the UK the mortality rate is just 2.2%. To see if the variation in mortality rates should be a cause for concern make the funnel plot.

Use the BINOMIAL distribution {C1} to find control limits. For example, if a surgeon whose work is compatible with the overall rate of 2.2% carries out 40 procedures there is a 95% probability of no more than

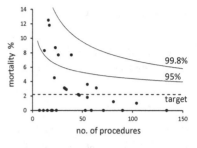

BINOM.INV(40,0.022,0.95) = 3 deaths

a mortality rate of 3/40 = 7.5%

The two lines show rates below which 95% and 99.8% of surgeons' mortality rates would be expected to fall. Of the 33 surgeons 6 (18%) have mortality rates higher than the 95% limit. This is more than the 5% expected. None has a rate higher than the 99.8% limit. There may be other factors such as differences in the underlying health of patients which mean that there probably is not any cause for concern (see below). You may wish to see more data, the results for the next period or the health of the patients for instance, to see if the 18% is reduced.

Rationale

A system to be monitored comprises a number of business units or teams or individuals, each delivering the same measurable output. In the Example the system was all AAA consultant surgeons in the UK. They worked at different hospitals but were doing the same job with the same purpose. Other systems might be

> all workers completing the same task in a business, measure task time
> business units in an organisation, measure staff turnover

Monitor the system by comparing the performance of people or teams or units to a common standard, most obviously the mean performance {G1,G3}.

If the system is in control and behaving normally performance variations around the mean will conform to an expected pattern. Control limits help you to decide this. When the system is in control there is no reason to draw attention to any of the individual performance levels; the system, *as a system,* is delivering as expected. There may be quite big differences between the performance of two people or units but this is not necessarily incompatible with the system being in control: the two measures may just be from opposite tails of the performance distribution. It is this whole system distribution which you are monitoring here.

On the other hand, if performance variation is greater than expected the system may not be behaving as assumed. You will want to identify those people or units which are exceptionally poor performers. Making a league table {G5} is a common way of doing this.

Being identified as a poor performer in a league table may encourage improved performance but also risks demotivation and reputational damage (think of the surgeons). Deciding whether and how to publish performance data should be done carefully. If you decide that the system is behaving as expected you have no justification for listing by performance. Present the data alphabetically by name of person or unit. If you think the system is not behaving as expected you may want to identify poor performance, perhaps by publishing a league table (but with confidence intervals {G5}). A funnel plot helps you decide what to do.

Therefore:

Make a chart showing performance plotted against number of cases. Show the mean and control limits. Use this funnel plot to support your decision that the system is or is not behaving as it should.

A funnel plot has two advantages:

it forces consideration of the system as a whole and provides an easy way to do so

it shows clearly the effect of different levels of information (the number of cases)

***

The idea of showing when a system is in control or out of control is common in process management where control charts {J4} show variation of the performance of a single unit over time. Funnel plots show the performance of the whole system at a single point in time. The role of control limits is the same in both: to identify how many extreme values you should expect.

The limits are calculated on the assumption that the data are an unbiased random sample from a population. But this may not be so. In the Example

some patients are healthier than others
potentially difficult cases may be allocated to more experienced surgeons

In small samples these differences may be important. They may account for the 18% of surgeons above the 95% control limit. Studies of the outcomes of medical interventions commonly use risk adjusted mortality rates to account for differences in patients' health. For AAA procedures the result is to reduce the proportion of results above the 95% line. The report gives details.

The probabilities chosen for the limits — 95% and 99.8% — are those used in the original study and also in other applications.

***

It will most usually be the case that potentially poor performance means either a too large or a too small value of the performance measure but not both, as in the Example. Sometimes potentially poor performance is associated with both extremes in which case the funnel plot is as shown at right. The principle of calculation is the same.

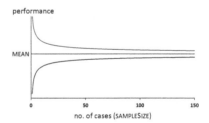

In **EXCEL**

How the control limits are calculated depends on the performance measure and this determines the appropriate statistical model:
BINOMIAL for proportion {C1}
POISSON for rate {C2}
NORMAL for mean {F9}

221

In the Example the BINOMIAL was used. For 40 procedures and a 95% control limit

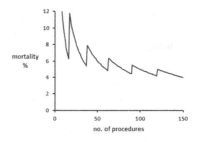

BINOM.INV(40,0.022,0.95) = 3

95% of case loads of 40 procedures should result in no more than 3 deaths, a mortality rate of 7.5%.

Workloads of from 38 to 62 procedures all have the same limit of 3 deaths, though different rates. This gives a saw-tooth line (top right).

Using the expected value {B7} rather than the integer number of deaths gives a smoother curve.

A linear interpolation gives a good approximation.

The probabilities of no more than 2 and no more than 3 deaths are

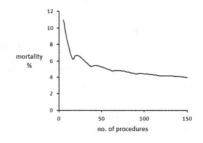

BINOM.DIST(2,40,0.022,TRUE) = 0.942

and   BINOM.DIST(3,40,0.022,TRUE) = 0.989

The interpolated value is for a probability of 0.95

2 + (0.95 – 0.942)/(0.989 – 0.942) = 2.170

and so a rate of 2.170/40 = 5.43%.

This curve is still a little irregular. Make a smoother presentation by fitting a *Power* trend line {I8}.

Finally, remove the interpolated (unsmoothed) series by right clicking on a point and then

Format Data Series / Line Color / No line

to leave just the smoothed line used in the Example.

The spreadsheet fragment (below) shows how the series was calculated for the Example.

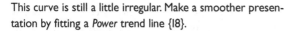

	A	B	C
1	rate =	0.022	
2	level =	0.95	
3			
4	no. of procedures	max. deaths	mortality %
5	5	1	10.983
6	6	1	10.577

cell B6: =BINOM.INV(A6,B1,B2)

cell C6: =(B6 – 1 +(B2-BINOM.DIST(B6 – 1,A6,B1,TRUE))/BINOM.DIST(B6,A6,B1,FALSE))*
        100/A6.

Significance and hypothesis testing

H 1. Hypothesis or target?
H 2. Significance test
H 3. Don't say "statistically significant"
H 4. $p = 5\%$: sound advice or automation of judgement?
H 5. Hypothesis Testing

---

overview

Finding out about the values of system variables given incomplete information — samples — is a basic task for which you need some statistical help. Mostly this will arise in the context of monitoring and other management tasks {sections F and G}.

There is a particular formalism which some people find helpful. The mechanics of data analysis are no different to that found elsewhere but the words used and the point of view implied are {H1}. This formalism is called significance testing {H2}.

The difficulties which can occur with unthinking use of the method are not to do with the calculations, which are uncontroversial, but with the presentation and interpretation of the results, which can be misleading {H3,H4}.

An alternative but related approach {H5} has the intention of being more decision oriented. The presentation is more formal and is popular, though often what is done is no different to significance testing.

H1. Hypothesis or target?

> Testing a hypothesis uses the same methods as monitoring against a target {G1}. The differences in terminology usually indicate a different mindset; academic enquiry rather than management problem.

Rationale

You have a question:

> is this performance target being met?
> has performance improved as a result of the new software?

In both cases the question has the form of a particular numerical value

> the average response time is no more than 5 minutes
> the difference between average project durations is zero

Managers use words such as target or standard. This reflects the reality of their work.

Statisticians, psychologists, social scientists and others tend to prefer the word hypothesis, probably reflecting that they are primarily interested in testing a theory.

**

Both use the same methods to test {F2} whether the data they collect should lead them to reject their hypothesis (view) or not.

If a manager decides that a standard is probably not being met or that a difference is found when it was not expected it makes sense to say "it is unlikely that what we have found is just due to random effects" {G1}.

Someone with a hypothesis testing mindset is likely to say that they have found a "statistically significant" result.

This is not just a question of semantics for two reasons:

1. When comparing two samples {F14} the result may be reported as being "statistically significant" which, to those unaware of the method, is easily interpreted as meaning that a usefully large difference has been found.
   A more accurate report would be that there is "probably not 'no difference'".

2. With enough data *all* differences become statistically significant and *all* hypotheses are rejected {H3}.

It is not the analysis which is problematic but the language used to report the conclusion.

**

There are two approaches to testing a hypothesis.

> *Significance testing* {H2} is just what is described above.
> *Hypothesis testing* {H5} is a framework which seems more decision oriented.

In practice most reported analyses are significance tests though they may use the language of hypothesis testing.

H2. Significance test

> You have a hypothesis that a variable will take a particular value.
>
> Collect some data and see how likely your data are if your hypothesis is true.
>
> The more unlikely the data the greater *may* be the evidence against your hypothesis.

Example

You want to test the hypothesis that there is no difference between the abilities of men and women as measured by a standardised aptitude test.

The test is taken by 200 men and 150 women with the results shown in the table {F14}.

	men	women	difference
SAMPLESIZE	200	150	
MEAN	7.2	6.8	0.4
STDEV	1.8	2.1	
SE	0.217	0.171	0.214

If your hypothesis, that the difference in population means is zero, is correct the likelihood {D1} of values of the difference in sample means is a NORMAL distribution with

MEAN = 0 (from your hypothesis)

and SE = 0.214 (from the data)

You are only interested in the size of the difference not whether the score for men is larger than the score for women or vice versa, so unusually large differences are in either tail {F2}

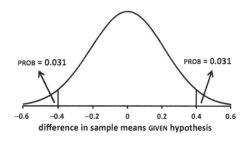

difference in sample means GIVEN hypothesis

PROB(–0.4 or smaller) = PROB(+0.4 or larger) = NORM.DIST(–0.4, 0, 0.214, TRUE) = 0.031

The probability of finding a difference at least as extreme as –0.4 or + 0.4 is 2 x 0.031 = 0.062 or 6%

In the language of significance testing this is called the *statistical significance*, p = 0.062.

What now do you think about your hypothesis?

Have you found a sufficiently unlikely result that you would reject, or at least doubt, your hypothesis that there is no difference and so now believe there is a difference in the aptitudes of women and men?

Rationale

You wish to test an idea by comparing what you think is true in a population (or populations) with some data {H1}. You cannot test a vaguely expressed view ("I think this is a bit bigger than that").

> Therefore:
> Formulate a hypothesis that the characteristic of interest to you has some particular value: In the Example that the difference in population means is zero.
> Find how unlikely the data are if your hypothesis is true.

All values described by the likelihood distribution are, by definition, possible. You are more likely to see some than others but *all are possible*. Whatever value you see, however unusual, is no basis for certain rejection of your hypothesis. You must make a judgement.

How will you make that judgement? Is 6% sufficiently unlikely that it counts as strong enough evidence for you to reject your hypothesis? This is a genuinely hard problem. A number of values have come to be used {H4}:

$p = 5\%$ indicates acceptable evidence against your hypothesis

to $\quad p = 0.1\%$ indicates strong evidence against your hypothesis

Using these criteria certainly gets over your problem of having to decide if your data are so unlikely that you are justified in rejecting your hypothesis.

But do not outsource your judgement and *unthinkingly* use these criteria. Treat them as guides {H4}.

***

If you decide that your p value is so low that you should reject your hypothesis all that the method allows you to say is just that: "reject the hypothesis". There is nothing here that gives you a guide for concluding anything else. If you take the $p = 5\%$ as a hard well-defined boundary you could only conclude from the significance test in the Example that there is not "no difference" between mean scores. This may be just the sort of result you want. Think of testing a new drug for harmful side effects. Being able to say there is no difference in the proportion of patients suffering these effects in the treatment group and the control group is good news.

On the other hand, if you have data such as that in the Example it seems a bit weak only to say that there is not "no difference".

But there is a way of saying something more: use a confidence interval {F19}. Some statisticians say that all you need is a confidence interval and that you don't need p at all. Others recommend that for testing a hypothesis you should give both the p value and the confidence interval. In the Example report

$p = 6\%$

and $\quad$ 95% confidence interval = −0.02 to 0.82

From the confidence interval say that plausible values vary from women having a mean score slightly higher than men, 0.02, to men having a mean score 0.82 higher.

The confidence interval gives a context for interpreting the p value {F2}. This works if differences in values of the variable you are testing are easily understood. The importance of differences in cost, for instance, have a clear impact. But what of the test scores used in the Example? You will need to have enough experience to make a sensible interpretation, or find someone who has.

However difficult it is to make a meaningful interpretation of the confidence interval do not rely only on the *p* value for your decision.

***

This statsNote has used as an example the comparisons of means of large samples. Exactly the same approach can be used for other problems {F8–F17}.

H3. Don't say "statistically significant"

You make a significance test {H2} to see whether your data provide evidence against a hypothesis.

Reporting a result as "statistically significant" risks confusion. You have not necessarily seen anything of practical significance.

Do not use this phrase. Do not rely only on p values. At the very least give a confidence interval too {H2}.

Example

As manager for a group of medical general practitioners you want to reduce the number of visits to your doctors by their patients without compromising the treatment they receive. For a particular condition two new drugs are available. They both claim to reduce the number of consultations needed during treatment. Two studies have been published, one for each drug. Both studies used as control groups patients given the currently standard drug for this condition.

The results are reported as confidence intervals for the reduction in mean consultations per patient {F14} and also as the p value in a two-tailed significance test with the null hypothesis that the drug has no effect, positive or negative {H2}.

	control	drug A	difference
SAMPLESIZE	200	150	
MEAN	1.8	1.7	0.1
STDEV	0.7	0.8	
SE	0.049	0.065	0.082

95% CI = −0.06 to 0.26; p = 0.222

	control	drug B	difference
SAMPLESIZE	20,000	15,000	
MEAN	1.8	1.78	0.02
STDEV	0.7	0.8	
SE	0.005	0.007	0.008

95% CI = 0.004 to 0.036; p = 0.015

Deciding on the basis of the p values alone is not a good guide. The test for drug B gives a much smaller p and so a more "statistically significant" result. But what is the *practical* significance.

Which drug, if either, would you recommend?

Rationale

These p values are determined by three things

  the difference in means
  the standard deviations of the data
  the sample sizes

The test for drug B gives a lower p value only because many more data were used. The effect is shown clearly by comparing the two confi-

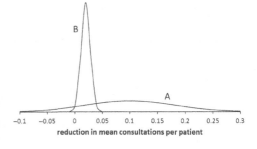

dence intervals and also the two distributions. The Example is extreme and made to illustrate the point, but the point is there to be made.

There is less uncertainty about the reduction offered by B but the reduction is much smaller.

***

See the effect of increased sample size. With enough data all differences, however small, will be "statistically significant". More data enable you to provide a more *precise* estimate of the effect (of the drugs in this case), however small and practically insignificant that might be. The increased precision gives a smaller confidence interval; a more straightforward and intuitively obvious effect.

***

p values do not measure significance in the normally accepted sense of something important. It is just too easy to fool yourself (and others) that by finding a "statistically significant" result you have something of use. You may have. But you may not.

Therefore:

Avoid saying that you have found something which is "statistically significant".

Do not give only a p value.

Give a confidence interval, think carefully before you decide to give a p value as well.

Assess all evidence and make a case for your decision.

In the Example the hypothesis tested does not have to be that there is no difference, though this is so common that it almost becomes a habit.

Thinking of a particular non-zero value of difference to test is hard and may be foolish: 0.05? 0.052? The precision implied is likely to spurious, which is why difference=0 is so often used.

There is no such difficulty in using a confidence interval.

H4. $p = 5\%$: sound advice or the automation of judgement?

> You must use your judgement in interpreting the result of a significance test given by the significance level p {H2}.
>
> Recommended criterial values for p are in common use. To use them (or not) as a guide you should know where they came from.

Example

You decide to use a significance test for the difference in aptitudes of men and women. The experiment returns $p = 6\%$ against the hypothesis that there is no difference {H2}. Do you decide to reject your hypothesis?

Rationale

Thinking and talking about probability is hard {B8}.

As part of what has become the significance testing orthodoxy certain p values have become accepted: 5%, 1% and 0.1% representing increasingly strong evidence against the hypothesis. This standardisation is necessary for the wide use of the method. These default values have been gratefully received and have become a sort of common language. As with any language we should be careful to use only those words whose meaning we understand.

But where did these values come from?

Sir Ronald Fisher, who promoted significance testing, wrote

> "If p is between .1 and .9 there is certainly no reason to suspect the hypothesis tested. If it is below .02 it is strongly indicated that the hypothesis fails to account for the whole of the facts. We shall not often be astray if we draw a conventional line at .05 ..."

R.A. Fisher (1890–1962)

Another statistician, Karl Pearson (1857–1936), discussing significance testing, described a probability of 0.1 as "not very improbable" and one of 0.01 as "very improbable".

And that seems about it.

The helpful suggestions of eminent men, no doubt, but how relevant are they for *your* problem which needs *your* judgement? What does the context of *your* problem require?

***

Confidence intervals help {H3}, though you will have to settle on a confidence level and this has the same difficulty; the popular 95% confidence level being the default as the complement to $p = 5\%$.

***

You must decide. Just remember that the method(s) you use are there to help you in making your decision. These default values may be a good starting point but you should not use them thoughtlessly. In the Example you would want to think carefully before deciding that $p = 6\%$ was so far above $p = 5\%$ that a different decision is justified.

H5. Hypothesis testing

> Hypothesis Testing is a framework for deciding whether to accept or reject a hypothesis.
>
> It offers a more formal decision oriented approach than significance testing {H2}.

Example

This illustration repeats the example in {H2}. Read that first.

The setup that follows is typical of hypothesis tests.

You want to test the hypothesis that there is no difference between the abilities of men and women as measured by a standardised aptitude test. Formulate two hypotheses:

> null hypothesis: population mean score for men = population mean score for women
> alternate hypothesis: population mean score for men ≠ population mean score for women,

or as you will more likely see it (μ stands for population mean)

$$H_0: \mu_m = \mu_w$$
$$H_A: \mu_m \neq \mu_w$$

You have to decide whether to accept or reject H_0 in favour of H_A. You may make one of the two errors, wrongly rejecting the null hypothesis or wrongly accepting it:

		In reality:	
		H_0 true	H_0 false
You decide to	accept H_0	✓	✗
	reject H_0	✗	✓

These are called Type I and Type II errors:

		In reality:	
		H_0 true	H_0 false
You decide to	accept H_0	✓	Type II error
	reject H_0	Type I error	✓

The probabilities of these errors are α (wrongly rejecting H_0 when it is true) and β (wrongly accepting H_0 when it is false). The probability of correct rejection, $1-\beta$, is called the *power* of the test.

		In reality:	
		H_0 true	H_0 false
You decide to	accept H_0	$1-\alpha$	β
	reject H_0	α	$1-\beta$

Most studies concentrate on α. You may set the value of α in advance and see if your data are more or less likely than your set value. If less likely (smaller α) accept H_0 otherwise reject.

The alternative is to calculate α from the data and then decide whether it is small enough to justify rejection. This is better because it more obviously invites interpretation. This is a straightforward significance test. In the Example {H2}, the difference in mean scores was 0.4 and standard error 0.214 and this gave $p = 0.062$. So $\alpha = 0.062$. If you reject H_0 there is a probability of 0.062 that you will make a Type I error.

Rationale

There is hypothesis testing and Hypothesis Testing.

Egon Pearson and Jerzy Neyman proposed the Hypothesis Testing apparatus as a more decision focussed model than Fisher's significance testing {H2}. Fisher hated it. He preferred his more flexible approach with its greater emphasis on interpretation of evidence rather than treating p (α) as an exact criterion as Pearson and Neyman's method encouraged.

***

Many reported analyses, however described, are significance tests with the H_0 vs. H_A formalism attached.

***

H_A is just "not H_0". If you reject H_0 you have nothing else to say. As with a significance test {H2, H3} using a confidence interval helps.

***

The Hypothesis Testing model does invite consideration of the power of a test. Setting the power $1-\beta$ in advance of data collection can help in determining sample size. This is especially useful with small samples.

Is there a relationship?

---

overview

The relationship between two variables is relevant either because their independence or correlation is itself of interest or because knowledge of one can be used to estimate the other {I9}. This is true, however many variables are involved. In these notes the simplest case of just two variables is described.

As usual with data analysis it is likely that you will only have a sample to analyse, so the familiar issue of inference (what can be said of the population from the sample) needs to be addressed.

If variables are categorical (man/woman, use product/do not use) data about them are collected in a table. This allows inference about whether in the population these variables are independent or not {I1}.

For other variables data are plotted as points on a graph. A numerical measure, the correlation coefficient, of the strength of the relation can help an appreciation of the pattern {I2, I9} and be used for inference {I3} in a way that a graph cannot.

If it seems plausible to believe that the relation is linear then fit a straight line model to the data {I4}. Measure the predictive usefulness of the model; the proportion of the variation in one variable that can be accounted for by variation in the other {I5}.

A full inferential analysis of the model is easily made using appropriate software, in this case EXCEL {I6}.

Predictions using the model are not perfectly accurate because the fit of model to data is imperfect and because the model will, in most cases, have been fitted to sample data. The effects of these sources of error are combined {I7} so that you can give appropriate interval forecasts.

There are cases where a nonlinear model better describes the relation between variables. Two examples are given {I8}.

I1. Is there structure in a table?

A table shows frequencies: in a sample how many data were seen in each category.

You want to decide whether this is evidence that the two variables are independent or not. Use a chi-squared test {C8}.

Compare the observed frequencies, O, with the frequencies you would expect, E, if the two variables really were independent

$$E = (\text{row sum}) \times (\text{column sum}) / (\text{SAMPLESIZE})$$

calculate $\quad \chi^2 = \text{SUM} [(O - E)^2 / E]$

and $\quad$ *degrees of freedom* $= (\text{no. of rows} - 1) \times (\text{no. of columns} - 1)$

Use the χ^2 (chi-squared) distribution to find the probability, p, that your sample, O, occurred by chance from a population in which the two variables really are independent.

Example

In its issue of 9 January 2007, the *Financial Times* contained an article headed *Bias Feared in Nutrition Research* which reported the results of an analysis in the online journal *Plos Medicine*. The *FT* piece was concerned with the possibility that studies funded by the food industry were more likely to have findings favourable to the industry than other studies. Marion Nestlé, Professor of Nutrition at New York University and a critic of the food industry, said "If industry could not use these studies in marketing, they would not do them". Here is the final paragraph of the *FT* piece:

"Among studies sponsored only by industry, 14 had favourable, five neutral and three unfavourable conclusions; while among those without industry support, 24 were favourable, eight neutral and 20 unfavourable."

Do you think that there is a bias due to funding?

1. Tabulate the data: observed frequencies, O.

	favourable	neutral	unfavourable	
sponsored	14	5	3	22
not sponsored	24	8	20	52
	38	13	23	74

2. Calculate expected frequencies, e.g. $E = 22 \times 38 / 74 = 11.297$

	favourable	neutral	unfavourable	
sponsored	11.297	3.865	6.838	22
not sponsored	26.703	9.135	16.162	52
	38	13	23	74

3. Calculate $(O - E)^2/E$, e.g. $(14 - 11.297)^2/11.297 = 0.647$

sponsored	0.647	0.333	2.154
not sponsored	0.274	0.141	0.911

$$4.460 = \chi^2$$

degrees of freedom $= (2 - 1) \times (3 - 1) = 2$

If sponsorship and result really are independent the probability of a value as large as $\chi^2 = 4.460$ or larger for this sample is CHISQ.DIST.RT$(4.460, 2) = 0.108$ or 11%.

This isn't that unusual, so you might conclude there is not enough evidence here that sponsorship matters. You may have other contextual evidence, of course.

Rationale

You are interested in examining the possibility of a relation between two variables:

> is brand preference different in men than in women?
> is the type of wine bought in supermarkets affected by music played (yes, really {B6})?
> is job turnover different for different shift patterns?

These variables are categorical. It is natural to show joint variation as a table the cells of which contain frequencies, how many times you saw that combination. These tables are called *contingency tables*.

The business implications of these relationships, if they exist, are clear. But you need evidence.

> Therefore:
> Collect data and make a contingency table. Even if you suspect there is a relation, test your data against what you would expect if there were no relation and the variables were independent. If your data are unlikely you might want to reconsider this assumption of independence.

This is a special case of testing a theoretical distribution against data {C8}. The theory or hypothesis here is independence. Why choose this?

To predict expected frequencies you need to know *exactly* what relationship is being tested, even though what you really want to know may be whether or not there is some kind, any kind, of relationship. But we cannot test "some kind". While there are many ways in which two variables may exhibit a relationship there is only one way in which they may show no relationship: when they are *independent* {B5, B6} so this is what we test.

If two variables are independent then the joint probability is found by simple multiplication {B6}. For instance,

PROB(*sponsored* AND *favourable*) = PROB(*sponsored*) × PROB(*favourable*) = $(22 / 74) \times (38 / 74)$

The *expected frequency* is just this probability multiplied by the SAMPLESIZE

expected frequency $= (22 / 74) \times (38 / 74) \times 74 = 22 \times 38 / 74 = 11.297$

In general, *expected frequency* = (row sum) × (column sum) / (SAMPLESIZE)

***

The formula *degrees of freedom* = (no. of rows − 1) × (no. of columns − 1) is easy to remember. There are two ways to think about what it means.

The marginal distributions, the row and column totals, are fixed. In the Example, once two cell values are decided the other four are also determined to ensure that the row and column sums of the expected frequency table are the same as for the observed. You are not free to choose all of them, just the first two. These are the two *degrees of freedom*:

	favourable	neutral	unfavourable	
sponsored	11.297	3.865	?	22
not sponsored	?	?	?	52
	38	13	23	74

***

The more general idea {C8, C9} is that *degrees of freedom* is the difference between the number of classes in the distribution and the number of values estimated *from the data* to get the expected frequencies.

In the Example there are six classes, the six cells in the table.

If you knew any four of the five row and column sums the fifth is easily found,

	favourable	neutral	unfavourable	
sponsored				22
not sponsored				52
	38	13	?	?

The assumed independence means that you can now calculate the expected frequencies in the table from the row and column totals.

So   *degrees of freedom* = 6 − 4 = 2

***

The assumptions and their implications which hold for the chi-squared test generally {C8} also hold here. The most important is that the test only works for **frequency** distributions, not percentages or proportions.

***

Deciding how to interpret the 11% probability can be a difficult. You can look for help by giving a confidence interval {F1}. Using the EXCEL function CHISQ.INV find that the 95% confidence interval for χ^2 as from 0.05 to 7.38. Because it is hard to think just what different values of χ^2 mean this interval is unlikely to be of much help. You may have experience in analysing lots of these tables to help you interpret the interval. But probably not.

What you have found is that a dissimilarity this big or bigger has an 11% chance of happening even if in the population the two variables really are independent. This gives you a measure of how unlikely your data are. If the data are very unlikely you may treat this as evidence against the assumption of independence {H2}.

The value of χ^2 is directly proportional to SAMPLESIZE {C8} so with a large enough sample any data are unusual {H3}. Bear this in mind when interpreting your result.

In **EXCEL**

Stage 3 of the calculation in the Example can be done using the function CHISQ.TEST. You will have to form the table of expected frequencies but then just access the function and highlight the two distributions, observed and expected.

12. Looking for correlation

Data showing the relation between two variables are plotted as points on a graph called a **scattergram**.

To describe numerically the pattern shown in a scattergram calculate the **correlation coefficient**, CORREL.

The value of CORREL corresponds to the pattern of points in the scattergram:

> CORREL = +1 → a perfect upwards sloping straight line
>
> CORREL = −1 → a perfect downwards sloping straight line
>
> CORREL = 0 → no discernible pattern

NOTE: the correlation coefficient is also written as *r*.

Example

You are considering investing in a leisure centre but are not sure about demand. You have some government forecasts about future income. You need to know what will be the impact on leisure spend.

Here are data from six households showing the relation between annual income and monthly expenditure on leisure activities:

X income (000)	Y leisure spend
18	200
22	240
26	210
28	300
35	470
36	370

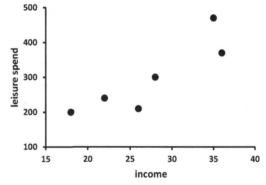

The data are in the first six rows of columns A and B in an EXCEL spreadsheet so

CORREL(A1:A6, B1:B6) = 0.879

This is quite close to 1 and so indicates a strong upwards sloping relation. This is just what the scattergram shows too.

(Of course, nobody would survey just six households. But this makes for an easily seen illustration.)

Rationale

You are interested in the relation between two variables. For example, it would be helpful to know if the movement of a particular stock is related to a market index {K2} to help in deciding your investment options. Looking at the scattergram will give you a good idea of the shape and strength of the relation: does the pattern of points conform closely to a straight line?

Deciding about a pattern of points on a graph is not always easy. Deciding whether a number is large or small is easier.

Therefore:

Plot the data as a scattergram and find the correlation coefficient. This measures how *linear* the data are, so it is important to look at the pattern too.

CORREL is bounded, with limits of +1 and –1 for perfect linear relations. When there is no relation the variables are said to be *uncorrelated* and CORREL = 0; they are *independent*.

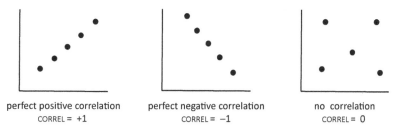

perfect positive correlation	perfect negative correlation	no correlation
CORREL = +1	CORREL = −1	CORREL = 0

It is important that you use both the scattergram and the coefficient for two reasons.

First, so that you get an appreciation of what a particular value of CORREL looks like. For example,

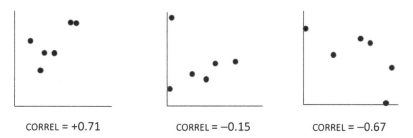

CORREL = +0.71	CORREL = −0.15	CORREL = −0.67

Second, CORREL measures the extent to which the two variables are lineally related. It may be that there is — and you would expect there to be — a nonlinear relation. A simple demand curve with constant elasticity is not a straight line.

In cases like this, even if the pattern of the observations perfectly corresponds to the model you expect from theory, the correlation, as measured by CORREL, would not be perfect.

Some alternatives are easily tested in EXCEL. Make a *Scatter* chart then right click on any point and select *Add Trendline* to see the options {18}.

***

When you have looked at the *scattergram* and calculated the correlation coefficient you may decide that on this evidence it is reasonable to say that the variables are correlated: that there is a pattern in the graph and so, for instance, that bigger values of X are associated with bigger values of Y. What you have not concluded is that X causes Y or *vice versa*. This argument must be based on some other reasoning from economics or psychology or whatever. The statistics helps you identify that a pattern exists, not why {19}.

***

It is likely that your data are a sample and so you will want to estimate the size of the correlation in the population. You can do this with a number, CORREL, but not with a graph {13}.

13. Inference for the correlation coefficient

> You have a correlation coefficient, CORREL, from a sample. To infer the population correlation either *report* a confidence interval or *test* against an assumed value (often CORREL = 0) {F2}.
>
> **Report**
>
> Transform values of CORREL to values of *w* using the EXCEL function FISHER.
>
> *w* is Normally distributed with standard deviation
>
> $$\text{STDEV} = 1/\sqrt{(\text{SAMPLESIZE} - 3)}$$
>
> Find a confidence interval for *w*. Transform back to CORREL values using FISHERINV.
>
> **Test**
>
> Test the hypothesis that in the population there is no correlation using a *t* distribution {F7} with
>
> $$t = \text{CORREL} \times \sqrt{[(\text{SAMPLESIZE} - 2)/(1 - \text{CORREL}^2)]}$$
>
> and   *degrees of freedom* = SAMPLESIZE − 2

Example

An assembly task is carried out by operatives in a plant. It is thought that performance increases with experience. A total of 30 operatives were surveyed and for each the throughput (no. of completed tasks per hour) and the number of months in the job were measured. The correlation coefficient {12} is CORREL = 0.56.

Report   Transform CORREL and make a confidence interval for *w* using a NORMAL distribution with

         MEAN = FISHER(0.56) = 0.633

     and   STDEV = $1/\sqrt{(30 - 3)}$ = 0.192

     The 95% confidence interval {F19} for *w* is

         0.633 ± (1.96 × 0.192) = 0.257 to 1.009

     Convert back to values of CORREL

         FISHERINV(0.257) = 0.25

     and   FISHERINV(1.009) = 0.77

     The 95% confidence interval for CORREL is 0.25 to 0.77.

     The population correlation is positive, between 0.25 and 0.77. Just how positive cannot be estimated with much precision due to the small sample.

Test $t = 0.56 \times \sqrt{[30 - 2)/(1 - 0.56^2)]}$ = 3.577

     degrees of freedom = 30 − 2 = 28

If the population correlation coefficient is 0 the probability of getting a sample value at least as big as +0.56 or at least as small as −0.56 is {F7, H2}

T.DIST.2T(3.577, 28) = 0.00129 = 0.13%

This is very low. Your data are very unlikely if in the population the variables are independent.

Rationale

You want to know whether two variables are lineally correlated or not and, if they are, how strongly. But you cannot collect data on all members of the relevant population.

Therefore:

Take a sample and find the sample correlation {I2}.

Report a confidence interval estimate for the population correlation.

You may also *test* to find how unlikely your data are if in the population the correlation is 0.

Always give the confidence interval. Give the test probability too if you wish {H2}.

***

Report

Any sampling distribution for the correlation coefficient will be skewed because CORREL is bounded between +1 and −1. A transformation is needed. This transformation was found by R A Fisher and is named for him.

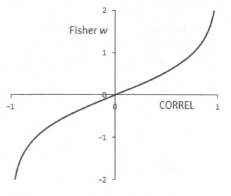

For this method to work well both variables should be Normally distributed and the sample size not very small.

The NORMAL approximation is better the larger the sample size and the closer to zero is the value of CORREL.

***

Test

The most common test value is that in the population the correlation is zero — the variables are independent. Sometimes this is because we really do have a firm idea that they are independent, but just as often we believe the variables are correlated and want to see if that belief is justified. As with tabular data {I1} variables may be correlated in a number of ways (different CORREL values) but there is only one way they can be independent (CORREL = 0) and so this is what we test.

14. Fitting a straight line

A straight line model relates changes in the value of one variable, X, to changes in the value of another, Y. The equation is

$$Y = a + bX$$

where a and b are the slope and the intercept.

In EXCEL use the SLOPE and INTERCEPT functions.

Alternatively, make a graph of the data and right click on one of the points. Choose the *Add Trendline* option.

Example

Use the data from {12} showing income and leisure spend for six households.

X income (000)	Y leisure spend
18	200
22	240
26	210
28	300
35	470
36	370

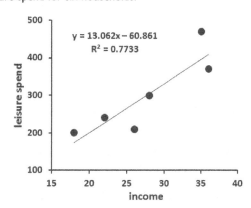

Plotting the scattergram and using the *Add Trendline* option gives the line and the equations as shown. The straight line is a pretty good model, as expected.

The straight line model is

$$Y = -60.861 + 13.062X$$

Expect a household with an income of 30,000 to have a leisure spend of

$$Y = -60.861 + (13.062 \times 30) = 331$$

Alternatively find this using the FORECAST function. If your data are in rows 1–6 of columns A and B

$$FORECAST(30, B1:B6, A1:A6) = 331$$

Add Trendline also shows $R^2 = 0.7733$. This measures how well the model performs {15}. For a simple two variable model CORREL $= \sqrt{R^2} = 0.879$.

Rationale

A linear model has two parameters, INTERCEPT, *a*, and SLOPE, *b*.

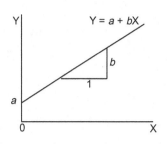

The SLOPE, *b*, is the increase in Y for an increase of 1 in X. Because this is a linear model this slope, or rate of change, is constant. In the Example a change of 1,000 in income is associated with a change of 13.062 in leisure spend.

The model does not establish causation (though it seems clear in this case). Say that variation in X accounts for variations in Y rather than X causes Y {19}.

The INTERCEPT, *a*, is just the value of Y when X = 0. Sometimes this has meaning (fixed cost in a model of total cost against volume) but in most cases, as here, it does not. Just treat it as a parameter needed for forecasts.

You decide that a relation exists by looking at the scattergram and the correlation coefficient {12}. You may be interested in the INTERCEPT or SLOPE or you may wish to have a model to predict values of Y from values of X.

> Therefore:
> Find the line which best fits the data by minimising the sum of squared errors.

The model is to predict values of Y from values of X and so error is the difference between the actual Y value and that predicted by the line given a value for X.

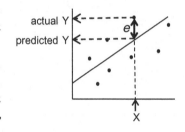

These errors in the Y direction, typically e, should be minimised. To prevent positive errors (those above the line) from cancelling the effect of negative errors (those where the point is below the line) minimise the sum of squared errors, SUM(e^2). This method is called *least squares regression*.

The software, EXCEL in this case, finds this line.

***

Although any shaped line can be fitted in this way it is most commonly a straight line that is used. This is called *linear regression*. Other nonlinear models may be useful; predicting using a constant annual growth rate, for example {18}.

***

The accuracy of predictions is described by R^2, the proportionate reduction in error variance as a result of using the linear model {15}.

***

Your data are likely to be a sample from a population. This has two consequences:

prediction error is increased because the INTERCEPT and SLOPE you have found are themselves subject to sampling error

if you want to estimate the population SLOPE or INTERCEPT make an appropriate inference.

These extra analyses can easily be done in EXCEL using the *Regression analysis* add-in {16}.

In EXCEL

Right click on any data point on the graph.

On the drop down menu click *Add Trendline* to get the panel below.

The top section lets you choose which model you want to use. The Example used a linear model.

The *Forecast* section allows you to plot the line outside the range of the data. Not needed here.

At the bottom of the panel choose to display the equation for the line and the R^2 value.

There is an option to force the line through the origin $X = Y = 0$ by setting the INTERCEPT = 0. Do not select this.

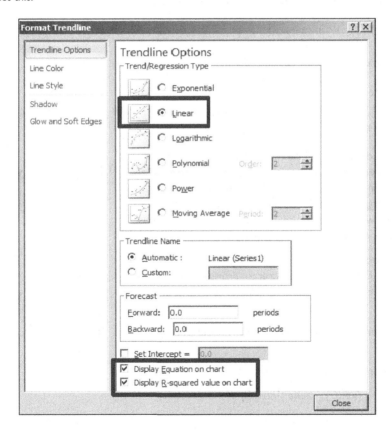

15. How useful is the model?

To decide how useful a regression model $Y = a + bX$ might be use the *coefficient of determination*

R^2 = proportion of variance of Y accounted for by the model

For a simple two variable model $R^2 = $ CORREL^2, the square of the correlation coefficient {12}.

$R^2 = 1 \rightarrow$ perfect model, all variation in Y accounted for

$R^2 = 0 \rightarrow$ useless model, no variation in Y accounted for
X and Y are independent

Example

In the model used to predict leisure spend from income {14} $R^2 = 0.7733$.

77% of the variation in leisure spend is accounted for by variation in income.

This makes sense: the more money you have the more you spend.

Rationale

You have a model to make predictions. You want to know how useful the model is.

Therefore:
Compare the errors you would have made without the model and those you still make with it. R^2 is a good summary.

With no model you would have made a prediction somehow. If you were predicting leisure spend for a particular household and had no other information and no model, the best you could do (the only thing you could do) would be to use the MEAN household spend. You would have to use this same value for all households. The error of the forecast is typically E.

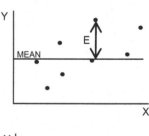

With the model in the Example, if you know the household income you can make a better forecast, provided the two variables are correlated. The error is reduced to e (see the table below).

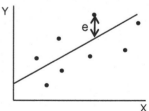

Square the errors to get an overall error measures: SUM(E^2) and SUM(e^2).

Find the proportionate reduction in error

$$R^2 = [\text{SUM}(E^2) - \text{SUM}(e^2)]/\text{SUM}(E^2)$$

$$= 1 - \text{SUM}(e^2)/\text{SUM}(E^2)$$

In the Example

$$R^2 = 1 - 12575.88 / 55483.33 = 0.7733$$

X	Y	without regression model			with regression model		
		estimate	error E	E^2	estimate	error e	e^2
18	200	298.33	-98.33	9669.44	174.25	25.75	663.17
22	240	298.33	-58.33	3402.78	226.49	13.51	182.40
26	210	298.33	-88.33	7802.78	278.74	-68.74	4725.31
28	300	298.33	1.67	2.78	304.86	-4.86	23.66
35	470	298.33	171.67	29469.44	396.30	73.70	5432.34
36	370	298.33	71.67	5136.11	409.36	-39.36	1548.99
				55483.33			12575.88

If the regression model was perfect SUM(e^2) = 0 and so R^2 = 1.

If there was no correlation the model would be useless. The regression line would just be the MEAN so that SUM (E^2) = SUM (e^2) and R^2 = 0.

***

This is quite a general idea about model performance. For a simple regression model, as here, numerically R^2 = CORREL^2. The two measures are founded on different ideas but give the same result in this case.

***

The discussion above used sums of squares. It could equally use variance, which is just an average sum of squares {A7}. It is common, and probably more easily understood, to talk of the reduction in variance and to think of R^2 measuring the proportion of the variance of Y accounted for by the variance of X.

Thinking this way will remind you of how the model works.

If there is no variation in X then, no matter how conceptually important you think X is, it would be of no help in predicting Y.

If there was no variation in Y no model would be needed.

16. Regression analysis in EXCEL

For a full analysis of a regression model in EXCEL use

   Data/Data Analysis/Regression

If this is not already installed on your computer go to the

   File/Options/Add-ins

section of the main menu and add in the *Analysis Toolpak*.

You can now make inferences about the population from your sample.

Preliminaries

This uses the data from {14}.

To access the regression analysis software use *Data/Data Analysis/Regression*

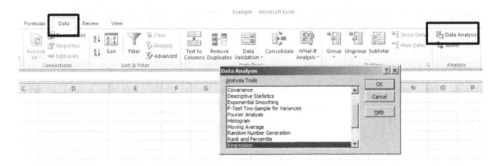

The options are clear (see screen image on next page).

Select the data. Check *Labels* if the first row contains variable names.

Decide where you want the output. Here it will be put in a new worksheet.

Residuals are the differences between given and predicted Y values. Decide what you want to see.

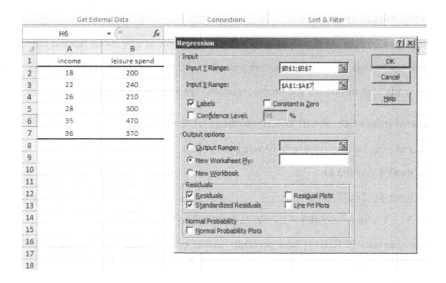

The result is shown below.

Cells in this output will be referenced using square brackets [ ].

	A	B	C	D	E	F	G
1	SUMMARY OUTPUT						
2							
3		*Regression Statistics*					
4	Multiple R	0.879					
5	R Square	0.773					
6	Adjusted R Square	0.717					
7	Standard Error	56.071					
8	Observations	6					
9							
10	ANOVA						
11		*df*	*SS*	*MS*	*F*	*Significance F*	
12	Regression	1	42907.455	42907.455	13.648	0.021	
13	Residual	4	12575.878	3143.970			
14	Total	5	55483.333				
15							
16		*Coefficients*	*Standard Error*	*t Stat*	*P-value*	*Lower 95%*	*Upper 95%*
17	Intercept	-60.861	99.889	-0.609	0.575	-338.197	216.474
18	income	13.062	3.536	3.694	0.021	3.245	22.878
19							
20	RESIDUAL OUTPUT						
21							
22	*Observation*	*Predicted leisure spend*	*Residuals*	*Standard Residuals*			
23	1	174.248	25.752	0.513			
24	2	226.494	13.506	0.269			
25	3	278.741	-68.741	-1.371			
26	4	304.864	-4.864	-0.097			
27	5	396.296	73.704	1.470			
28	6	409.357	-39.357	-0.785			

The basic model result

In the *Regression Statistics* see that there are six data points and that $R^2 = 0.773$. [B5 and B8].

Regression coefficients are just the INTERCEPT and SLOPE, -60.861 and 13.062 [B17 and B18].

Forecasts made with this model and errors (residuals) are in cells [B23:C28].

Errors and inference about the usefulness of the model

An analysis of errors and calculation of R^2 was given in {I5}:

$\text{SUM}(E^2) = 55483.33$

$\text{SUM}(e^2) = 12575.88$

so $\quad R^2 = 1 - \text{SUM}(e^2)/\text{SUM}(E^2) = 1 - 12575.88/55483.33 = 0.7733$

The error quantities [C12:C14] have particular names often written in the language of Sum of Squares (SS):

Total SS $= \text{SUM}(E^2) = 55483.33$

Residual SS $= \text{SUM}(e^2) = 12575.88$

Regression SS $=$ Total SS $-$ Residual SS $= \text{SUM}(E^2) - \text{SUM}(e^2) = 42907.46$

As well as partitioning the sum of squares, in this way *degrees of freedom* can also be partitioned [B12:B14].

The model requires an estimate for the intercept (or, equivalently, the mean of Y {I7}). The estimate is made from the data leaving $6 - 1 = 5$ *degrees of freedom*.

The slope parameter is estimated by the regression model leaving $5 - 1 = 4$ *residual degrees of freedom*.

To see if in the population there is likely to be a reduction in error variances use an F test {F16}. The variances are $MS = SS/df$ [D12, D13] and the ratio is $F = 42907.455/3143.970 = 13.648$ [E12]. The chance of getting a value this large or larger if in the population there was no difference in the variances (F=1) is only 2.1% [F12]. This is not very likely. You may feel justified in concluding that the model gives a real reduction in error variance

Inferences about slope and intercept

Just as inferences are made about population means and proportions from a sample {F7–F11} so inferences can be made about regression parameters. Row 18 shows the analysis for the SLOPE.

The best estimate is 13.062 with standard error 3.536 {F5}.

Using a t distribution {F7} with *degrees of freedom* $=$ SAMPLESIZE$-2 = 6 - 2 = 4$

Report   95% confidence interval {F19} is 3.245 to 22.878 [F18, G18]
The population slope is certainly positive though we cannot be sure of its value
There is a positive relation

Test $p = 0.021$ (the same as for the F test, no coincidence) [E18]
There is only a 2.1% probability of a slope this different from 0 if the two variables were independent

Make the same analysis for the intercept if this is relevant.

Sampling

It is assumed that errors have the same NORMAL distribution, whatever the value of X.

The model is unbiased (mean error = 0) and errors have a common variance

$$\text{SUM}(e^2)/(\text{SAMPLESIZE} - 2) = 1275.88/4 = 3143.970 \ [\text{D13}]$$

so standard error $= \sqrt{3143.970} = 56.071$ [B7]

A second sampling effect is that R^2 is adjusted to

$$1 - [(1 - R^2) \times (\text{SAMPLESIZE} - 1)/(\text{SAMPLESIZE} - 2)] = 1 - [(1 - 0.773) \times 5/4] = 0.717 \ [\text{B6}]$$

to give a better estimate of the population R^2.

Residuals

The residuals [C23:C28] have a mean of 0 (the model is unbiased) and a standard deviation of 50.15.

The *Standard Residuals* [D23:D28] are the raw residuals divided by 50.15 so that they have a standard deviation of 1. This makes it easier to interpret how important each is by reference to z or t values {C4, F7}.

17. Prediction error with a regression model

A forecast made using a linear regression for Y given some value of X is a t distribution {F7} with

> *degrees of freedom* = SAMPLESIZE − 2
>
> MEAN = $a + b$X
>
> STDEV = SE × $\sqrt{[1 + (1/\text{SAMPLESIZE}) + (X − \text{MEAN}(X))^2 × (\text{SAMPLESIZE} − 1)/\text{VAR}(X)]}$

where SE is the standard error of the regression. Use this equation to predict Y for a **particular** individual.

To predict the **mean** value of Y for some X

> STDEV = SE × $\sqrt{[(1/\text{SAMPLESIZE}) + (X − \text{MEAN}(X))^2 × (\text{SAMPLESIZE} − 1)/\text{VAR}(X)]}$

Example

Use the data and results from {12, 16}.

X income (000)	Y leisure spend
18	200
22	240
26	210
28	300
35	470
36	370
mean 27.5	298.33
variance 50.3	11096.67

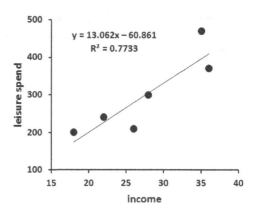

Find from regression analysis {16} SE = 56.071 or, remembering R^2 is the proportionate reduction in variance {15}

> SE = $\sqrt{[(1 − R^2) × \text{VAR}(Y) × (\text{SAMPLESIZE} − 1)/(\text{SAMPLESIZE} − 2)]}$
>
> = $\sqrt{[(1 − 0.7733) × 11096.67 × 5/4]}$ = 56.071

To predict leisure spend for a **particular household** with income 30,000, X = 30, use a t distribution {F7} with

> *degrees of freedom* = 6 − 2 = 4
>
> MEAN = −60.861 + (13.062 × 30) = 331
>
> STDEV = 56.071 × $\sqrt{[1 + 1/6 + (30 − 27.5)^2 × (6 − 1)/50.3]}$ = 77.65

For a 95% confidence interval {F19} use t = T.INV.2T(0.05, 4) = 2.77

For X=30 the 95% confidence interval forecast is

> Y = 331 ± (2.77×77.65) = 331 ± 215 = 116 to 546

This wide interval is in part due to the artificially small SAMPLESIZE for this illustration.

To predict the **mean spend** of **all** households with income X = 30 use

$$\text{STDEV} = 56.071 \times \sqrt{[1/6 + (30 - 27.5)^2 \times (6 - 1)/50.3]} = 49.77$$

The 95% confidence interval estimate is 331 ± 137.86 = 193 to 469

The prediction of the mean is more precise than the prediction for an individual, of course.

Rationale

The mathematics of the least squares calculation {I4} ensures that the regression line passes through the centroid of the data.

If you fit a model to the whole population the prediction error for an individual is just the standard error, SE = 56.071 in the Example.

But if you are using a sample there is additional uncertainty because the slope and centroid are subject to sampling error. The model forecasts Y from X so X values are assumed to be error-free: all errors are in Y and it is this which leads to uncertainty about the centroid and the slope.

Here are three effects:

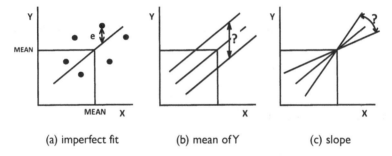

| (a) imperfect fit | (b) mean of Y | (c) slope |

The three components are:

source of uncertainty or error	variance
(a) imperfect fit, e	SE^2
(b) the mean of Y	$SE^2/\text{SAMPLESIZE}$
(c) the slope	$SE^2 \times (X - \text{MEAN}(X))^2/\text{SUM}[(X - \text{MEAN}(X))^2] =$ $SE^2 \times (X - \text{MEAN}(X))^2 \times (\text{SAMPLESIZE} - 1)/\text{VAR}(X)$

The variance of the total error is just the sum of these variances {E10}:

to estimate the population mean value of Y use $\quad$ VAR = (b) + (c)
to estimate a particular value of Y use $\quad\quad\quad$ VAR = (a) + (b) + (c)

18. Nonlinear models

> The EXCEL *Add Trendline* option {I4} allows you to fit a number of nonlinear models.
>
> For a constant growth rate use the *Exponential* option.
>
> For a general nonlinear curve use the *Power* option.

Example 1. Constant growth rate

Time	Sales
0	22.7
1	27.2
2	27.8
3	35.5
4	46.2
5	58.3

$y = 21.512e^{0.1871x}$
$R^2 = 0.9583$

You have sales data for the most recent six accounting periods. A constant growth rate model seems plausible and is in common use

$$\text{Sales at time } t = S_t = S_0(1 + r/100)^t$$

where S_0 is sales at time $t = 0$ and r is the percentage growth rate per period.

Plot the data. Click *Add Trendline* {I4} and select *Exponential*.

The model is $S_t = 21.512e^{0.1871t}$ which is almost as you expected.

use $\quad e^{0.1871} = \text{EXP}(0.1871) = 1.206$

so $\quad S_t = 21.512 \times 1.206^t$

The growth rate is 20.6% per time period.

Example 2. Demand curve

Price (P)	Sales Volume (Q)
13	56
15	33
16	23
19	22
21	16

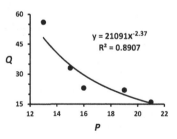

$y = 21091x^{-2.37}$
$R^2 = 0.8907$

A company has altered the price of its product a number of times recently. This gives data for a model of the relation between demand, Q, and price, P.

Economists measure the sensitivity of this relation by the elasticity

$$E = \frac{\%\ \text{change in demand}}{\%\ \text{change in price}}$$

The data look curvilinear which is consistent with a constant elasticity model

$$Q = aP^E$$

Click *Add Trendline* and select *Power* to get

$$Q = 21091.4 \times P^{-2.37}$$

The elasticity is –2.37 and is constant at all price and demand levels.

19. Correlation doesn't have to be causal to be useful

> The existence of correlation signals consistent covariation of two variables. It does not prove causation. But if you believe the correlation is (a) big enough and (b) can be plausibly explained it may still be useful.

Example 1

A study[1] was recently (January 2015) reported that found a positive correlation between some over the counter drugs and dementia. Dr. Simon Ridley, head of research at Alzheimer's Research UK, said that while the study was interesting there was no evidence that the drugs caused dementia.

Dr. Doug Brown of the Alzheimer's Society said, "We would encourage doctors and pharmacists to be aware of this potential link".

Example 2

In her Business Life column in the *Financial Times* of 26 November 2012, Lucy Kellaway cited a piece on "thought leadership" by experts at Credit Suisse who wrote that big companies with more than one woman on the board outperform by 26% companies with entirely male boards. The message was pretty clear: having more women on boards is good for company results. But Lucy suggested that given the publicity about the apparent under-representation of women on boards better companies had been quick to appoint women non-execs in order to avoid criticism.

Example 3

In a post of 5 December 2014 *Focus Economics*, a provider of economic forecasts, wrote this about the Venezuelan economy[2]:

> In the 12 months up to November, car sales reached just 21,392 units, which was 79.5% lower than in the same period last year ...

> Meanwhile, the government and the Central Bank continued not to deliver relevant economic data for several indicators, including the scarcity index, inflation, GDP estimates for 2014, balance of payments and external debt.

> Given the limited availability of timely data for the real sector, analysts often use car sales as a proxy for private consumption.

Rationale

Correlation describes the degree to which the occurrence of certain values of one variable are consistently associated with certain values of another. The strength of this relation is shown in a table {I1} or by a graph {I2}. If a useful correlation does seem to exist how should it be interpreted?

If a causal link can also be established this can lead to useful action. In Example 1 it may be that more research will establish a neurological or other mechanism which will lead to revised prescribing guidelines. But that has not yet happened. In the meantime, doctors and pharmacists should be cautious.

What if correlation is found but the cause is not only not established but could be argued either way, as in Example 2? Again, more research. You may have found a plausible mechanism (or two or more) for causation but it could take some skill to devise an experiment which tested the validity of the argument. And alternative explanations are not necessarily mutually exclusive. Even if women were appointed to avoid criticism their presence could still have the beneficial effect effect claimed.

In 1926 George Taylor, an economist at the Wharton School of Business, suggested that skirt length was an indicator of the state of the economy. In the good times women wore short skirts to show their expensive silk stockings. When the economy took a dive they wore long skirts to hide that they could no longer afford the stockings. Hmm. It was a different time. But ...

Some proxy measures are more plausible (Example 3). If data on the state of the economy are not available or take a long time to collect and publish or are not trusted then immediately available data on car sales, housing starts and the like might well be good and useful proxies. They are often used as indicators of GDP. But GDP is itself only a partial and imperfect measure, though widely accepted, of the state of the economy.

It is the nature of a proxy measure that it stands for something else not that it causes that something else. Changes in car sales (or skirt lengths!) do not cause changes in GDP. Both are a function of economic activity.

***

You see a correlation between two variables. The existence of the relationship could prove useful but you have no established causal link.

> Therefore:
>
> If you believe there is a plausible link use carefully. This may mean act cautiously and wait for more analysis. It may mean using one indicator as a proxy for another even though there is no direct causal link between them.

Even though you can see a plausible link the correlation, to be useful, has to be large enough: it has to be practically significant, not just "statistically significant" {H3}. The square of the correlation coefficient measures how much the variation of one variable is accounted for (not caused) by the variation in the other {I5}. This needs to be big enough to be useful for your problem. Quite a small correlation may signal the need for caution in prescribing. A much higher correlation would be needed to justify the use of proxy measures of the economy.

Production and operations

overview

The successful management of operations and processes is often associated with manufacturing, for that is where much of the theoretical developments originated, but these methods are useful in managing any process with a measurable output.

Project planning is a common management task. The contribution of statistical thought is to provide a method for allowing estimates of the uncertainty of project duration {J1}.

Systems are made from a number of components and sub-systems. Their performance is variable and so is measured statistically. It is important to be able to relate the reliability of the whole to that of its parts {J2} and to improve that reliability if needed {J3}.

System performance is monitored to take account of variation in output and also to identify unwanted dynamic shifts in that output {J4}.

Process variability is vital. When a process does not meet output standards defined by acceptable tolerances waste or other costs are the result. To identify if this is likely to be a problem use a simple measure {J5}. To drive the change needed for process improvement embed a statistical approach in a change management programme {J6}.

J1. Uncertainty and project duration

> The duration of a project is determined by the activities in the critical path, the longest sequence of activities.
>
> Estimate the MEAN and variance, VAR, of each activity. For all activities in the critical path, sum means and variances. Use a NORMAL distribution to describe uncertainty about project duration.
>
> If you need to make a judgement about activity duration use three points, **L**ow, **M**ost likely and **H**igh then
>
> MEAN = $(L + 4M + H)/6$
>
> VAR = $(H - L)^2/36$

Example

A European company is to establish a facility overseas in which to relocate its purchasing and logistics function. Some new staff will be recruited locally. A site, an existing office space, must be found and acquired following which it must be refurbished. This will mainly consist of equipping the space with modern IT and other systems. To speed the project both equipping the new facility and training the new staff will be carried out in two phases. The first phase of training will take place at the company's European base to ensure that the new recruits are fully aware of the company's culture and its expectations. After the first phase of equipping the new office is completed the new staff will return home to complete their training.

An activity diagram shows the project. The link from 3 to 5 shows a logical requirement: it has no duration.

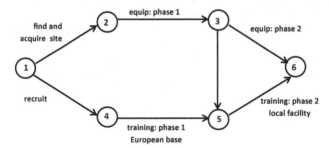

The judgemental estimates of activity times (weeks) and of the three paths, A, B and C, from start, node 1, to completion, node 6, are:

| activity | activity duration | | | path A: 1–2–3–6 | | path B: 1–4–5–6 | | path C: 1–2–3–5–6 | |
| | low | likely | high | MEAN | VAR | MEAN | VAR | MEAN | VAR |
		most							
1–2 find and acquire site	3	6	12	6.50	2.25			6.50	2.25
2–3 equip: phase 1	8	10	15	10.50	1.36			10.50	1.36
3–6 equip: phase 2	12	15	18	15.00	1.00				
1–4 recruit	3	4	5			4.00	0.11		
4–5 training: phase 1	9	10	13			10.33	0.44		
5–6 training: phase 2	9	10	11			10.00	0.11	10.00	0.11
				32.00	4.61	24.33	0.67	27.00	3.72

Path A is the critical path. The estimated MEAN is 32 weeks, longer than B or C, and standard deviation is STDEV = $\sqrt{4.61}$ = 2.15 weeks.

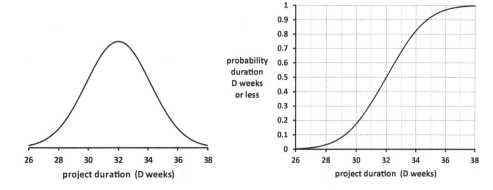

Rationale

You are planning a project consisting of a number of activities which are linked and so can be drawn as a network. If you know how long each activity will take the project duration is determined by the longest path through the network. This is called the critical path because any delay to activities on this path will cause the project to be delayed. This is the basis of the Critical Path Method (CPM).

Estimating activity durations may be straightforward (using a database of previous work) or not (a completely new activity for which you must use your judgement). Whichever method you use there will inevitably be some uncertainty about task duration. Measure this by the variance of the data in the database or by the imprecision of your judgement.

If you are making judgemental estimates it is likely that your best estimate will be based to some extent on recollection and so will be the most likely value, the MODE, but what you need to estimate path durations is the MEAN. This problem is more severe the more skewed your estimate.

Your lowest and highest estimates describe your pessimistic and optimistic judgements.

You want to take account both of uncertainty and of possible bias.

Therefore:

Estimate the mean and variance of each activity. Sum the means and variances of all activities in a path and use a NORMAL distribution to describe the uncertainty about project duration.

This is an application of the Central Limit Theorem {F4}. The averages to add or subtract must be mean values, not modes, which is where the three point estimate is useful. Simple summation works provided that the uncertainties about activity duration are independent {B5}. This is probably a reasonable assumption in most cases but is not inevitable:

some phases of a construction project may all be subject to the same weather conditions

a project is running behind schedule because some activities took much longer than expected so resources are reallocated to make good the deficit

The method is a way of making an assessment of project duration for planning purposes, adjustments during execution are to be expected.

***

Finding critical paths uses methods and software which have been in use for some time. The Program Evaluation and Review Technique, PERT, introduced the modelling of uncertainty, in particular the use of the three point method for modelling estimates of task duration.

The basic idea is that estimates of duration may be skewed and that durations must by definition be bounded. The BETA distribution {C5}, which need not be symmetric, better describes this than the NORMAL {C3}. But the NORMAL is often a good approximation to the BETA.

The formula for variance is based on the idea that you are almost certain that the duration will be between L and H. For a NORMAL distribution MEAN ± 3STDEV defines a 99.8% interval. The range is 6 standard deviations so $(H - L) = 6STDEV$, and so $STDEV = (H - L)/6$ and $VAR = (H - L)^2/36$.

There has been quite a bit of work examining the accuracy of these formulae and providing alternatives,[1] but the two given here seem to be the most popular (a case of first mover advantage, perhaps).

For alternatives models for your judgement see {C11–C13}.

***

It may be that the path with the highest expected duration has a lower variance than another path with lower mean. This may complicate your decision about just which is the critical path or in evaluating the risk of overrun. Of the two paths shown at right, A is the path with the longer expected duration

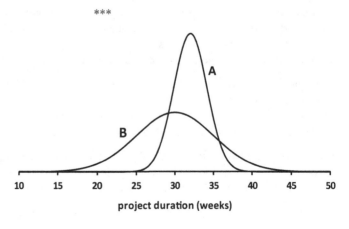

project duration (weeks)

and so the critical path, but B poses the greater risk of extended project overruns, longer than 40 weeks, for instance.

Information about both may be helpful in planning and scheduling, provided you have software which generates these alternatives in realistically large networks.

***

This note has concentrated on judgemental estimates, which may be necessary. But if you have a database — use it.

J2. System reliability

A system consists of a number of components, A, B…. The reliability of each component, $P_A, P_B, \ldots$, is the probability that it will function as specified. These probabilities are assumed *independent*.

For the system to function all components must function. The system reliability is

$$P_{system} = P_A \times P_B \times \cdots$$

If there are n components each with reliability P

$$P_{system} = P^n$$

If you require a level of system reliability, P_{system}, the reliability for each component should be

$$P = (P_{system})^{1/n}$$

Example

An electric lawn mower has five key components (motor, switch, …) which function independently of each other. The reliability of each is 98% so system reliability is

$$P_{system} = 0.98^5 = 0.904$$

The mower is 90% reliable. Not good enough. For the mower to have a reliability of 98% each component must have a reliability, P, to ensure that

$$P^5 = 0.98$$

so $\qquad P = 0.98^{1/5} = 0.98^{0.2} = 0.996$

The reliability of each components must be at least 99.6%.

Rationale

In many cases the proper functioning of a system requires that all components function successfully.

Your goal is that the system as a whole has an acceptably reliable performance but this depends on the reliability of the components. You need to specify component reliability that will enable you to meet your goal.

Therefore:

Decide the system reliability you want. If justified, assume that the performance of components is independent and use the calculation above to find the necessary component reliability.

If component reliabilities are not all the same you will need to use $P_{system} = P_A \times P_B \times \cdots$.

***

The important assumption is independence {B5,B6}. This makes the modelling much easier but you will need to check that this is how your system works. For many reasons it is a desirable design goal to have independence of components. It is a precondition for successful modular design and

266

manufacture. In manufacture different teams, possibly at different companies, can work on just their component. It is the responsibility of the manufacturer to manage this and the assembly of the components into a finished product.

Dependencies between components require modelling using conditional probabilities {B6}. Positive correlations can result in increased probability of failure {E11} and so degrade system reliability.

***

Systems become complex as the number of components increases. A car has about 15,000 to 20,000 components. An airliner has about two million. Ensuring system reliability requires very high component reliability.

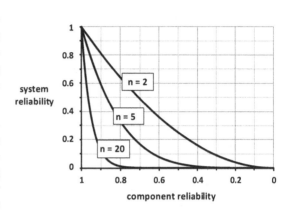

This is especially difficult when components are made by sub-contractors. The initial problems with the lithium batteries in the Boeing Dreamliner causing fires and the recall of cars by major manufacturers because of faulty airbags are just two examples. The reputational damage is to the manufacturer.

Any supply chain is liable to these problems. The horse meat scandal in the UK in 2013 resulted from poor management by supermarkets of their meat product supply chain. The result was that while some consumers were paying for beef they were getting horse.

J3. Backups for improved reliability

> The reliability of a system can be improved by installing more than one component or sub-system to accomplish a task so that if one fails there is another to do the job.
>
> The reliability of each sub-system — the primary, A, and the backups B, C... — is P_A, P_B, ···, the probability that each will function as specified. These probabilities are assumed *independent*.
>
> The system reliability is
>
> $$P_{system} = 1 - (1 - P_A)(1 - P_B) \ldots$$
>
> If there are n systems each with reliability P
>
> $$P_{system} = 1 - (1 - P)^n$$

Example

A hospital in a remote rural settlement is powered by a generator. The electricity is needed for, among other things, lighting in the operating theatre. The generators are likely to breakdown about once every six months. A generator can be repaired in a day. The hospital wishes to increase the reliability of the electricity supply by having one or more standby generators which will automatically cut in once power is lost.

$1 - P = \text{PROB}(\text{generator breaks on a particular day}) = 1 - P = 2/365 = 0.0055$

with no backup, system reliability $= P_{system} = 1 - P = 1 - 0.0055 = 0.9945 = 99.45\%$

Here are the results for up to 3 generators:

no. of generators n	PROB(all generators fail) $(1 - P)^n = (2/365)^n$	system reliability $1 - (1 - P)^n$ (%)	expected days per year without electricity $365 \times (1 - P)^n$
1	0.00547945	99.45205	2
2	0.00003002	99.99700	0.01
3	0.00000016	99.99998	0.00006

One backup generator (n = 2) looks enough. Two backups would all but eliminate the risk but would be expensive and impossible to justify given the improvement in reliability with one backup.

Rationale

You need to ensure the correct functioning of a system. You know the reliability of a critical component.

Therefore:

Decide on the level of system reliability that you need. Install backups to meet your target.

Backup systems are common. Usually, the extra capacity is needed when process failure is likely to be catastrophic: for example, hospital power systems or aircraft braking systems. Data security is an increasingly relevant case. Banks will have backup systems for their data. We all backup data from our laptop or other device and keep the copy safely in a different place (don't we?).

***

Using backup systems introduces a degree of redundancy. Redundancy may sometimes be taken as the cue for cost saving by cutting out that which is thought unnecessary. But one person's redundancy is another person's safety. Redundancy can be useful, even necessary, as a method of performance improvement but you will have to pay for this improvement.

***

Often just one backup will do but in safety critical situations this may not be enough. A Boeing 747 can fly on just one of its four engines. There was some initial concern when Airbus introduced long range aircraft with only two engines, but such was engine reliability that this has not proven to be unduly risky.

In the recent (November 2014) crash of the Virgin Galactic spacecraft there was speculation that the usual requirement that spacecraft be "two failure tolerant" — the spacecraft can survive two independent failures, mechanical or human or both — had not been met (*Financial Times*, 7 November 2014).

***

The calculation of system reliability is just the application of the multiplication rule for independent probabilities {B6}. The probability of single component failure is (1 − P). The system will fail if all n components fail with probability $(1 - P) \times (1 - P) \times \cdots = (1 - P)^n$. The probability that the system will not fail is therefore $1 - (1 - P)^n$, the system reliability.

***

Whatever be the reliability of any component or sub-system, the reliability of the whole may be increased dramatically by duplication. The graph illustrates this:

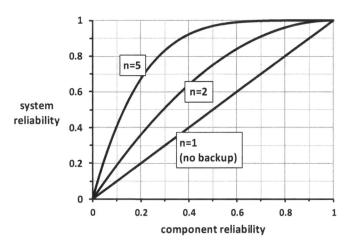

J4. Control charts

A continuous process has a measurable but variable output.

To monitor system performance set expected **control limits** for the output so that extreme values are easily identified. For example, if control limits are set such that values outside those limits are expected only 5% of the time then about 1 in 20 measurements should be outside the limits.

Make a *control chart* by plotting output value against time.

Drawing the *control limits* on the chart enables an easy monitoring of the output and also provides a visual indication of any unwanted trend towards unacceptable performance.

Example

A plant manufactures small electrical components in batches of one thousand. The number of rejects in each of the last twenty batches were

10, 11, 5, 7, 12, 8, 11, 10, 17, 8, 14, 7, 13, 9, 9, 10, 12, 6, 10, 9

The MEAN number of rejects per batch was 9.9.

Assume faults occur randomly and independently of each other. A POISSON distribution {C2} describes this process so

$$\text{MEAN} = 9.9$$

and $\quad\text{STDEV} = \sqrt{\text{MEAN}} = \sqrt{9.9} = 3.146$

The NORMAL distribution {C3} is a good approximation to the POISSON when means are not small. Set limits at MEAN ± 2×STDEV. About one batch in 20 should be outside these limits if the process is behaving as expected. Show three values on the chart:

centre line = CL = 9.9
lower control limit = LCL = 9.9 − (2×3.146) = 3.61
upper control limit = UCL = 9.9 + (2×3.146) = 16.19

Statisticians often use the Greek letter σ (sigma) for population standard deviation. These limits are frequently called 2σ limits. Wider 3σ limits are also used. About one batch in five hundred will fall outside these limits.

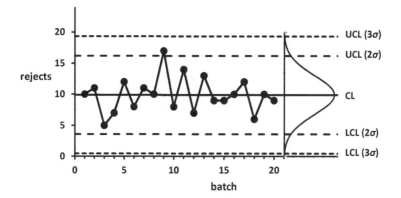

The process is behaving as expected. One batch is outside the 2σ limits. None are outside the 3σ limits. There is no obvious trend.

Rationale

You need to monitor a system or process {G2}. As well as identifying unusual results you want to see if the process is stable through time, not drifting out of acceptable range.

Therefore:

Decide what you want to monitor. Collect data and plot results against time. Plot limits to help you identify unusual system behaviour.

This analysis assumes that the process is stable over time: the mean and variance do not change. If either do change, the system is out of control. Looking at the control chart should help you spot this.

In this next chart it seems as if the mean of the last few batches is high and variance low. Has there been a step change which you should investigate?

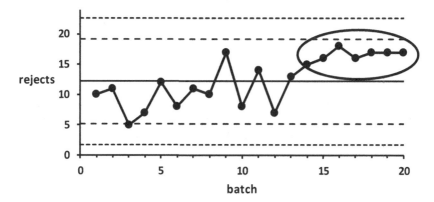

In this chart the system might be drifting out of control: there seems to be a trend.

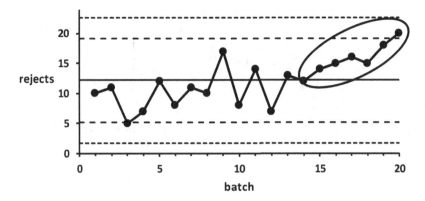

***

Control charts are also used for output variables other than counts. Proportions, means and ranges are obvious applications.

It is commonly recommended for counts and proportions that 2σ and 3σ limits are used with the NORMAL distribution. While this usually works well, if the MEAN number of counts is small or the proportion extreme, the lower limits may be negative. Textbooks recommend that in those cases the lower limit is ignored (set to zero). This presumably dates from the time when access to the true distributions — GAMMA {C6} or BETA {C5} — was difficult. In EXCEL it is easy to use them.

***

The Example uses a POISSON distribution {C2}. Only an estimate of the MEAN is needed. The variance is set, no separate estimate of process variability is necessary.

***

These charts show variation over time. The same idea can be used to monitor single outputs from a number of business units at a single point in time {G7}.

***

Choosing the limits (2σ, 3σ, something else) needs careful thought. 3σ limits minimise the risk of wrongly concluding that the system is out of control but may miss the chance to identify non-random behaviour. 2σ limits will show more data beyond limits but you will need to be more careful in inferring out of control behaviour. It is easy to show both, as in the Example.

J5. Process capability

Can a process meet required specification?

Specification is measured by tolerance. Output must be between **Low** and **High** bounds to be acceptable.

Output produced is variable. Variation is measured by standard deviation STDEV.

As an indicator use

$$\text{process capability ratio} = C_p = (H-L)/6\text{STDEV}$$

Values greater than 1 indicate that the process is capable of meeting specification.

Look for values a little higher. $C_p = 1.3$ is often used as a minimum goal.

Example

Wooden legs for flat pack dining tables are required to be 73cm long. Some adjustments are possible on assembly which can accommodate variations of ± 2mm. The standard deviation of leg lengths is 0.5mm.

$$C_p = 4/(6 \times 0.5) = 1.33$$

The process is capable of meeting requirements.

Rationale

If process variability is small enough, waste can be reduced to almost nothing.

Process variation is described by a probability distribution, usually a NORMAL distribution {C3}. It is then easy to find the proportion of output which is within tolerance and the proportion that is not and must be discarded, reworked or sold as scrap.

Analysts in production engineering and quality management sometimes prefer to use a simple ratio of the specification width, $H - L$, to the process width, the range of the output. Assuming a NORMAL distribution, a range 3 standard deviations either side of the MEAN accounts for most output {C3} and so this measure, 6STDEV, is taken as the process width. So,

$$\text{process capability ratio} = C_p = \text{specification width/process width} = (H-L)/6\text{STDEV}$$

This leads to processes being classified either as capable of meeting specification, or not capable.

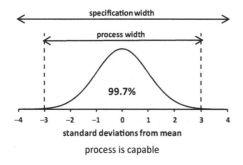

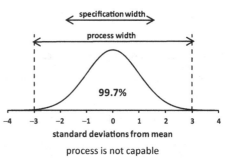

process is capable

process is not capable

***

This simple ratio works on the assumption that the mean of the process width and the mean of the specification width are the same: there is no consistent bias in the process.

This may not be the case.

Modified calculations are sometimes made. Split the process width in two and consider separately:

$$(\text{MEAN} - \text{L})/3\text{STDEV}$$

and $(\text{H} - \text{MEAN})/3\text{STDEV}$

Take the smaller value for C_p.

***

If you have a problem because of excess waste the obvious solution is to see if process width can be improved by reducing the standard deviation of the output. This is the main idea behind the Six Sigma movement {J6}.

But you may also be able to increase tolerance. In the Example tolerance is not just the result of a judgement about how customers might react to wobbly tables but also considers the fixing of leg to table top. It may be possible to increase the range of adjustment, for example, by redesigning the bracket used to join leg to table top to give more scope for adjustment.

J6. Six Sigma

> Output must be between **L**ow and **H**igh bounds to be acceptable.
>
> To ensure practically zero non-conformance of process to requirement the standard deviation of the process should be no more than $(H-L)/12$.

Example

To be of use in a particular car the width of a dashboard must be within the limits 1430mm and 1434mm. For there to be no rejected dashboards the variability in the production process must have a standard deviation of no more than $4/12 = 0.33$mm.

Rationale

Reducing non-compliance reduces cost due to waste, rework and complaints.

Therefore:

Improve process capability by reducing process variation so that just about all output is acceptable. Ensuring that standard deviation is no more than a twelfth of the tolerance does this.

This is a stringent application of the idea behind process capability {J5}. Setting the standard deviation ("sigma", σ) in this way reduces defects due to non-compliance to 0.002 per million, about as close to zero as you will ever need. Using the far less stringent $\pm 3\sigma$ gives a rate of 2,700 per million.

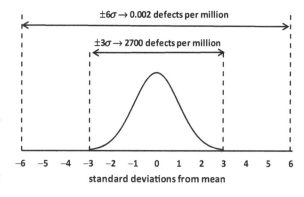

The key idea behind the Six Sigma movement is that the benefits of eliminating defects far outweigh the costs of improving the process.

But improving system performance may itself be very costly. This has led some to question whether this very high level of performance is needed.

***

The Six Sigma (6σ) movement for business process improvement began at Motorola but is probably most associated with Jack Welch when he was CEO of GE. These companies produce at high volumes so 2,700 defects per million probably is unacceptable. Judge for yourself the level of non-conformance you need. This will be a function of output volume and the consequences of non-compliance (think drugs or air safety).

***

Six Sigma programmes contain much more than this calculation. They are a way of effecting process improvement by the application of statistical thinking and analysis, but they are also programmes for change management more broadly. Like any programme of management change there is a fairly large rhetorical component.

***

At Motorola it was observed that during process change not only was STDEV reduced but that there was also a tendency for the MEAN output level to drift by as much as 1.5σ. The result of this process shift is that the area in one tail of the distribution is reduced to practically zero while in the other it is increased to 3.4 defects per million, more than 0.002 but still a lot less than 2,700.

Finance

---

overview

Much of finance theory and practice is concerned with considerations of risk and reward {K1}, which are based on the mean and variance of share price movements over a period. It is hoped that these will give a good indication of which investment options best fit the demands of an investor and that investor's appetite for risk.

Share price movements are to some extent a function of the state of the market and the economy overall and to some extent due to the performance of individual companies. Comparing returns from a particular share and the market {K2} will help you assess relative volatility.

Most investors don't just back one share, they have a portfolio of shares. The aim is to find a mix of return and risk which meets your needs. Applying a little basic statistics will let you find the characteristics of the portfolio from the characteristics of the shares you have chosen {K3}.

To decide the shape of your portfolio you have to have an objective. Minimising risk is probably a good place to start {K4}.

Accounting for risk when evaluating investment in different projects has traditionally involved increasing the discount rate but this fails to account for future decisions which managers might make. Real options valuation attempts to take account of these actions and their uncertain outcomes {K5}.

Finance is, of course, a huge business and academic discipline. This section shows how the application of some basic statistics helps in the analysis.

There is much, much more.

K1. Risk and reward

> The return on a share is the percentage difference in closing prices over an interval, typically a day or week.
>
> The standard deviation of returns over a period is a measure of risk.
>
> A simple description of the relation between the expected return (MEAN) and the associated risk, measured by standard deviation, STDEV, is given by the return:risk ratio,
>
> return:risk = MEAN/STDEV
>
> This is also known as the reward:risk ratio.

Example

The daily closing share prices for the insurance group AVIVA on the London Stock Exchange on 30–31 October 2014 were 518p and 521p.

$$\text{RETURN} = 100 \times (521 - 518)/518 = 0.579\%$$

The distribution of daily returns from 1 January to 31 October 2014 is shown in the chart.

$$\text{MEAN} = 0.078$$
$$\text{STDEV} = 1.408$$

The reward:risk ratio is

$$0.078/1.408 = 0.055 = 5.5\%$$

Rationale

The return on a share varies over time. The variation is described by the distribution of returns. This is a guide for your investment decision. When considering alternatives it is easier to compare numbers than comparing charts showing distributions.

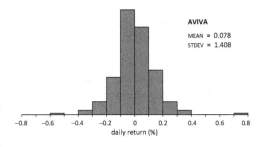

Therefore:

Use the ratio of mean/standard deviation as a single figure summary for an initial comparison of alternative investments.

These two elements, standard deviation and expected value {B7}, are basic to an appreciation of any sort of variation, including share price movements.

Using standard deviation as a measure of risk is a blunt instrument. It is certainly a measure of variation but variation can have good outcomes too if share prices rise more than expected. Risk is usually associated with undesirable outcomes, unexpectedly low prices in this case, so use the probability of particularly low prices to give a value at risk (VaR) {E9}.

***

It is commonly believed that as risk increases so does return. Some investment options are for all practical purposes free of risk; a bank account, for instance (though the events of 2008 have made this not quite the safe bet it once was). This leads to an alternative measure of the relation between expected return and risk based on the difference between the return obtained from a share and the risk-free return. This is called the *Sharpe Ratio*:

Sharpe Ratio = [expected return − risk return] / risk

or, to emphasise the statistical underpinning,

Sharpe Ratio = [MEAN(return) − risk-free return] / STDEV(return)

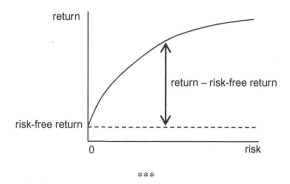

***

The reward:risk ratio or the Sharpe ratio give a single figure summary of return compared to risk — the higher the ratio the greater the return as a proportion of risk. This should help in deciding between alternative investments.

A single figure summary is a useful simplification. But remember that it is a simplification.

***

Think carefully about how frequently you may trade. This will help you decide the interval between closing prices (daily, weekly, …) and the time period for collecting data which you will use in your analysis.

K2. Beta: systematic and unsystematic risks

> The beta value — Greek letter β — describes the volatility of the return on a share compared to that obtainable from the market as a whole.
>
> The value of β is just the SLOPE of the regression line of the return on a share and the market return. Calculate the returns using share prices and values of an appropriate market index such as the S&P 500 or the FTSE 350.
>
> If $\beta = 1 \rightarrow$ share is as volatile as the market
>
> $\beta > 1 \rightarrow$ share is more volatile than the market
>
> $\beta < 1 \rightarrow$ share is less volatile than the market

Example

The graph shows the percentage daily returns {K1} for shares in the insurance group AVIVA and of the FTSE 350 index for the first ten months of 2014.

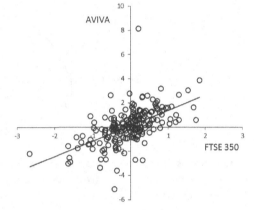

The regression line {I4} is

$$\text{AVIVA} = 0.108 + 1.269 \times \text{FTSE350}$$

so $\beta = 1.269$

The AVIVA shares are more volatile than the market. They both rise and fall more than the market.

The correlation {I2,I5} is $R^2 = 0.334$.

Conclude that

(a) for every 1% change in the market the expected return on shares in AVIVA will change by 1.269%.

(b) 33% of the variation in returns on AVIVA are due to market movement so 67% of the variation must be due to company specific factors (the state of the insurance market, company competitiveness and performance …).

Rationale

The volatility of a share is the result of two factors

        systematic risk, changes in the market generally

        unsystematic risk, which is company specific

Knowing about the relative size of these effects should help you when making investment decisions.

Therefore:

Plot returns of the share against those of a market index. The slope of the line describing the relation will tell you how volatile the share is compared to the market. The correlation will show the relative effect of systematic risk.

An obvious way to measure volatility is to calculate the standard deviation of a returns {K1}. This makes no distinction between share price volatility and market volatility as a whole. Using β as well does make that distinction.

***

The slope is called beta because the linear equation fitted to population data is sometimes written as

$$Y = \alpha + \beta X$$

where α and β are population INTERCEPT and SLOPE {I4}.

This has nothing to do with the BETA probability distribution {C5}.

***

Suppose that all the share returns had been exactly doubled. The slope would then be $\beta = 1.269 \times 2 = 2.538$ but R^2 would not change. The *proportion* of share volatility due to the market is the same but the *magnitude* is not.

***

For any regression line {I4} fitted to data for variables X and Y it is a standard result that

$$\text{SLOPE} = R \times \text{STDEV}(Y)/\text{STDEV}(X)$$

In this application you can think of the two effects as

$$\beta = \left(\begin{array}{c}\text{correlation between} \\ \text{share and market}\end{array}\right) \times \left(\dfrac{\text{volatility of share}}{\text{volatility of market}}\right)$$

***

If you use a different set of returns, just the last three months for instance, you would, of course, get different results.

Analysing the data used in the Example in the *Regression Analysis* tool in EXCEL {I6}, the 95% confidence interval for β is from 1.015 to 1.523.

K3. Portfolio

You have a portfolio of shares A,B ... The proportion of shares in each are P(A), P(B) ... which sum to 1.

The expected return is

$$[P(A) \times \text{RETURN}(A)] \quad + \quad [P(B) \times \text{RETURN}(B)] + \cdots$$

and the variance is

$$[P(A)^2 \times \text{VAR}(A)] \quad + \quad [P(B)^2 \times \text{VAR}(B)] + \cdots +$$
$$2 \times \text{SUM} [\text{CORREL}(A,B) \times P(A) \times P(B) \times \text{STDEV}(A) \times \text{STDEV}(B)]$$

Where the SUM is of all pairs of shares.

The Beta {K2} of the portfolio is

$$\beta(\text{portfolio}) = [P(A) \times \beta(A)] + [P(B) \times \beta(B)] + \cdots$$

Example

A portfolio consists of shares in three companies:

> AVIVA (insurance)
> BAE Systems (technology)
> J Sainsbury (retail)

Using data from the first ten months of 2014 find the percentage daily returns {K1}, correlations between them {I2} and Beta values {K2}:

Returns and Beta

	AVIVA	BAE	SAINSBURY
MEAN	0.078	0.032	−0.168
STDEV	1.408	1.228	1.721
β	1.269	0.875	0.916
P(.)	0.5	0.4	0.1

Correlations

BAE	SAINSBURY	
0.214	0.113	AVIVA
	0.076	BAE

A portfolio with 50% AVIVA, 40% BAE and 10% SAINSBURY has

$$\text{MEAN} = (0.5 \times 0.078) + (0.4 \times 0.032) + (0.1 \times -0.168) = 0.035$$

and

$$\text{VAR} = (0.5 \times 1.408)^2 + (0.4 \times 1.228)^2 + (0.1 \times 1.721)^2$$
$$+ 2 \times [\ (0.214 \times 0.5 \times 0.4 \times 1.408 \times 1.228) +$$
$$(0.113 \times 0.5 \times 0.1 \times 1.408 \times 1.721) +$$
$$(0.076 \times 0.4 \times 0.1 \times 1.228 \times 1.721) \ ]$$

$$\text{VAR} = 0.767 + (2 \times 0.094) = 0.955$$

so $\quad \text{STDEV} = \sqrt{0.955} = 0.977$

Also $\quad \beta = (0.5 \times 1.269) + (0.4 \times 0.875) + (0.1 \times 0.916) = 1.076$

Rationale

You decide to construct a portfolio of shares. Share price movements are likely to be correlated: shares of firms in the same sector will to some degree move together depending on what the market thinks of that sector; shares in oil users will go up as oil price falls but shares in oil producers will go down. For any pair of shares the correlation coefficient CORREL {I2} describes the relation between movements. You need to assess the risk and return {K1} of the portfolio.

Therefore:

Find the risk and return of your portfolio as a special case of *Correlated risks* {E11} and use the method described here.

You now have the main characteristics of your portfolio, but how to choose the shares and the proportions? Think of your attitude to risk and the purpose of the investment.

You may want to choose the proportions of shares to minimise risk {K4}.

Choosing some negatively correlated shares reduces risk even more.

If you want quick big returns invest heavily in a growth sector.

There is much literature (and many brokers) who might help.

***

In summarising your options you may like to consider the Beta for the portfolio. In the Example $\beta = 1.076$: the portfolio is about as volatile as the market.

K4. Minimum risk portfolio

> You have a portfolio of two shares, A and B.
>
> The proportions of shares are P(A) and P(B), which sum to 1.
>
> The correlation between the returns is CORREL and the covariance is
>
> $$COVAR = CORREL \times STDEV(A) \times STDEV(B)$$
>
> Give a weight for each share
>
> $$W(A) = VAR(A) - COVAR$$
>
> and $\quad W(B) = VAR(B) - COVAR$
>
> To minimise the standard deviation (risk) of the portfolio choose
>
> $$P(A) = W(B) / [W(A)+W(B)]$$
>
> and $\quad P(B) = W(A) / [W(A)+W(B)]$

Example

A portfolio consists of shares in two companies

> AVIVA (insurance)
> BAE Systems (technology)

Using data from the first ten months of 2014 the percentage daily returns {K1} have means and standard deviations shown in the table.

The correlation between returns is CORREL = 0.214 and so COVAR = 0.214 × 1.408 × 1.228 = 0.370.

	MEAN	STDEV	VAR	W = VAR − COVAR	P
AVIVA	0.078	1.408	1.982	1.612	0.414
BAE	0.032	1.228	1.508	1.138	0.586
				2.750	1.000

The proportions of each share in the portfolio are

P(AVIVA) = 1.138 / 2.750 = 0.414
P(BAE) = 1.612 / 2.750 = 0.586

Your minimum risk portfolio {K3} has returns with MEAN = 0.051 and standard deviation STDEV = 1.108.

Rationale

Having decided the shares for your portfolio {K3} you have to decide an investment strategy. This will depend on your attitude to the relative importance of risk and return {K1}.

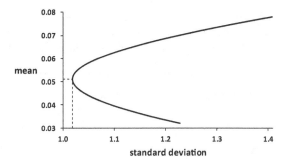

As you change the proportions in your portfolio risk and return vary (right).

There is a point of minimum risk and you may consider this as a strategy, or at least a start for thinking about a strategy.

This note shows the simple calculation for a two share portfolio. For more shares the calculations are not so easy but the principle is the same.

K5. Real options

The value of an investment depends on what happens after you have invested. This will be a combination of external events, management decisions and their chance outcomes.

Use a decision tree {E14} with appropriately discounted costs and benefits.

Calculate the expected value of the investment.

Example

A small business develops ideas for new drugs which it sells to pharmaceutical companies. It can sell at different stages of development at prices which reflect how much work has been done at that point. Even a failed trial contains information. After the discovery stage there are two developmental stages. After a successful first stage the drug and all intellectual property rights could be sold for $2m. Even if the drug failed the test at the end of this stage it could still be sold for $0.7m to a company who could reformulate and re-test. After the second stage these figures are $6m and $0.2m.

The company could sell the drug and its intellectual property rights now for $1m.

At this time it is estimated that there is a 70% chance that stage 1 will be successful and an 80% chance for stage 2. Here is the tree.

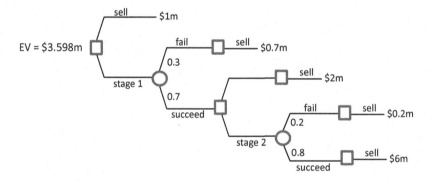

This problem is analysed in {E14}. The expected value {B7} is EV = $3.598m.

Each stage takes one year. Using a discount rate of 5% a price of $2m at the end of stage 1 has a discounted value of $2m/1.05 = 1.90m. A price of $6m at the end of stage 2 has a discounted value of $6m/1.05^2 = $5.44m.

Using these discounted values an investment in this project has an EV of $3.273m.

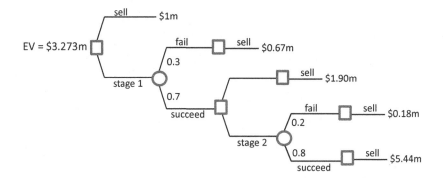

Rationale

One way of dealing with the risk inherent in any project with a time stream of costs and benefits is to increase the discount rate. This has the effect of decreasing the value of positive returns which are forecast to occur but perhaps not for a long time. The longer into the future they are forecast to occur the more speculative (the more risky) they are. Increasing the discount rate devalues these distant prospects.

Costs too would be discounted (think spent nuclear fuel).

The sum of these discounted costs and benefits is called the Net Present Value (NPV). The effects of varying the discount rate are illustrated in the table. There are incomes of 1,4 and 8 in each of three years starting now.

		discount rate	
year	none	5%	10%
0	1	1	1
1	4	3.81	3.64
2	8	7.26	6.61
NPV	13	12.07	11.25

Discounting at a rate not inflated for risk models your preference for money sooner rather than later.

Simply increasing the rate to account for risk seems a blunt instrument. You want to take account of what might really happen over the life of the project as best as you can foresee it.

Therefore:

Make a decision tree which describes your view of what might happen. Find the expected discounted value as a measure of the worth of the project.

You will have a useful evaluation to help decide whether to invest or not and, if so, how much.

***

As with all models you will have made assumptions, of actions and probabilities in this case. Use sensitivity tests {E8} to see if alternative plausible assumptions would alter your decision.

4

Why do statsNotes look like that?

You may have wondered why I chose to make statsNotes in that particular form. Why not just write a book with chapters and sub-headings and the rest? Some of the answer is given in the Introduction. The motivating idea was that a modular form would make it easier for you to find what you want and so encourage you to use a little statistics when you need to.

We do not often have bright ideas all on our own. We find ideas that others have had then react to them and adapt them, so that we have something that works for us. Call it knowledge transfer or useful analogy or just grateful borrowing.

My background is in engineering and urban planning with a little computer science so it was natural for me to borrow ideas from those areas. The main source was the concept of design patterns and a pattern language. To me statsNotes are patterns. But it wasn't just the form but the thinking behind the form which was important.

In this section I describe this background and give references in case you want to read more both of the history and origins of the patterns idea and some of the subsequent developments.

You don't have to know about any of this to use the statsNotes, of course, but I hope your curiosity is roused enough to make you read on.

A design problem

Software developers have long had a problem with re-use, many programmers writing the same code as solution for the same problem. Why not use another programmer's code? Because there might have been assumptions and limitations which you do not share and this makes you nervous.

What are the context and rationale for the successful use of a recommended method? You need to know why it seems a good thing to do and what its limits are so that you can with confidence decide if your problem really is the same as that solved by others. You need to see how good is the fit before you adopt the solution.

Just like the problems managers face. Should you copy a practice from another organisation? How much of its success was because of the particularities of that organisation? If you import the practice, at some time and money cost, can you be sure it will be a success for you too?

Programmers naturally think in terms of breaking a problem into a number of components (sub-programs or routines) and then recombining them to form the whole program. Perhaps the same form could be used to structure advice on programming methods and related issues of project management? It could.

A previous attempt had been made in another field entirely; architecture. The way to give design advice was to use a modular form. People could see why and how it was thought to be good advice and how much to take. Perhaps a little subset of modules would be helpful for you just now.

The argument was, to me, compelling which is why the statsNotes are modular. This is a design decision.

Modularity

For centuries designers did not think about a design method in which formal analysis of the design process itself could help in generating good alternatives and improving the management of that process.

The idea of a design method seems to date from a 1947 paper by Franz Zwicky[1] in which he proposed a scheme for disaggregating an object (the propulsive system of a jet engine) into its components (analysis). For each component a list of alternative solutions is given (imagination). These combinations of component/solution are shown in a table, rows for components or functions and columns for alternative solutions for each function. Picking one alternative for each component generates a new object for evaluation. This makes for easy customization too (think automobiles).

This morphological analysis encourages ideas generation.[2] Evaluating all possible configurations of a large problem object can be arduous but computer assistance can make the task more manageable by eliminating incompatible combinations.[3–5]

This is clearly an interesting way to generate alternatives. Modular disaggregation is also a way of managing difficult large problems.

The key idea is that a large problem may be just too big to be comprehended but that it can be subdivided into a set of sub-problems or modules each of which has a sufficiently reduced scope so that they can be solved (which might mean designed or decided in some way). Ideally the solution of the whole problem is just the sum of the solutions of the modules. This means that a big task can be divided into a number of manageable subtasks. If they really are independent the solutions to the subtasks are the solution to the whole task with no more work needed. That is the ideal. In software design it might be achievable (the motivation in object orientation[6]). When you use the EXCEL function to find, say, the average of some data and then use another function to find the maximum value it is clear that the chunks of code work independently: the calculation of the average does not affect the calculation of the maximum.

This ideal is made difficult — in the extreme impossible — by interaction between the modules. If the modules are independent there is no interaction and all is well. The greater the interaction the more problematic the disaggregation. For example, you will know from your experience as managers that this desirable state of affairs is not typical of project management. You need coordination meetings and the rest to ensure that what one team does is known by other teams in case assumptions or functionality have changed and to which other teams need to respond. This is much more typical of the problems you face.

Think of the ideal disaggregation as a tree. This becomes undermined by the interactions between the modules not accounted for in the tree. The result is better thought of as a network; either as a picture or as a mathematical representation with, at its simplest, elements 1 if a link exists and 0 if it does not.

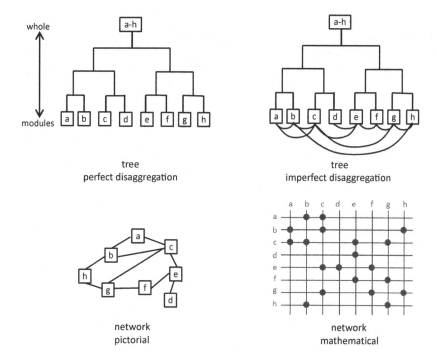

tree
perfect disaggregation

tree
imperfect disaggregation

network
pictorial

network
mathematical

These ideas have been around for a long time.

Tree disaggregation has long been used by taxonomists as a means of classifying plants and animals and this has resulted in a number of mathematical methods for creating taxonomies or clusters.[7]

Network models have also been used for a long time as models of social interaction and group definition[8] which now has developed a large literature[9] (think small world networks[10]).

Modular disaggregation and the problem of interaction has a long history[11,12] which has influenced many areas of design both of objects and organisations.[13–17]

Modularity is a prerequisite for task partitioning and sharing[18,19] and for customization.[20]

The year after Zwicky's paper Claude Shannon established information theory.[21,22] Psychologists saw that this could help in the study of the capacity of humans to process information. In his famous paper Miller[23] showed that modularity underpinned the chunking strategy used to overcome human information processing limits: we break tasks which are too large for our cognitive limits into smaller tasks that we can manage.

These developments and others (not least the increasing availability of computers) resulted in much discussion of design and design methods.[24] It was in this environment that Christopher Alexander found himself thinking about architecture and design.

Christopher Alexander and the Pattern Language

Christopher Alexander is an architect but one with a very particular view of design. His Bachelor's degree in architecture was quickly followed by a Master's in mathematics. This gave him an interest in form not just from the standpoint of the aesthetics of places and buildings but also in the structural relationships between different components of a design. He attempted a mathematical disaggregation based on information theory.[25–28] A design problem (designing a village) was decomposed into 141 requirements (access to railway station, security for women and children …). A link connected a pair if the solution of one affected the solution of the other.

A tree defined clusters of highly connected sub-problems. Each cluster a suggestion that the constituents be treated as one design problem.

As with any cluster analysis different, perhaps equally plausible, algorithms give different clusters (modules). This was seen by some as a strong argument against the hierarchical decomposition of design problems.[29]

A different shortcoming was seen by Alexander. He realised that the results of this computational model missed some of the interactions which are so important to our enjoyment of the physical environment.[30] The city is not a tree (the title of Alexander's paper). Strict modular segregation can result in arid spaces. It is the interactions between design elements which are pleasing and so interactions between the solutions to design sub-problems should be recognised.

As an architect Alexander would have been aware of the centuries old use of pattern books to disseminate good design (which probably meant approved or fashionable) from the opinion forming elite to others who needed to know what was a good design. These books enabled designers and makers (architects, furniture makers and others) to know what might please their clients. For example, at right is a page from a renaissance pattern book by Heinrich Voghterr[31] showing alternative designs of table pedestals.

And so Alexander rejected the hierarchical tree of design tasks and instead provided a pattern book.[32] The collection of 253 patterns he called a pattern language. He and his colleagues certainly did not lack ambition, covering a vast range of physical design problems from planning a city region to locating a bench.

The pattern language was still a modular decomposition but now the modules were not tasks for teams of designers but patterns of advice for solving particular design tasks. The advice was not simply prescriptive but contained an argument stating what the problem was and why the proposed solution provided good advice. There were also links to other patterns.

This was a *network* of patterns not a *tree* of tasks. The form of a pattern was

Name

A picture showing an example of the pattern

Context: how this pattern helps complete larger patterns

***

Headline: the essence of the problem

The problem (background, evidence for solution)

Solution: what is needed to solve the problem

diagram showing solution

***

links to other patterns

The *** separator marks the start and finish of the solution. In **bold** are the problem statement and the suggested solution.

Alexander's patterns have been influential for a number of reasons.

The setting of a problem in a context showed how a problem can arise. It does not just appear, it is there for a reason and that reason is usually because of conflict between a number of requirements or forces. This recognition that "the art of designing is the art of reconciliation"[33] is at the heart of these patterns.

The names given to a pattern is a signpost to the sort of problem for which a solution is offered

sacred sites
public outdoor room
road crossing
reception welcomes you

so that when thinking about a particular design project a user can quickly see which patterns might be needed.

Patterns were given as solutions to problems which have been used repeatedly and so are worth having. Solutions are justified by satisfactory repetition, sometimes backed by a little theory. The argument is given in the solution section of the pattern so that you can see why the solution is offered and make what use of it you think best fits your problem.

Time passes, and over in the software world Alexander's patterns struck a chord.

Software and the Gang of Four

The development of programming concepts and languages to support them has always been characteristic of the software community. One particular development was the use of Object Oriented

Programming, OOP.[34] The important idea was that software is seen as a data structure, a set of objects and relations between them rather than as an extension of older formula-like procedural languages. The intention is that the OOP model helps in maintaining software and, importantly, helps code sharing.

This is very obviously a modular design into which the idea of patterns as a way of disseminating reusable solutions fitted easily. These software design patterns were being written independently of Alexander's work but soon were influenced by it.

The patterns idea was enthusiastically pursued by some programmers[35] four of whom became known as the Gang of Four and produced the first published collection.[36] Four other books added to the Pattern Languages of Program Design series.

Many more books followed, notably that by Coplien and Schmidt,[37] but the list is long. There are also many patterns to be found on the web.

The form and detail of software design patterns varies a lot, some having as many as fifteen sections[38] and others just two.[39] Here, for example, is the influential form used by Coplien[40]:

context	describes why and where the problem arises
forces	shows which conflict(s) are responsible for the problem and are to be reconciled
discussion	sets out thinking about the problem and possible solutions
solution	gives the recommended course of action
new context	this advice is likely to solve much of the problem but will necessarily leave a situation which has new and, it is hoped, more tractable difficulties
see also	gives links to other patterns which may also be of interest

The same elements are here as were present in Alexander's original but in a much more structured form. This is itself a recognition of altered context: programmers are not architects.

One suggestion is that a pattern should have at least the three elements — *context/problem/solution* — but may contain more[41]:

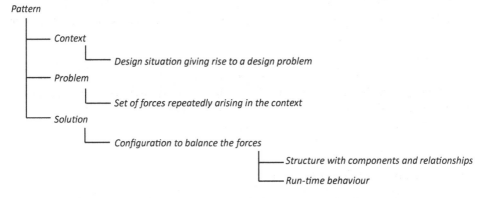

The structure depends on purpose, of which three have been distinguished[41]:

Architectural Patterns specify the fundamental structure of an application
Design patterns refine and extend the fundamental architecture
Idioms specify implementation, by giving some computer code, for example

It is likely that idioms, or application patterns, will need the most categories because of the greater detail they must contain, and architectural patterns the fewest.

There are, as you might expect, patterns about writing patterns.[42]

The structured form of Coplein[37] works well as an aid to discussion when you are building your own patterns. It is interesting that the project management patterns he gives in that paper have been reformulated[43] and written in the style of Alexander's original. The same pattern may be viewed and understood in different ways for different purposes. The structure best suited to writing a pattern is not necessarily the best for communicating it (as I later found to my cost).

Perhaps even more than with Alexander software design patterns are for knowledge transfer. The validity of the advice is meant to be ensured in two ways. First, track record: the solutions have been used successfully several times. Second, by group acceptance. In pattern workshops constructive criticism is given and the pattern amended if necessary. This process is perhaps best known via a series of conferences on Pattern Languages of Programs (PloP) organised by the Hillside Group,[44] who are also the source of much else and a gateway to pattern collections. Hillside is a continuation of the work of the Gang of Four whose patterns are also used and developed by Microsoft.[45]

Patterns for other purposes

Patterns have been proposed for the solution of other problems, mostly, but not only, by and within the software community. For example,

business improvement and related matters,[46–48]
project management,[43]
team working,[38,49,50]
the design and implementation of systems for human–computer interaction.[51–53]

Closer to the purpose of this book are patterns for educators to help in teaching and learning[54] and the design of tutoring systems.[55–56]

The statsNotes

The statsNotes in this book are a revised version of an earlier set which were based on the highly structured Coplein scheme described above. An example is shown on the next page.

I used these for one of my MBA classes. The reception was mixed but it was clear that the majority of students found the notes unhelpful.

Those in the class with prior knowledge of the subject mostly found the form interesting and useful. Those with little prior knowledge (the majority; this was an introductory class) found they had two new things to cope with: statistics (which they were expecting) and this new thing called a pattern language (which they were not). It was too much.

pattern **7**	**picturing many distributions**
PROBLEM	We need visually to compare a number of distributions.
CONTEXT	The variability or uncertainty of a number of systems is known and needs to be compared by using appropriate graphics.
FORCES	Each variability may be described by a frequency distribution or a probability distribution {3}. However, looking at a lot of these graphs is sometimes confusing because of the amount of information presented.
DISCUSSION	This problem arises in many situations:

we wish to compare the fluctuations in a number of share prices;

the risky outcomes of a number of investment plans must be shown;

the variability of production data from a number of plants must be assessed.

Simply plotting the distributions may give a graph so complex that it is difficult to interpret:

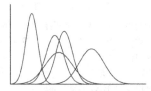

Making a simplified picture of each distribution will permit visual comparisons. It is necessary to retain the key features of a distribution but in a more compact form. A *box plot* allows this (here it is derived from the cumulative distribution {6}):

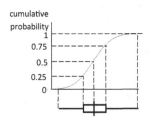

The box shows the interquartile range {9}, where the middle 50% of values fall, and the line the whole range. The vertical line shows the median {8}. The box plot retains the main features of the distribution but in a more compact display.

SOLUTION To show a number of distributions so that easy comparisons can be made represent each by a box plot and arrange them in an informative way, by order of increasing median, for instance. Here we show the fluctuations of some share prices:

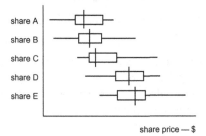

I had found the Coplein headings a good way of thinking about writing the notes, prompts for a consideration of why and when as well as how. I had assumed that students would see this but they did not. What they wanted was to know first what to do. Once they had the security of that knowledge they were then able to think of the wider issues of justification and application. *How* took precedence over *why*.

I had made an elementary mistake but still thought the modularity of patterns would be helpful.

Reading more about patterns it was clear that the narrative form of Alexander's model was increasingly being used for communication with non-specialists (rather than programmer to programmer). This was shown by the reformulation of Coplein's project management patterns described above.

There is also the question of urgency. Managers and management students do not have much time and so appreciate a form that gets to the point. The environment in which software design patterns are written (and used?) seems not so rushed as the environments in which managers work. Or perhaps the reports as published just make it seem that way.

All this has resulted in the statsNotes in this book. Compare the first version shown here with {A11}.

Software design patterns claim validity because of repeated successful use. Statistical patterns can rely on theory to some extent but must also address the concerns of practice, as when making a good fit between business problems and statistical methods.

The structured form of the first set of patterns was intended to convey, from the start, something of the problem situation and the subtleties and ambiguities which are present even in a basic statistics course. But managers and management students are much more likely to find a concrete example helpful preparation for a discussion of principle. The revised statsNotes recognise this.

***

You will have noticed that this book does not come with a Pattern Language label. As should now be clear it seems to me that these notes are a set of patterns but, learning from my students, I was keen not to lose focus. That is why this discussion of patterns comes at the end of the book for you to read (as you must have done if you are reading this) if the design issues are of interest. You will not have had to know anything about patterns to use the notes. This is as it should be.

5

A quick guide to definitions, functions and charts

The listing of statsNotes in Section 2 should help you find what you want. The index will help too.

This brief listing shows the notes where you can find some important definitions and also EXCEL functions and charts.

Definitions

Functions

Some functions have several versions for different tasks but all using basically the same calculation or distribution. These can usually be found in the statsNotes listed.

AVERAGE	A6
BETA	C5
BINOM	C1
CHISQ	C8, F12, I1
CONFIDENCE	F7, F19
CORREL	I2
F	F16
FISHER	I3
FREQUENCY	A3
FORECAST	I4
GAMMA	C6
MEDIAN	A6
MODE	A6
NORM	C3
PERCENTILE	A7
POISSON	C2
QUARTILE	A7
REGRESSION	I2, I6
SKEW	A10
STDEV	A7
T	F7, F15
VAR	A7

Charts

bar chart for frequency distribution	A2
cumulative distribution from data	A5
distributions: boxplots	A11
distributions: intervals	G5
diverging stacked bar chart (for attitudes)	A13
histogram	A3
scattergram and regression	I2, I4

•

Attribution of images

Section 3. The statsNotes

B. Probability: the language of uncertainty

B9. Daniel Kahneman. http://commons.wikimedia.org/wiki/File:Daniel_KAHNEMAN.jpg.

D. Evidence and judgement

D2. Thomas Bayes. http://commons.wikimedia.org/wiki/File:Thomas_Bayes.gif.
D6. Laplace. http://upload.wikimedia.org/wikipedia/commons/9/91/Pierre-Simon-Laplace_(1749–1827).jpg.
D7. Edwin Jaynes. http://commons.wikimedia.org/wiki/File:ETJaynes1.jpg.

E. Risky decisions

E7. John von Neumann. http://commons.wikimedia.org/wiki/File:JohnvonNeumann-LosAlamos.gif, accessed 7 September 2015.

F. Using Information from samples

Friedrich Bessel (1784–1846). https://upload.wikimedia.org/wikipedia/commons/1/16/Bessel,_Friedrich_Wilhelm_1839.jpg, accessed 7 September 2015.

G. Monitoring

G4. Poster image courtesy of Ladbrokes International plc.

H. Significance and hypothesis testing

H4. Fisher. Copyright photograph by AC Barrington Brown, reproduced by permission of the Fisher Memorial Trust.

Section 4. Why do statsNotes look like that

Christopher Alexander and the Pattern Language. Image courtesy Corbis.

Notes and References

Section 3. The statsNotes

A. Describing data

1   Lu H, While AE & Barriball KL (2007). Job satisfaction and its related factors: A question-naire survey of hospital nurses in Mainland China. *International Journal of Nursing Studies*, **44**(4), 574–588.

B. Probability: the language of uncertainty

1   Uncertainty is used very particularly in some decision situations {E5}. For the rest it is used as in this statsNote.
2   Solomon S, Qin D, Manning M, Chen Z, Marquis M, Averyt KB, Tignor M & Miller HL (eds.) (2007). *Contribution of Working Group I to the Fourth Assessment Report of the Intergovernmental Panel on Climate Change, 2007*. Cambridge: Cambridge University Press. http://www.ipcc.ch/publications_and_data/ar4/wg1/en/tssts-2.html#box-ts-1.
3   O'Brien BJ (1989). Words or numbers? The evaluation of probability expressions in general practice. *Journal of the Royal College of General Practitioners*, **39**, 98–100.

C. Probability models: the shapes of uncertainity

1   http://www.slideshare.net/enterpriseresearchcentre/erc-lep-dashboard-presentation-bristol-28-november-2014.
2   The function EXP just raises the exponential constant, e = 2.718, to a given power: $e^2 = 2.718^2$ = EXP(2) = 7.389.
3   You may first need to install *Solver* from the *File/Options/Add-Ins* menu in EXCEL.

D. Evidence and judgement

1   For probability distribution (p1, p2, ...),   entropy = −[p1log(p1) + p2log(p2) + ⋯]

E. Risky decisions

1   Cosack S, Guthridge M & Lawson E (2010). Retaining key employees in times of change. *McKinsey Quarterly*, August. http://www.mckinsey.com/insights/organization/retaining_key_employees_in_times_of_change.
2   NHS 24 Risk Management Strategy 2012/13. http://www.nhs24.com/aboutus/nhs24board/agendasandpapers/2012/~/media/nhs24/agendas%20and%20papers/2012/mar/20120329%20board%20item%2073b%20risk%20management%20strategy%20201213.ashx.

3 Knight Frank H (1921). *Risk, Uncertainty, and Profit.* Boston: Hart, Schaffner & Marx; Houghton Mifflin Co.

4 Skidelsky R (2011). The relevance of Keynes. *Cambridge Journal of Economics*, **35**(1), 1–13.

F. Using information from samples

1 This sampling was simulated in EXCEL using the function RANDBETWEEN (0, 10).

G. Monitoring

1 Mintzberg H & Waters JA (1985). On strategies, deliberate and emergent. *Strategic Management Journal*, **6**(3), 257–272.

2 Health and Social Care Information Centre.

3 The National Vascular Registry (UK), *2013 Report on Surgical Outcomes: Consultant-level statistics*.

I. Is there a relationship?

1 http://www.bbc.co.uk/news/health-30988643.

2 http://www.focus-economics.com/news/venezuela/retail/car-sales-record-softest-drop-11-months-november.

J. Production and operations

1 For example by Keefer DL & Verdini WA (1993). Better estimates of PERT activity time parameters. *Management Science*, **39**, 1086–1091.

Section 4. Why do statsNotes look like that?

1   Zwicky F (1947). Morphology and nomenclature of jet engines. *Aeronautical Engineering Review*, **6**(6), 49–50.

2   Ritchey T (2006). Problem structuring using computer-aided morphological analysis. *Journal of the Operational Research Society*, **57**(7), 792–801.

3   Harary F, Jessop N, Luckman J & Stringer J (1965). Analysis of interconnected decision areas: An algorithm for project development. *Nature*, **206**, 118.

4   Luckman J (1967). An approach to the management of design. *Operational Research Quarterly*, **18**(2), 345–358.

5   Friend JK & Jessop WN (1969). *Local Government and Strategic Choice: An Operational Research Approach to the Process of Public Planning*. London: Tavistock Publications.

6   West D (2004). *Object Thinking*. Richmond: Microsoft Press.

7   Everitt BS, Landau S, Leese M & Stahl D (2011). *Cluster Analysis* (5th edition). Chichester: Wiley.

8   Luce RD & Perry AD (1949). A method of matrix analysis of group structure. *Psychometrika*, **14**(1), 95–116.

9   Wasserman S & Faust K (1997). *Social Network Analysis: Methods and Applications*. Cambridge: Cambridge University Press.

10 Watts DJ & Strogatz SH (1999). Collective dynamics of 'small world' networks. *Nature*, **393**, 440–442.

11 Simon HA (1969). *The Sciences of the Artificial.* Cambridge: The MIT Press.

12 Kauffman S (1995). *At Home in the Universe: The Search for Laws of Complexity.* Harmondsworth: Viking.

13 Papalambros PY & Wilde D (2000). *Principles of Optimal Design: Modelling and Computation.* Cambridge: Cambridge University Press.

14 Baldwin CY & Clark KB (2000). *Design Rules: Volume 1. The Power of Modularity.* Cambridge: The MIT Press.

15 Hoetker G (2006). Do modular products lead to modular organisations? *Strategic Management Journal,* **27**(5), 501–518.

16 Sanchez R & Mahoney JT (1996). Modularity, flexibility, and knowledge management in product and organisation design. *Strategic Management Journal,* **17**(Special Issue: Knowledge and the Firm, Winter), 63–76.

17 Brusoni S & Prencipe A (2006). Making design rules: A multidomain perspective. *Organization Science,* **17**(2), 179–189.

18 Benkler Y (2002). Coase's penguin, or, Linux and the Nature of the Firm. *Yale Law Journal,* **112**(3), 369–446.

19 von Hippel E (1994). "Sticky information" and the locus of problem solving: implications and innovation. *Management Science,* **40**(4), 429–439.

20 Voss CA and Hsuan J (2009). Service architecture and modularity. *Decision Sciences,* **40**(3), 541–569.

21 Shannon CE (1948). A mathematical theory of communication. *The Bell System Technical Journal,* **27**, 379–423, 623–656.

22 Gleick J (2011). *The Information* (Chapter 7). London: Fourth Estate.

23 Miller GA (1956). The magical number seven, plus or minus two: Some limits on our capacity for processing information. *Psychological Review,* **63**(2), 81–97.

24 Jones JC & Thornley DG (eds.) (1963). *Conference on Design Methods.* Oxford: Pergamon.

25 Alexander C (1963). The determination of components for an Indian village. In Jones JC & Thornley (eds.), *Conference on design Methods.* Oxford: Pergamon Press.

26 Alexander C (1964). *Notes on the Synthesis of Form.* Cambridge: Harvard University Press.

27 Chermayeff S & Alexander C (1966). *Community and Privacy: Towards a New Architecture of Humanism.* Harmondsworth: Penguin Books.

28 Alexander C and Manheim ML (1962). *HIDECS 2: A Computer Program for the Hierarchical Decomposition of a Set with an Associated Linear Graph.* Cambridge: MIT School of Engineering Report No. 160.

29 Batty M (1971). An approach to rational design. *Architectural Design,* **41**, 436–439, 498–501.

30 Alexander C (1966). A city is not a tree. *Design,* **206** (February), 46–55.

31 Vogtherr H (1539). *Libellus artificiosus omnibus pictoribus, statuarijs, aurifabris, lapidicidis, arcularijs, laminarijs & cultrarijs fabris, sumopere utilis, nec à quae antea uisus, nec prius editus.* Strasbourg: Cum priuilegio Cesareo impressus Argentorari per Heinricum Vogtherren. https://archive.org/details/libellusartifici00vogt.

32 Alexander C, Ishikawa S & Silverstein M (1977). *A Pattern Language.* New York: Oxford University Press.

33 Archer LB (1965). *Systematic Method for Designers.* London: Design Council [Reprinted in Cross N (ed.) (1984). *Developments in Design Methodology.* Chichester: Wiley].

34 Coad P & Yourdon E (1991). *Object-Oriented Analysis.* Englewood Cliffs: Prentice-Hall.

35 Gabriel RP (1996). *Patterns of Software: Tales from the Software Community.* New York: Oxford University Press.

36   Gamma E, Helm R, Johnson R & Vlissides J (1994). *Design Patterns: Elements of Reusable Object-Oriented Software*. Reading MA: Addison-Wesley.

37   Coplien JO & Schmidt DC (eds.) (1995). *Pattern Languages of Program Design*. Reading: Addison-Wesley.

38   Harrison NB (1996). Organizational patterns for teams. In Vlissides JM, Coplien JO & Kerth NL (eds). *Pattern Languages of Program Design 2*. Reading: Addison-Wesley.

39   Cunningham W (1996). EPISODES: A pattern language of competitive development. In Vlissides JM, Coplien JO & Kerth NL (eds), *Pattern Languages of Program Design 2*. Reading MA: Addison-Wesley.

40   Coplien JO (1995). A generative development-process language. In Coplien JO & Schmidt DC (eds). *Pattern Languages of Program Design*. Reading MA: Addison-Wesley.

41   Buschmann F, Meunier R, Rohnert H, Sommerlad P & Stal M (eds.) (1996). *A System of Patterns*. Wiley: Chichester.

42   Meszaros G & Doble J (1998). A pattern language for pattern writing. In Martin R, Riehle D & Buschmann F (eds.), *Pattern Languages of Program Design 3*. Reading MA: Addison-Wesley. See also http://hillside.net/index.php/a-pattern-language-for-pattern-writing.

43   Coplien JO & Harrison NB (2005). *Organizational Patterns of Agile Software Development*. Upper Saddle River: Pearson Prentice Hall. See also http://orgpatterns.wikispaces.com/ProjectManagementPatternLanguage.

44   http://www.hillside.net/.

45   Microsoft http://www.gofpatterns.com/.

46   Slywotzky AJ, Morrison DJ, Moser T, Mundy KA and Quella JA (1999). *Profit Patterns: 30 Ways to Anticipate and Profit from Strategic Forces Reshaping Your Business*. Chichester: Wiley.

47   Laurier W, Hruby P & Poels G (2009). Business plan conception pattern language. Conference: EuroPLoP 2009: 14th Annual European Conference on Pattern Languages of Programming, Irsee, Germany, 8–12 July 2009.

48   Manns ML and Rising L (2005). *Fearless Change: Patterns for Introducing New Ideas*. Boston: Addison-Wesley.

49   Taylor P (1996). Capable, productive, and satisfied: Some organizational patterns for protecting productive people. In Vlissides JM, Coplien JO and Kerth NL (eds.), *Pattern Languages of Program Design 2*. Reading MA: Addison-Wesley.

50   Weir C (1998). Patterns for designing in teams. In Martin R, Riehle D and Buschmann F (eds.), *Pattern Languages of Program Design 3*. Reading MA: Addison-Wesley.

51   Dearden A and Finlay J (2006). Pattern languages in HCI: A critical review. *Human-Computer Interaction*, **21**(1), 49–102.

52   University of Kent HCI patterns. http://www.cs.kent.ac.uk/people/staff/saf/patterns/gallery.html.

53   http://www.hcipatterns.org/.

54   Pedagogical Patterns Editorial Board (2012). *Pedagogical Patterns: Advice for Educators*. Joseph Bergin Software Tools.

55   Harrer A and Martens A (2006). Towards a pattern language for intelligent teaching and training systems. In Ikeda M, Ashley K and Chan T-W. (eds.), *Intelligent Tutoring Systems (ITS) 2006*. Berlin: Springer-Verlag.

56   Goodyear P and Retalis S (eds.) (2010). *Technology-Enhanced Learning: Design Patterns and Pattern Languages*. Rotterdam: Sense Publishers. https://www.sensepublishers.com/media/1037-technology-enhanced-learning.pdf.

Index

Printed in the United States
By Bookmasters